D0215430

Violence and the
Prevention of Violence

Violence and the Prevention of Violence

EDITED BY
Leonore Loeb Adler and Florence L. Denmark

FOREWORDS BY
Lenore E. A. Walker and
Benjamin B. Wolman

Westport, Connecticut
London

Library of Congress Cataloging-in-Publication Data

Violence and the prevention of violence / edited by Leonore Loeb Adler
and Florence L. Denmark ; forewords by Lenore E. A. Walker and
Benjamin B. Wolman.
    p. cm.
    Includes bibliographical references and index.
    ISBN 0–275–94873–0 (alk. paper)
    1. Violence. 2. Violence—Prevention. 3. Family violence.
4. Family violence—Prevention. I. Adler, Leonore Loeb.
II. Denmark, Florence.
HM291.V457   1995
303.6—dc20   94–28007

British Library Cataloguing in Publication Data is available.

Library of Congress Catalog Card Number: 94–28007
ISBN: 0–275–94873–0

First published in 1995

Praeger Publishers, 88 Post Road West, Westport, CT 06881
An imprint of Greenwood Publishing Group, Inc.

Printed in the United States of America

The paper used in this book complies with the
Permanent Paper Standard issued by the National
Information Standards Organization (Z39.48–1984).

10 9 8 7 6 5 4 3 2

This book is dedicated to all the people who study the causes of violence, and to those who search to find ways to prevent violence.

Contents

Foreword

Lenore E. A. Walker

Violence still exists around the world today despite the many attempts to erad-
icate it from our lives. Most violence is used to obtain power and control over
other people. Sometimes the violence is state sponsored and used to obtain
control over territory as well as people. Sometimes it is used randomly to assert
one's individuality. Sometimes it is used to terrorize those who are also loved
within one's family. Those who use violence may bully, intimidate, verbally
insult, sexually coerce, and physically harm others into submission. Various
forms of violence are described in this book.

During the past twenty years feminist psychology has analyzed violence from
a perspective different from that of other psychological theoretical frameworks.
Women now recognize that they are more likely than men to be battered and
raped by men. United States Federal Bureau of Investigation (FBI) statistics
indicate that 95 percent of all reported domestic violence is committed by men
against women (Straus & Gelles, 1988). Sexual abuse is more likely to be committed by an adult male against an adult female. Only in the case of child abuse
are more males than females reported abused; and when the abuse is sexual,
over 90 percent of perpetrators are males who abuse both male and female
children. When women began to believe the system would do something to help
stop the violence, they reported the crimes. Once police began making arrests
in domestic violence cases, the jails became overflowing (Walker & Corriere,
1991). Gender analysis of violence is critical to understanding and controlling
world violence.

Those studying child abuse and battered women have found that a little boy
who watches his father batter his mother is 700 times more likely to use violence
in his own life than is the child who has no abuse in his or her home. If that
little boy is also abused himself, the risk for his learning to use violence is
raised to 1,000 times the norm (Straus, Gelles, & Steinmetz, 1980). Such a boy

has difficulty learning how to feel empathy for another person's pain. Patterson (1982) and his colleagues, Reid, Taplin, & Lorber (1981), studied the behavioral interactions in the homes of children who were identified as aggressive boys. Their family behaviors were coded and compared with those in homes where boys were not reported as using aggressive behavior. The results were interesting: Those in homes without aggressive boys exhibited many more positive than negative behaviors toward each other.

The data divided the homes with aggressive boys into two groups. One group centered on reported family violence, the other on relationships that were dysfunctional. As might be expected, those in the dysfunctional homes that produced an aggressive boy engaged in many more negative behaviors toward each other. However, the group with the aggressive boys from homes with family violence was most interesting. Here there were more negative than positive interactions, but they occurred in a special pattern of *chaining and fogging*. That is to say, one negative act quickly followed the last one, one after the other, so that there was no time to make an effective response. This caused sufficient cognitive confusion, further reducing the possibility of making an effective response. And most importantly from a gender perspective, the negative behavioral interactions were directed mostly from males to females. Patterson suggests that coercive families train boys and men to use violence as a learned response to obtain domination.

Research on men who batter women indicate that they learn to use verbal intimidation and aggression punctuated by physical assaults in order to get women to do what they want them to do (O'Leary & Arias, 1988; Walker, 1984). Sexual abuse is also used to humiliate the woman and render her more powerless to male demands (Herman, 1992; Walker, 1979, 1989a, b & c). Men who believe they are entitled to a woman's services usually seek to gain power and control over the woman. Often these aggressive behaviors turn to violence when she does not comply with what the man demands. Although there are many different theoretical explanations for why men batter women, the most parsimonious one is that "no one stops them." Those who work with men ordered by the court into treatment say that men who abuse women (1) believe they are not doing anything wrong; (2) if they understand that their behavior is wrong, do not believe they will be caught; (3) if they get caught, believe they will talk their way out of any trouble; (4) if they can't talk their way out completely, believe the consequences will be light. Most men who commit violence who believe these points would be correct.

Feminist psychologists believe that violence in the home is the underbelly of all violence in the streets and in society (Pagelow, 1984; Walker, 1979). Disconnected and alienated from their own families (Hansen & Harway, 1993), often victims of racial and class oppression with no belief in a future, many males and some females learn to use violence as an attempt to survive (Barnett & LaViolette, 1993). Kilpatrick (1990) found that the single most important factor in women using alcohol and drugs is prior history of abuse. Most women and men in prison have witnessed and experienced violence in their own lives. Men who are exposed to violence learn to use it; women exposed to violence are more likely to be victims, although more are now fighting back. Why is there such a gender difference? Violence exists throughout our societal institutions, as is described throughout this book. Violence in the community supports and facilitates the perpetuation of violence for those who have witnessed or experienced violence in their own homes. It is important to place the transmission of violence from one generation to another in a social context rather than deal with individual pathology (Herman, 1992).

During her lifetime one out of two women will be beaten by a man who loves her! If the battered woman tries to leave her abuser, she increases the four-to-one risk that he will kill her. Twenty-five percent of all women will be sexually assaulted, usually by someone they know. Over one-third of all girls will be sexually abused by the time they are 18; over 25 percent before age 14. Ten to twenty-five percent of all boys will also be sexually abused, usually by a man. The polls show that over 90 percent of all American women have been sexually harassed on the job. Sexual harassment rates for European countries approach one-half of all working women. Men's violence against women appears to be the norm in all countries. Feminist psychology suggests that these different forms of violence by men against women have the same core: men who expect to have power and control over women.

Psychologists who work with abused women suggest that many develop a Post Traumatic Stress Disorder (PTSD) as a result of the trauma they have experienced. Battered Woman Syndrome (Walker, 1984, 1989a, 1989b, 1991), Rape Trauma Syndrome (Burgess & Holmstrom, 1974), and Battered Child Syndrome (Walker, 1990) are various subcategories. Any normal person who is exposed to PTSD would be expected to demonstrate its mental health symptoms. The predominant symptoms are high arousal and anxiety, high avoidance and numbing of feelings and depression, and intrusive memories with cognitive distortions. New psychotherapy techniques have been designed to help women who were victimized to become survivors (Walker, 1994). But not all victims need therapy to become survivors; many need lots of genuine caring and support of friends and family.

The contributors to this volume put forth many contemporary theoretical ideas about violence in society. All agree with the editors, Leonore Loeb Adler and Florence L. Denmark, that finding ways to prevent violence is critical given the escalating reports of violence around the world. Our studies of family violence assure us that unless we eliminate sexism, racism, classism, and other forms of oppression, one group will continue to want power and control over another group, and some members of that group will condone the use of violence to get power and keep it. Living in peace means acceptance of diversity. Women and men must work together to promote a nonviolent world.

REFERENCES

Barnett, O. W., & LaViolette, A. D. (1993). *It could happen to anyone: Why battered women stay.* Newbury Park: Sage.

Burgess, A. W., & Holmstrom, L. L. (1974). Rape trauma syndrome. *American Journal of Psychiatry, 131,* 981–986.

Dutton, M. A. (1992). *Healing the trauma of woman battering: Assessment and intervention.* New York: Springer.

Hansen, M., & Harway, M. (Eds.). (1993). *Battering and family therapy: A feminist perspective.* Newbury Park: Sage.

Herman, J. L. (1992). *Trauma and recovery.* New York: Basic Books.

Kilpatrick, D. G. (1990). Violence as a precursor of women's substance abuse: The rest of the drugs-violence story. Presented in the symposium *Critical Issue-Substance Abuse and Violence: Drugs and Violent Crime.* American Psychological Association Convention, Boston.

O'Leary, K. D., & Arias, I. (1988). In G. Hotaling, D. Finkelhor, J. T. Kirkpatrick, & M. A. Straus (Eds.), *Family abuse and its consequences: New directions in research* (pp. 218–227). Newbury Park: Sage.

Pagelow, M. (1984). *Family violence.* New York: Praeger.

Patterson, G. (1982). *Coercive family processes.* Eugene, OR: Castaglia Press.

Reid, J. B., Taplin, P. S., & Lorber, R. (1981). A social interactional approach to the treatment of abusive families. In R. B. Stuart (Ed.), *Violent behavior: Social learning approaches to prediction, management and treatment.* New York: Brunner/Mazel.

Straus, M. A., & Gelles, R. J. (1988). How violent are American families? Estimates from the National Family Violence Resurvey and other studies. In G. T. Hotaling, D. Finkelhor, J. T. Kirkpatrick, & M. A. Straus (Eds.), *Family abuse and its consequences* (pp. 14–36). Newbury Park, CA: Sage.

Straus, M. A., Gelles, R. J., & Steinmetz, S. (1980). *Behind closed doors: Violence in America.* New York: Doubleday.

Walker, L. E. (1979). *The battered woman.* New York: Harper & Row.

Walker, L. E. A. (1984). *Battered woman syndrome.* New York: Springer.

Walker, L. E. A. (1989a). *Terrifying love: Why battered women kill and how society responds.* New York: Harper & Row.

Walker, L. E. A. (1989b). Psychology and violence against women. *American Psychologist, 44,* 695–702.

Walker, L. E. A. (1989c). When the battered woman becomes the defendant. In E. Viano (Ed.), *Crime and its victims: International research and public policy. Proceedings of the Fourth International Institute on Victimology* (pp, 57–70). NATO Advanced Research Workshop, Il Ciocco, Tuscany, Italy. New York: Hemisphere.

Walker, L. E. A. (1990). Psychological assessment of sexually abused children for legal evaluation and expert witness testimony. *Professional Psychology: Research and Practice, 21* (5), 344–353.

Walker, L. E. A. (1991). Post-Traumatic Stress Disorder in women: Diagnosis and treatment of Battered Woman Syndrome. *Psychotherapy, 28*(1), 21–29.

Walker, L. E. A. (1994). *The abused woman and survivor therapy: A practical guide for the psychotherapist.* Washington, DC: American Psychological Association.

Walker, L. E. A., & Corriere, S. (1991). Domestic violence: International perspectives on social change. In E. Viano (Ed.), *Victims' rights and legal reforms: International perspectives. Proceedings of the Sixth International Institute on Victimology, (1990). Onati Proceedings, No. 9* (pp. 135–150). Onati, Spain: University of Onati Institute on Sociology and the Law.

Foreword

Benjamin B. Wolman

Violence is a physical or verbal behavior that aims at harming and/or destroying someone or something. Violent behavior is a part of nature, and nature is violent.

There are two main sources of violence, namely, the fear of death by starvation and the fear of death by being killed. The fear of having nothing to eat leads to offensive violence, and the fear of being eaten up leads to defensive violence. To eat and not to be eaten, this is the question.

Animals practice both offensive and defensive violence. Animal violence is usually interspecific: The predators practice offensive violence, whereas their victims practice defensive violence to prevent being eaten. Intraspecific violence is usually related to fight for access to food, water, and sex. Most often intraspecific fights are not murderous, and the intraspecific competition is usually settled by pecking order. However, in several species the intraspecific violence is murderous. Hippopotamus, deer, musk, for example, kill in intraspecific violence. Human beings are ahead of all other species in intraspecific murderous violence. In war and in peace people are killed by people.

HUMAN VIOLENCE

All living organisms are vulnerable and mortal, but only human beings are painfully aware of the inevitable end and are therefore eager to fight. Being capable of anticipating and imagining future dangers, they are almost always ready to fight offensive as well as defensive wars.

The fear of death by starvation and the fear of being killed are the main causes of human belligerence. The fear of not having food motivates hatred of those who have plenty, so that underprivileged, poor, and hungry human beings tend to hate the wealthy ones. The fear of being harmed, enslaved or killed motivates hatred to the powerful true or imagined enemies. People do not fear or hate butterflies, but they hate powerful and potentially dangerous adversaries.

xvi • Benjamin B. Wolman

The feeling of insecurity is a most frequent cause of hatred and violent behavior, for usually people do not fear or hate their poor and weak relatives, but they may envy, resent, and even hate their rich and powerful ones.

POWER

Fight for survival is the chief motivation of human behavior. The chances for survival depend mainly on one's *power,* that is, the ability to get food and shelter and to fight off one's enemies. Power can be defined as the ability to satisfy one's own needs and the needs of others, or to prevent the satisfaction of the needs of others. Preventing the satisfaction of one's own needs—through self-imposed starvation, martyrdom, and suicide, for instance—does not belong to the category of power.

Elation and depression originate in true or exaggerated feelings of strength and weakness. People are elated when they feel powerful, and they are depressed when they feel weak and powerless. Elation carries the message of power; depression is a psychological corollary of feeling weak and angry at oneself for being weak (Wolman & Stricker, 1990).

Violent behavior can give people an illusion of power they do not have. Several people toil to build a building, but one half-wit can set it afire. It takes years of tender love and care to bring up a child, but one terrorist can kill many children. It takes plenty of power to create, but it takes little to destroy. Small wonder that many young people and immature adults are an easy prey for fanatics and gang leaders. Benito Mussolini's fascistic *arditi,* Adolf Hitler's SS and SA gangs, Joseph Stalin's henchmen, the Irish Republican Army, the Palestine Liberation Organization—all have attracted the young and involved them in terrorist activities that kill innocent people.

There is a magnetic attraction to terrorist gangs. Joining a dictatorial cult or a terrorist gang suspends individual responsibility, obliterates guilt feelings, and removes moral inhibitions. Some people tend to assault, mug, kill, but it has always been easy to incite average people to a robbery, to a pogrom of Jews, to the lynching of blacks, or to kidnapping of businesspersons and diplomats. The main attractiveness of violent behavior is the psychological attractiveness of power.

THE PROLIFERATION OF VIOLENCE

The proliferation of drug abuse and violent crime is a dangerous sign of cultural regression. Civilization as we understand it started when God and/or wise men said, "Thou shall not . . . !" The decline in self-discipline and disinhibition is a dangerous sign of deculturation, reminding us of what happened in 1933 to the land of Kant, Goethe and Beethoven.

The present social climate of excessive hedonism, with its widespread "have fun" attitudes encourages alcoholism and drug abuse and the "do whatever pleases you" mentality. This selfish social climate fosters sociopathic personality (Wolman, 1987).

Every day someone is mugged, raped, or killed. Shoplifting and burglaries are matched by extortion, dope pushing, and holdups. So far nothing has stopped crime, and antisocial and antihuman acts go on and on. The judicial and penal systems are unable to put an end to the spread of criminal behavior. Jailing has never been an adequate deterrent, and in many instances penitentiaries have turned out hardened criminals, individuals more vicious and more determined than ever before. Leniency and permissiveness have not fared better, and the "soft" system of justice has often given the impression that one can "get away with murder."

WEAKNESS ENCOURAGES VIOLENCE

The apparent increase in violence is the result of several factors, among them the abundance of lethal weapons and the apparent weakness in the control of violence. Criminals armed with automatic weapons can attack anybody and everybody, and courts and police have thus far been inadequate in protecting innocent citizens. At the present time violent people do indeed get away with murder. Consider violent gangs in the United States. Their easy success is quite apparent in the fight against terrorism. Today terrorist groups are more numerous and better armed than ever before, and there is no end in sight to terrorism. (Kupperman & Kamen, 1989)

Moreover, the United Nations, the hoped-for international guardian of peace, is not very successful in assuring peace and preventing violence. Internal conflicts and external confrontations, little and big, go on unabated in Ireland, Africa, the Middle East, Latin America, and many other places. Despite agreed-upon and highly publicized international rules, countries like Iraq and North Korea are still armed with chemical, biological, and potentially atomic weapons.

LOVE IS NOT ENOUGH

There is a widespread belief that love can cure hostile and violent behavior, for love inspires people to do whatever they can for the loved person. However, no one can love everyone else. "Love thy neighbor" and "love thy enemies" as precepts for civilized life have not resulted in success. The question is how to prevent hostile behavior toward people whom one does not love.

Benedict de Spinoza (1677) related morality to love. According to Spinoza, *Summa ethica* is *summus amor*. However, the question is not how to avoid hostility in love; the question is to be fair and ready to help the people that one does *not* love. (Kohlberg, 1979).

MORAL DEVELOPMENT

One can distinguish four levels of moral development. At the lowest level, *anomous*, antisocial behavior can be contained by retaliation and/or fear of retaliation. The fear of punishment coming from without is the single, powerful restraining factor. Morality, at the second level, *phobonomous,* is based on fear.

The substitution of religious or symbolic punishment for the physical threat of retaliation is a significant step in human progress. The idea of a loving and punishing God enables people to internalize moral restraint. Love for God and fear of losing His love, the desire to be loved and the fear of being punished, enables people to develop self-restraint. Moral behavior then becomes *heteronomous,* or related to the moral authority of God.

A similar process takes place in children's development: The introjection of a parental image leads to the formation of self-restraint Sigmund Freud called the superego. Moral restraint that comes through acceptance of external authority is heteronomous. Heteronomous morality, which is based on the love of parents and/or other authority figures, is a combination of love and a fear of rejection.

The third phase of moral development is *socionomous.* This phase starts with the voluntary acceptance of social norms. It entails "some freedom for all," instead of the licentious "all freedom for some." Members of a society take part in determining and sharing equal rights and obligations. In child development it is a process of identification with one's group that leads to the formation of *we-ego,* which is tantamount to the individual's sharing of collective responsibility.

The highest level of moral development has been exemplified in Henrik Ibsen's play *An Enemy of the People,* in which an individual accepts moral responsibility even when he is alone. This is the highest, or *vectorial,* level of morality. It is the moral commitment of an individual.

REGRESSION

Hostile behavior can easily be provoked, for it is much easier to go down the ladder than to climb up. Hatred is biologically older than love, and destructive acts do not require much power or intelligence. Anything can stir up hostile behavior. "To eat or be eaten" guides not only animal behavior but that of the human race, governing practically every aspect of human life under the guise of patriotism, proselytism, fanaticism, glorification, jealousy, pride, frustration, Lebensraum, and anything else.

PREVENTIVE ACTION

One may indulge in lofty dreams of peace on earth, but neither preaching nor punishing can produce any significant change. Prevention is the only rational approach that could bring a substantial reduction in antisocial acts.

The most basic preventive method is exterior restraint. Not the after-the-fact-punishment, but a strong and determinate protection of the population can deter potential muggers, rapists, and murderers. Forceful and efficient protective force can secure peace and freedom and safety for millions who are not criminal. The wars against Hitler and Saddam Hussein were the moral obligation of humanity, for morality must be defended. Moreover, antisocial behavior requires a long-range preventive action that must start at home and be supported by schools, enabling children to develop heteronomous morality. Mass media, youth centers, and religious, cultural, and political organizations must embark on a far-reaching program of moral education leading to socionomous and, hopefully, vectorial morality.

WHERE ARE WE NOW?

The era of territorial conquests, colonial empires, and military splendor is over. Wars have become too expensive to wage, and victories too futile to aspire to. The great upheavals of the past have become obsolete, and the biggest protest marches cannot feed even one hungry mouth. The cemeteries are full of Napoleons, Caesars, and Alexanders who believed they were indispensable, but history no longer bows her head to generals.

The world does not need naive dreamers, prophets, and world saviors. The facts are clear: Wherever there is life, the fight for survival goes on. Animals kill other animals to eat, and animals fight against being killed for food. Nature knows no morals, no manners, no consideration; the big ones eat the smaller ones, the smaller eat the smallest, and all living organisms fight for survival. But human beings can get whatever they need without fight: They can produce whatever they need, and the democratic way of life can offer equal opportunities for all people.

Self-styled elitism, the idea of being extra-ordinary human beings, must be countered by a universal repudiation and condemnation of terror and terrorists. Terrorists crave publicity, recognition, and glamor; they are actors on a big stage and they applaud themselves and expect public applause. A universal disrespect, disgust, and condemnation will frustrate their hopes. A united, determined, and forceful attitude will make them realize the futility of the game they play.

We need not passively wait for destruction of our democratic way of life. Democracy as we know it was not born overnight. Humanity struggled for centuries along a tortuous road toward the system of law and justice that we call democratic. Weakness invites aggression, and we must not repeat the errors of the past. We are for freedom of speech, but not for freedom of action. We are willing to listen to everyone's words, but we shall not allow anyone to be killed by swords.

Two hundred years ago Edmund Burke declared, "The only thing necessary for the triumph of evil is for good men to do nothing." The International Organization for the Study of Group Tensions is calling on all men and women of good will to join us in the search for solutions—to prevent and to stop the growing wave of violence. We do not promise an easy victory, but we are here, ready to do our job. We shall never surrender.

NOTE

This Foreword is based on the keynote address delivered on November 9, 1991, at Molloy College, Rockville Centre, NY, at the Conference on Violence and Prevention of Violence, chaired by and cosponsored by the International Organization for the Study of Group Tensions, the Institute for Cross-Cultural & Cross-Ethnic Studies and Queens County Psychological Association, by the Academic and Social Psychology Divisions of the New York State Psychological Association, and by Leonore Loeb Adler and Florence L. Denmark.

REFERENCES

Kohlberg, L. (1979). *The meaning and measurement of moral development.* Clark, MA: Clark University Press.

Kupperman, R., & Kamen, J. (1989). *Final warning.* New York: Doubleday.

Spinoza, B. (1677). *Ethica in ordine geometrico demonstrata.* In *Works.* Heidelberg: Heidelberg University Press.

Wolman, B. B. (1971). Sense and nonsense in history. *Pyschoanalytic interpretation of history.* New York: Basic Books.

Wolman, B. B. (1973). Violent behavior. *International Journal of Group Tensions, 3,* 127–141.

Wolman, B. B. (1987). *Sociopathic personality.* New York: Brunner-Mazel.

Wolman, B. B., & Stricker, G. (Eds.). (1990). *Depressive disorders.* New York: John Wiley.

Preface

Leonore Loeb Adler and Florence L. Denmark

In recent years there has been a tremendous increase in the occurrence of violence worldwide. *Violence and the Prevention of Violence* takes a thorough account of this phenomenon and investigates the many conditions that may lead to violent actions and behaviors. It is currently believed that many of these antecedent variables are wide-ranging and interactive. Factors such as biology, the socialization process, observational learning, cognitive reasoning, and the presence, absence, or distortion of moral judgment have been posited as contributory. In spite of attempts at explanation, however, causes are often multifaceted and uncertain, making them difficult to clearly measure or identify. Despite this obstacle to our understanding the causes of violence, a growing awareness of the conditions that precipitate explosive episodes may lead us to ways to avoid and/or eliminate violence.

Renowned scholars with expert knowledge in specific areas of violence have contributed to this volume. Their expertise gives high credibility to their exploration of different types of violence. The reader is therefore presented with the latest information from the current experts in the field.

There are many forms and expressions of violence. The topics in this book, while written from a North American perspective, make comparisons with similar violent behaviors that occur in other countries and among different cultures in present societies. The need for the prevention of violence and crime on a global level is appreciated and addressed.

Part I focuses on violence as a societal phenomenon. In the first chapter, Sergei V. Tsytsarev and Charles V. Callahan discuss the motivation of violent behavior cross-culturally. The next chapter, by Robert S. Lee, also has as its focus the causes of crime, comparing geographical regions in the United States of America with machismo values frequently held by U.S. westerners. In the following chapter, Harold Takooshian and William M. Verdi outline a new survey scale they developed to measure attitudes toward terrorism. Their scale has a wide range of attitudinal choices, from abhorrence and disdain to acceptance and social approval.

Part II, "Violence Involving the Young," presents specific aspects of violence toward and by children. June Chisholm's chapter investigates family strife and child-rearing practices that may be precursors to later aggression by and among youth. Chapter 5, by Jack L. Herman and Barbara A. Mowder and their colleagues, deals with specific traumas in children's lives (i.e., physical violence against children), the deleterious effects of which can permanently alter a child's life physically and psychologically. Herman and Mowder and their coauthors discuss the critical need for psychological treatment for the individual and the family. Dan Meyer continues this discussion of treatment in the next chapter, emphasizing therapy for the victim as well as punishment for the offender. He further advocates the development of prevention programs that train young people in nonviolent dispute resolution and in the control of anger and frustration. Next Joseph O'Donoghue addresses the global pattern of school violence, comparing the manifestations of such in the United States of America and in Japan. He also discusses school violence in other countries as well, including Australia, Canada, and Sweden. Punishment is the focus of Joan M. Reidy Merlo's chapter. While not allowed in most states of the United States, J.M.R. Merlo cites cases in which the death penalty for juvenile offenders is made by jury decision.

Part III, "Violence in Adulthood," broadens our perspective on the types of crimes committed, focusing on women, who according to Nancy Felipe Russo, Mary P. Koss, and Lisa Goodman are most often the victims of domestic violence. Preventive measures for domestic violence are discussed by Herbert H. Krauss and Beatrice J. Krauss in the next chapter, followed by a more extensive exposition on marital violence by Gwendolyn L. Gerber. G. L. Gerber proposes a connection between gender-stereotyped traits, the power factor, and ensuing violence. Although a more androgynous behavior pattern may alleviate or prevent marital violence, such a pattern may or may not deter women from criminal activities. Barbara Cowen deals further with this topic in Chapter 12, elaborating on the issues concerning women and crime. Whereas alcoholism generally has the family as its focal point, in Chapter 13 Jean Cirillo offers suggestions for the rehabilitation of the female alcoholic specifically. Finally, the topic of abuse against the elderly is presented by Margot B. Nadien in Chapter 14. This chapter describes multifaceted home situations, relying on theoretical evaluations to come to grips with this increasing problem.

The need for the prevention of violence and crime is universal, and the readers of this book are exposed to a self-searching look at our society and our world. It is the ardent hope of the editors, Leonore Loeb Adler and Florence L. Denmark, that this book will help to lay the cornerstone in the construction and development of programs for the prevention of violence. To this end, Benjamin B. Wolman's voice is heard in his Foreword, who asks that everyone come forth and join in the search for the prevention of violent actions. Lenore E. A. Walker, a long-time advocate for women's issues in domestic violence, expresses similar sentiments in her Foreword. The final word, given in the Epilogue by Uwe P. Gielen, shows that a nonviolent society *can* exist as evidenced by his report "Traditional Buddhist Ladakh: A Society at Peace." It is our hope that these chapters will enhance recognition of the need for drastic measures to remedy as well as prevent the overwhelming incidence of violence as it occurs worldwide.

PART I

VIOLENCE: A SOCIETAL PHENOMENON

1

Motivational Approach to Violent Behavior: A Cross-Cultural Perspective

Sergei V. Tsytsarev and Charles V. Callahan

Many theories of violent behavior have been developed and elaborated from psychodynamic, social learning, cognitive, and family system perspectives. Previous studies espousing such positions, however, have given relatively meager consideration to a motivational analysis of violent behavior. Meanwhile, the dramatic increase in the report of all manner of violent behaviors urgently raises the issue of psychological causality and the determinants of violence and begs for answers from the community of behavioral and social scientists. Moreover, the motivational analysis of violent conduct plays an important role in predicting the dangerousness of a potentially violent individual, a task faced with increasing regularity by most mental health professionals (Hillbrand, Foster, & Hirt, 1988).

Research investigations that deal with violence often contain systematic weaknesses or inadequacies in the realms of methodology and experimental design. A good deal of the time control groups are not employed at all; indeed, such controls often appear to be impossible. Often, inadequate control subjects are selected, and *violence* itself is not operationally defined. This underlying confusion over what constitutes violence further complicates efforts to research the topic systematically, since some very common forms of violent behavior (e.g., verbal violence in the family) are not usually perceived as such by a majority of people, whereas other, obviously violent behaviors (e.g., homicide) are very infrequent occurrences even among angry, violence-prone individuals. Convicted murderers, for instance, are nonviolent in most of their transactions with other people. In fact, not more than 2 percent of violent individuals commit violent crimes (Hillbrand, Foster, & Hirt, 1988), and most of them are able to find alternative, socially accepted, institutionalized ways to express violent behavior at work, at home, and so forth. Such realities are not usually considered in the empirical research on violence.

Another difficulty in doing research in this field is that violent behavior can be considered in isolation as a psychological phenomenon only from a purely academic perspective. In real life, violence is occasioned not only by social determinants, precipitating events, and psychological predispositions but also by such factors as alcohol and/or drug intoxication. In New South Wales, Australia, 22 of 85 murderers and 59 of 100 perpetrators in assault and robbery cases were "addicted to drink." Similarly, studies conducted in Poland and the Netherlands reveal that offenders and probationers in homicide cases frequently are alcoholics or were drinking alcoholic beverages at the time of the crime. Donald W. Goodwin (1973) investigated 233 parolees and probationers from Missouri correctional facilities and found that 43 percent of the sample were alcoholic and an additional 11 percent were "possibly" alcoholic. In Russia, according to the 1990 Annual Report of the Police Commissioner of St. Petersburg, 72 percent of violent crimes there were committed by alcoholics or nonalcoholics who were severely intoxicated. Over 60 percent of murderers had no other explanation of their criminal conduct than that they were "drunk and angry."

In modern criminal psychology several attempts have been made to create a comprehensive model of violent and criminal behavior. One of the better efforts in this area is presented in *Criminal Behavior: A Process Psychology Analysis* by Pallone and Hennessy (1992). The authors contend that the emission of a criminal behavior requires that "four process elements that interact with and potentiate each other in varying ways" be present and active in the behavioral situation. These elements include (1) an "inclination or predisposition . . . to behave in ways . . . construed . . . to be formally and legally criminal, whether aggressive or not," (2) the opportunity to act "without direct deterrence" by an observer who might intervene, (3) "the expectation of reward . . . either tangible or symbolic" for the criminal act, and (4) the anticipation that the act will go unpunished and undetected.

Even in this insightful analysis little attention is concentrated on the motivational mechanisms involved in criminal conduct. This chapter elucidates a motivational approach to violent behavior that appears broadly applicable in both theoretical studies and empirical research. Violent behavior is an extremely complex, multiaxial phenomenon. To understand its nature one must explore the meaning of violent behavior both for the individual behaving violently and for his or her social environment. The psychological meaning of violent behavior depends upon its overt and covert functions, that is, upon the underlying needs that to some extent are satisfied by, and may be developed through, violent behavior.

An approach previously developed as a methodology for the motivational analysis of sexual behavior (Kon, 1988), psychopathology (Guldan, 1987), and addictive behavior (Nyemchin & Tsytsarev, 1989) appears applicable to the analysis of violent behavior as well. In the United States, a similar approach has been developed by Cox and Klinger (1990). The central concept in this model is *craving*. In earlier research (Nemchin & Tsytsarev, 1989; Boky & Tsytsarev, 1987) it was found that all cravings usually develop along the way as the motivational process unfolds: from the individual's basic *need,* to the *goal object* capable of satisfying it, then to *need satisfaction,* and finally to motivational *tension reduction.*

To be defined as craving, the motivation should meet following requirements:

1. A significantly higher level of *motivational tension* than what the individual typically experiences as affective tension, frustration, discomfort, and the like, such that the basic need produces considerable strain;

2. A great *attractiveness of the goal object* deemed capable of satisfying the need, and a wealth of opportunities to do so;

3. *Two groups of obstacles* impeding access to the goal object: *objective* barriers arising from the overt situation or environment, and *subjective* barriers resulting from personality traits or problems.

If the object is natural and adequate to the need, and if the individual is capable of coping with both objective and subjective obstacles and finally reaches the object of his or her need, then a *normal craving* can be formed. These normal cravings result in real need satisfaction and motivational tension reduction and play a very important role in personality growth because the individual involved is compelled to change either the social environment (coping with objective obstacles) or his or her own personality (coping with subjective obstacles).

If the object is not adequate to the basic need, that is, if the normal object is supplanted by another that is unable to provide real need satisfaction, then a certain discharge of motivational tension associated with the strained need occurs. However, the individual achieves no real satisfaction and becomes frustrated, and the basic frustrated need is repeatedly recycled into a state of tension. In time, the individual is unable to follow a normal course of need satisfaction and gradually becomes dependent upon the substitute object. The motivation underlying such behavior can be defined as an *abnormal craving.*

Within the present model the ultimate goal of the psychological study of violent behavior is the investigation of the various psychological mechanisms involved in the development of violent behavior as well as the basic frustrated needs underlying cravings and related motivations. We must therefore evaluate the subjective and objective meanings of violent behavior and how they derive from the needs being satisfied with violent conduct. From this perspective violent behavior could be considered in the following ways:

1. As a means of *tension reduction:* Anger and violence are elicited by inner impulses that demand to be discharged by any means, and violent behavior is just one possibility.

2. As a means of temporary *self-esteem:* Violence toward others may provide a strong feeling of self-confidence, and even omnipotence and grandiosity.

3. As a means of *emotional state transformation* and *sensation seeking,* obtaining unusual affective experience, escaping from emotional emptiness and boredom.

4. As a means of *compensation* or *substitution:* A profound frustration of any basic need (e.g., the need for love, affiliation, power, or social achievement) results in excessive motivational tension and anger that can be directed toward others or, rarely, at the subject himself.

5. As a means of *communication:* Violence is an integral part of certain specific subcultures (e.g., criminals or drug and alcohol abusers) wherein violent behavior serves as a sign of affiliation with the group and as a means of establishing a hierarchy of interpersonal relations. Moreover, violent, aggressive behavior substantially simplifies the complex emotional relationships within these groups. Physical or psychological violence is commonly employed as a means of *manipulation* of others and is aimed at achieving goals that are otherwise unattainable.

When analyzing different types of violent behavior, it is important to bear in mind that initially some kind of motivation (i.e., one of the basic frustrated needs) plays the role of a psychological predisposition to violent or other abnormal behavior and facilitates violent manifestations. But later, reaching no satisfaction, it may become progressively stronger and result in more intense aggressive or destructive motivations and their respective expressions. Moreover, the individual who becomes accustomed to using violence to "satisfy" one of these needs, thereby reducing the associated tension and frustration, may subsequently employ the same mode of gratification for the remainder of his or her frustrated needs.

Thus, violent behavior may become a "process addiction," as characterized by Schaef and Fassel (1988). Compulsive craving, with massive denial as a prevalent defense mechanism, and confusion, self-centeredness, dishonesty, perfectionism, "frozen feelings," and ethical deterioration (up to spiritual bankruptcy) may predominate. Other significant features may be present as well, including crisis orientation, depression, stress, abnormal thinking processes, forgetfulness, dependency, negativism, defensiveness, projection, tunnel vision, and fear (Schaef, 1987).

The common stereotypes of a society tend to be reflected in the mass media of communication. People prejudiced against one sex, age, ethnic, or social group display some likelihood to be prejudiced against others. This stereotyping of certain groups appears to be similar across the society, among various social groups, and often within the stereotyped group itself. Certain characteristics of those groups are employed to justify violent behavior against them, as is so often the case with ethnic, social, or sexual minorities, for example. Rieber and Kelly (1989) refer to this process of enemy making as "enmification." And indeed, the target of violent behavior, whether a stranger, a relative, or even an offender (as in case of autoaggressive behavior) must have a number of qualities eliciting a fear-hatred feeling. According to Rieber and Kelly (1989), "Enmification is a process that goes beyond objective and historical conditions. It entails psychological processes that run very deep and which rapidly acquire their own momentum. . . . Having an enemy goes far deeper than merely having a competitor or an adversary."

Prevention of violence is clearly one of the major functions of a society and its government and has an obvious presence in most cultures and countries. At the same time, modern history provides a number of examples of violent cultures and subcultures. The dramatic history of Russia from the 1920s through the 1950s, the present criminal terror and the violent ways of doing practically any type of business in the former Soviet Republics, the ruthless ethnic wars, and the penetration of criminal (violent) values into all parts of modern society are perfect examples of the use of violence to solve political, economic, and ethnic problems. Many of the same examples can be found in other cultures in different historical periods (e.g., the United States in the 1920s, Germany in the 1930s and 1940s, Japan in the 1940s, China in the 1960s, and Latin American countries throughout this century, to name just a few).

However, most psychologists do not appear to be interested in the cross-cultural analysis of violent behavior. Even a brief review of the *Journal of Cross-Cultural Psychology* reveals that psychologists would rather concentrate their attention on more "innocent" types of behavior and/or psychological processes rather than on aggression and violence. According to one cross-cultural scientist, John E. Williams, there are at least three reasons why these "mainstreamers" are not as interested in cross-cultural psychology as he thinks they should be.

Some adhere to the view that culture merely provides the contents of psychology; so they are interested in psychological processes that are assumed to operate in a similar manner everywhere. Other psychologists may believe that cultural variables are much more powerful than they are usually found to be and fear that if they attempt to test their pet theory in other cultural contexts it will fall apart and be stripped of its power to explain or predict. Some other mainstreamers may prefer not to be reminded of the sizable similarities in psychological processes across cultural groups because this is taken, incorrectly, as an indication that such similarities must be genetically or biologically based. (Williams, 1991)

At the same time it should be clear that discovering cultural differences and similarities underlying important variations in human behavior across cultures provides priceless information for better understanding the social and psychological meanings of various behaviors within our own cultures and subcultures. Moreover, in conducting empirical cross-cultural research, we construct conceptual bridges between different ethnic schools of psychology and facilitate better understanding among not only interested professionals but also the general population as it is apprised of our research in popular books and journals. This is especially true when we study various forms and motives of violent behavior in different cultures. Unfortunately, there is precious little truly cross-cultural scientific psychological research on these phenomena. We should therefore focus on some methodological issues surrounding research in the field.

From the present psychological perspective, a comparative analysis of violent behavior across cultures should include several critical issues. First of all we must study the specific needs that are "pseudo-satisfied" in violent conduct and that underlie abnormal cravings. We should raise the important question: Are those needs all the same, somewhat similar, or totally different in the cultures being studied and/or compared? We must also examine the nature of the cravings' goal objects. Is the craving solely for a substance (alcohol, drug, etc.) but accompanied by violent conduct, or for the violent, aggressive behavior itself? Further, is the craving associated primarily with certain stable personality traits or with more temporary states?

We must explore the objective obstacles to need gratification that seem to be inviolable in the particular culture or subculture. Depending upon the cultural, social, and economic conditions that prevail, these objective obstacles could be entirely different in various societies. In some cultures, for example, they may act to block higher psychological and/or spiritual needs. This may occur when, for example, access to trustworthy information is quite limited and cognitive needs cannot be satisfied, or when selection of spouses is determined by older relatives and it is impossible for the individual to date and then marry a loved person. Some additional examples include situations where the individual is unable to satisfy his or her affiliation need because of individualistic cultural values or, conversely, where the self-actualization need cannot be satisfied because of pressure from the group-oriented culture, and so forth. In other cultures, objective obstacles might block basic security needs if, for example, food is not available, a personal freedom is in jeopardy, and so on.

We should also be able to describe those personality patterns typical for the particular culture that could be considered major subjective obstacles in the process of normal need gratification. These could include, for example, extremely poor self-esteem, strong dependency needs, and shyness as typical personality patterns in a particular culture or subculture, or narcissism, self-centeredness, and rigidity resulting in chauvinistic attitudes in some other cultural circumstance.

We also need to study the types of objects that are sufficient for the normal need gratification (fulfillment) but are in fact unavailable for subjects displaying violent behavior. Two common avenues are available in different cultures to provide their members with goal objects to satisfy their needs and normal cravings. The first is well known and widely used in free societies wherein individuals are granted access to the choices and opportunities that allow them to fulfill their lives by searching for and finding appropriate goal objects. The second is commonly observed in so-called addicted societies (Shaef, 1987), where various opportunities are replaced by some form of "harmless" substitute such as gambling or excessive work that "pseudo-satisfy" the individual's needs.

We must also identify the psychological qualities of the "satisfaction" achieved with violent acts. According to the Tsytsarev's practical experience with testifying in court on criminal cases, at least 60 percent of perpetrators were unable to explain their violent behavior in rational terms, but upon psychological examination most could describe a variety of emotional states experienced while their violent acts were committed. Numerous studies of the violent offenders (e.g., serial killers) offer such accounts, but curiously, no comparisons across cultures have been included. A cross-cultural analysis of the emotional gratification occurring *before, during,* and *after* such violent acts would seem a timely topic for future research.

We should investigate the culture's or subculture's positive reinforcers (rewards) for violent behavior. One can differentiate several types of cultures with respect to reinforcing violent behavior. Some, which could be termed *repressing violence cultures,* reinforce nonviolent modes of behavior and directly punish or extinguish violent behavior. The alternative type could be termed *permissing violence cultures,* where violent ways of resolving conflicts and achieving goals are highly valued and respected. Between these two extremes are intermediate variations, and in each a certain amount of violent behavior is allowed and positively reinforced under certain circumstances (e.g., military combat, police work, sports, or some workplace activities). Such permitted violence is a ready source for the overwhelming violence in a society where the aforementioned conditions arise; violent behavior serves as a mean of "pseudo-satisfaction" of the frustrated basic needs.

In conclusion, it could be argued that cross-cultural motivational analyses of violent behavior may effectively be employed for understanding the major similarities and differences among cultures and subcultures. Violent behavior reflects many, if not most, of the problems in the societies being explored. Studying violence from the motivational perspective advocated in this chapter would provide us with important information regarding the "psychopathology of everyday life" in different cultures.

REFERENCES

Berelstone, B., & Steiner, G. (1964). *Human behavior: An inventory of scientific findings.* New York: Harcourt, Brace & World.

Boky, I. V., & Tsytsarev, S. V. (1987). Pathological craving for alcohol in alcoholic patients during remissions: A clinical psychological analysis. In I. V. Boky, Rybakova, T. G., & Yeryshev, O. F. (Eds.), *Remission in alcoholism: Collected scientific papers* (pp. 7–19). Leningrad: Bechterev Institute.

Cox, W. M., & Klinger, E. (1990). Incentive motivation, affective change, and alcohol use: A model. In W. Cox (Ed.), *Why people drink: Parameters of alcohol as a reinforcer.* New York: Garden Press.

Forrest, G., & Gordon, R. (1990). *Substance abuse, homicide, and violent behavior.* New York: Gardener Press.

Goodwin, D. W. (1973). Alcohol, suicide and homicide. *Quarterly Journal of Studies on Alcohol, 34,* 144–156.

Guldan, V. (1987). Motivation of criminal behavior in psychopathic individuals. In V. Kudriavtsev (Ed.), *Criminal motivation* (in Russian). Moscow: Nauka (The Science).

Hillbrand, M., Foster, H., Jr., & Hirt, M. (1988). Variables associated with violence in a forensic population. *Journal of Interpersonal Violence, 3,* 371–380.

Kon, I. (1988). *Introduction to sexology* (in Russian). Moscow: Medicina.

Nyemchin, T. A., & Tsytsarev, S. V. (1989). *Personality and alcoholism* (in Russian). Leningrad: Leningrad University Press.

Pallone, N., & Hennessy, J. (1992). *Criminal behavior: A process psychology analysis.* New Brunswick, NJ: Transaction Publishers.

Rieber, R., & Kelly, R. (1989). Substance and shadow: Images of the enemy. In R. Rieber (Ed.), *The psychology of war and peace.* New York: Plenum Press.

Schaef, A. (1987). *When society becomes an addict.* San Francisco: Harper & Row.

Schaef, A., & Fassel, D. (1988). *Addictive organization.* San Francisco: Harper & Row.

Williams, J. E (1991). A note from the incoming editor. *Journal of Cross-Cultural Psychology, 22*(1), 9–10.

2

Machismo Values and Violence in America: An Empirical Study

Robert S. Lee

It has often been noted that the homicide rate for the United States of America is higher than that for any other major industrialized nation.[1] In attempting to understand this phenomenon, it may be useful to examine homicide rates among the various states within the United States, which are far from uniform. In the 1980–84 time period, for example, the state highest in homicide, Texas, had a rate nine times that of the lowest state, North Dakota. Homicides in the United States tend to be committed by offenders who are young (53 percent between age 15 and 29), male (86%), and disproportionately black (49 percent). The average annual black one-on-one homicide rate of 33.10 per 100,000 between 1980 and 1984 was more than seven times that for whites. Most homicide is intraracial, with victims mainly family members (24 percent) or acquaintances (51 percent).[2] Stranger homicide, about half the time connected with another crime, is nearly always committed by males (Bachman-Prehn, Linsky, & Straus, 1988; Straus & Williams, 1988). Homicide rates tend to be especially high in the South, a phenomenon first noted by Redfield in 1880.

COMPETING EXPLANATORY POSITIONS

Attempts to explain homicide in the United States have given rise to a large number of research studies and analyses that focus not so much on individual motivation but on broad social and cultural conditions that might tend to foster or inhibit homicidal acts in a population. The various theories offered generally derive from two often competing explanatory positions—structural versus cultural. The most prominent structural explanation is economic, viewing homicide as a function of severe poverty (Huff-Corzine, Corzine, & Moore, 1991; Loftin & Hill, 1974). The general relationship of homicide and poverty has, of course, been well established but is not very satisfying in terms of the functioning causal dynamics. One attempt to elaborate the relationship puts the emphasis on blocked opportunities, inequality, and a sense of relative deprivation rather than on low income per se as accounting for high homicide rates (Parker, 1989; Williams, 1984). Other investigators see homicide as an outgrowth of stressful life conditions and often make use of a frustration-aggression model to link such conditions to high rates of homicidal behavior (Dollard, 1937; Bachman-Prehn, Linsky, & Straus, 1988; Huff-Corzine, Corzine, & Moore, 1991; Linsky, Straus, & Bachman-Prehn, 1988). High homicide rates in metropolitan areas, especially in central cities, have been noted and analyzed by Crutchfield, Geerken, and Gove (1982), Messner (1982), and Parker (1989).

The cultural approach to explaining violence was initially developed by Wolfgang and Ferracuti in their seminal book *The Subculture of Violence* (1967). These authors postulated that certain segments of society exist with a low threshold or willingness to resort to violence. Within these subcultures are normative supports and values that tolerate or even endorse violent behavior under certain circumstances. Because such violent behavior is not viewed as immoral, those who commit the violence do not have to deal with feelings of guilt about their aggression. Within such subcultures is an increased likelihood that violent impulses will result in homicidal behavior. It should be noted that one cannot define a subculture of violence by simply showing that there is a high level of violence in that subculture. Various structural factors such as poverty, weak social controls, and the widespread availability of guns may be at work. To identify a subculture of violence, we need evidence that links the violence to independent measures of value preferences, norms, attitudes, institutions, and traditions that foster such violence. In this study we shall do this by using a measure of machismo values that will allow us to identify certain states as possessing a machismo subculture. We will then examine both contemporary and historical data connecting this subculture to high levels of homicide and other forms of violence in the United States.

PREVIOUS ATTEMPTS TO CONFIRM
THE SUBCULTURE THESIS

One attempt to test the subculture thesis was a study by Sandra Ball-Rokeach (1973), where the Rokeach values instrument was administered as part of a national sample survey of 1,429 adults. Focusing on the machismo concept, the author postulated that violence can be used as a symbol or defining characteristic of masculinity and that men who identify with machismo values are quick to resort to physical combat as a measure of daring or as a defense of their status or honor. She then went on to define seven values as likely machismo indicators: an exciting life, freedom, pleasure, social recognition, being courageous, independent, and giving low importance to being forgiving. Using an index of past participation in violent episodes (as either assailant or victim), the author found no pattern of convincing evidence that male high participants are more machismo than low participants. She also found no convincing evidence that high participants adhere more to characteristically male values than do low participants. For a more stringent test, the values instrument was administered to 363 imprisoned male felony offenders in Michigan to compare the values profiles of violent crime offenders with the profiles of those convicted of nonviolent crimes. The author found no significant differences in values. Furthermore, there was no compelling evidence even when she compared murderers with those convicted of all other crimes. Rokeach concluded that violent men do not have a stronger commitment than others to machismo values and that her research provides no support for the Wolfgang-Ferracuti culture of violence hypothesis.

Another research attempt to tie violence to culture was based on the hypothesis that a subcultural preference for football in a group or subculture reflects a more general support for violent behavior. To test this, Messner (1981) computed the per capita football player production rate for each state and correlated this with the state's 1970 homicide rate. The correlation was only moderate (r = .25) and dropped to nearly zero when controlling for percent black or percent poor.

Most attempts to link cultural factors to violence, however, have focused on the high homicide rates found in the South. As mentioned above, the extensive literature on this phenomenon goes back over a century to Redfield's (1880) analysis of Northern and Southern homicide rates. Redfield concluded that Southern violence antedated the Civil War. In his 1969 paper "Southern Violence," the historian Sheldon Hackney reviewed the various causal explanations that had been proposed in the scholarly literature to account for the pattern of Southern violence. In his analysis Hackney questions the adequacy of various noncultural explanations such as the rural nature of Southern society, severe child-rearing practices, poverty, anomie, the frustration-aggression hypothesis, and the ready availability of guns. He prefers, instead, a historically based cultural explanation.

In Hackney's view, the South was created by the need to protect what he calls "a peculiar institution" from threats outside the region. He states that

in search for a valid explanation of Southern violence the most fruitful avenue will probably be one that seeks to identify and trace the development of a Southern world view that defines the social, political, and physical environment as hostile and casts the white Southerner in the role of the passive victim of malevolent forces. When scholars locate the values that make up this world view and the process by which it was created and is transmitted, the history of the South will undoubtedly prove to have played a major role. The un-American experiences of guilt, defeat, and poverty will be major constituents of the relevant version of that history, but perhaps they will not loom so large as the sense of grievance that is at the heart of the Southern identity. (Hackney, 1969, p. 401)

Hackney agrees with Dollard (1937, Ch. 3) that as black aggression against whites was extremely dangerous, frustrated blacks committed violence against other blacks. Looking toward future scholarship on Southern white violence, Hackney stresses the need for survey data on attitudes toward violence, perceptions of the environment, feelings of efficacy, and other measures of alienation.

Following up on Hackney's focus on the South, Gastil (1971) argued that Southern culture accounts for most of the difference in homicide rates between the United States and comparable countries such as Canada and Australia. He claimed that the U.S.A. rate for whites alone in 1966 was about three times what we should expect in terms of the general experience of the developed world (p. 413). Gastil further argued that the "Southernness" of a state's culture was a more important causal influence than various socioeconomic factors and that this culture, which was already developed before 1850, has been spreading via Southern migration throughout the country. To test this regional subculture of violence thesis, Gastil developed an index of Southernness to measure the extent of Southern influence on a state's culture. Based primarily on the percentage of the population born in the South, Gastil also took into account historical information about state elites, as well as religious and linguistic considerations. Each state was given a Southernness rating on a six-step scale with scores ranging from five for the least Southern states to thirty for states under overwhelming Southern influence. As Gastil did not provide detailed rules as to how he classified the fifty states, his Southernness Index cannot be validated or updated. Gastil then performed various multiple-regression analyses on 1960 homicide data controlling for a variety of structural variables. He concluded that "the degree of 'Southernness' in the culture of the population of the states accounts for more of the variation in homicide rates than do other factors such as income, education, percent urban, or age. It is suggested that high homicide rates in the United States today are related primarily to the persistence of Southern cultural traditions developed before the Civil War and subsequently spreading over much of the country" (Gastil, 1971, p. 412).

Loftin and Hill (1974) severely criticized the Gastil-Hackney methodology and presented a replication of Gastil's study using improved measurement and control procedures. Their results strongly favored a structure of poverty explanation for Southern violence. Gastil's Southernness Index showed no relationship to homicide independent of the effects of situational variables. Interestingly, however, because culture cannot simply be equated with region, the authors did not conclude that the subculture of violence thesis was refuted. They noted that *neither* study made use of an independent measure of culture and that "unless culture can be measured distinctly and independently of region, the validity of our studies will always be threatened" (p. 723). This point has been made time and again by other researchers even when they too find themselves trying to test the regional subculture of violence thesis without being able to make use of a direct measure of culture.[3]

The study by Baron and Straus (1988) is a notable exception. These authors attempted to develop a direct measure of a state's cultural support for violence— the Legitimate Violence Index. No previous study of homicide rates employed a measure of cultural support for violence that is conceptually and empirically independent of Southern region. Components of the index include circulation rates of magazines that feature violence, ratings of violent TV shows, the existence of laws permitting corporal punishment by school teachers, death sentences per 100 people arrested for homicide, executions per 100 homicide arrests, hunting licenses per 1,000 population, number of college football players produced per 100,000 population, National Guard enrollment per 100,000, National Guard expenditures per capita, and lynchings per million during the years 1882–1927. The alpha reliability of the index is .72.

Using multiple regression, the authors presented results showing that the Legitimate Violence Index is a significant predictor of homicide once the effects of situational variables like poverty, income inequality, percent black, family integration, percent age 18–24, and Confederate South are held constant. Urbanity, poverty, and income inequality were also shown to have independent predictive power. The Confederate South dummy variable, however, had no significant independent relationship with homicide rate. Furthermore, as a straightforward comparison shows the West to have a higher level of acceptance of legitimate violence than the South, the authors concluded that their study provides no support for a distinctive Southern culture of violence. The Baron and Straus study was strongly attacked by Gilles, Brown, Geletta, and Dalecki (1990), who questioned the validity of six of the twelve components used to construct the Legitimate Violence Index. For example, they questioned the idea of including the hunting license measure and the duplicative use of two highly correlated National Guard variables, enrollment and expenditures. They also strongly criticized Baron and Straus for their selection of control variables. (See Straus & Baron, 1990, for a rejoinder to these criticisms.)

At this point it seems fair to conclude that research on the hypothesized Southern subculture of violence had become a quagmire. Some researchers used states as the unit of analysis, whereas others used metropolitan area or county data. Some measured Southernness simply as membership in the old Confederacy, whereas others preferred Gastil's Southernness Index or percent born in the South. There were strong disagreements about the choice of control variables and how to construct indices. Findings about the existence of Southern regional effects beyond structural factors were inconsistent. And although there has been strong consensus on the need for independent measures of cultural factors to properly test the subculture hypothesis, the one team that tried to do this was strongly criticized for methodological inadequacies.

Despite all this, recent work by Nisbett and his associates at the University of Michigan is especially promising and may finally clarify our understanding of Southern violence. Going beyond the analysis of various homicide statistics, the Michigan researchers made use of attitude studies and also conducted controlled laboratory experiments. Their findings are that Southerners are more inclined than others not toward violence in general but specifically where issues of protection or insult are involved. Nisbett concludes that Southern violence is rooted in a "culture of honor" that is especially characteristic of rural Southern whites (Nisbett, 1993).

THE MEASUREMENT OF MACHISMO

In the following sections, we shall examine machismo as a subcultural factor and its relationship to homicide. The measure of machismo we shall use for this analysis is taken from a factor analytic study that investigated variation in magazine circulation rates across the fifty states (Lee, forthcoming). The dataset used in the factor analysis consists of state circulation figures on forty-eight magazines as certified for the years 1983 or 1986 by the Audit Bureau of Circulations and expressed as rates—usually circulation per 100,000 population. On the basis of a scree analysis (Cattell, 1966), three factors were extracted using the principal components method with oblimin rotation. The three factors account for 72 percent of the total variance.

The first factor, titled Urbane Cultivated Interests, is represented by magazines such as *Business Week, House and Garden, Vanity Fair, Gourmet,* and *New Yorker.* Factor 2, Mainstream Magazine Readership, identifies broader-interest, very high circulation mass-audience magazines such as *Reader's Digest, Mc-Calls,* and *Good Housekeeping.* For the purpose of the present study however, our interest centers on Factor 3, which we shall call Machismo. This factor is dominated by magazines such as *Shooting Times, Playboy, Cosmopolitan,* and *Muscle and Fitness,* where physical strength, self-defense, weapons, combat, and sex are prominent themes. There are overtones here of toughness, self-sufficiency, independence, and individualism. Table 2.1 lists the magazines with loadings of .60 or higher on the factor. Standardized factor scores with a mean of zero and a standard deviation of one were computed based on factor score coefficients for all forty-eight magazines. Machismo scores for each of the fifty states are given in Table 2.2.[4]

The map in Figure 2.1 and the variables shown to be strongly correlated with Machismo in the previous study portray the classical U.S. American West: vast spaces, high elevation, low population density, many states with an arid climate, an influx of newcomers, boomtown conditions, much drinking in bars, a shortage of women, and the presence of Indians. The states that score one standard deviation or more above the mean are Alaska, Nevada, Hawaii, Wyoming, New Mexico, Colorado, and Arizona.[5] The correlation between Machismo scores and years since admission to statehood is −.76. The frontier spirit is evidently still with us, but in modern form.

The high associations of Factor 3 with *Cosmopolitan* and *Playgirl* as well as *Playboy* and *Penthouse* magazines suggest that the relations between the sexes may be more eroticized in the high-Machismo states than in states with lower scores on this factor. It is possible that women as well as men in the high-scoring states might exhibit Machismo values. Governor Ann Richards of Texas, when speaking of President George Bush and Ross Perot in May 1992 was

Table 2.1
Magazines with Loadings of .60 or Higher on Factor 3: Machismo

Magazine	Factor loading
Shooting Times	.84
Muscle & Fitness	.79
Consumers Digest	.78
Azimov's SF + Analog groups	.77
Motor Home	.77
Penthouse	.75
Playboy	.72
Car Craft	.66
Cosmopolitan	.65

Note: The previous study documents a shortage of housing in the high Factor 3 states as indicated by an influx of newcomers, crowded living conditions, high home values, much new home construction, and high sales of major appliances. This may explain why *Motor Homes* and *Consumer's Digest* have high loadings on the factor. It should be noted that *Car Craft* frequently displays a shapely young female as well as a "muscle car" on its cover. Data on a few magazines became available after the factor analysis was completed. *Survive!* has a correlation of +.82 with Factor 3 scores, *Soldier of Fortune* has a correlation of +.76, and *Playgirl* has a correlation of +.79.

quoted by the *New York Times* as saying, "They will try to out-tough each other. You have to prove your manhood down here whether you're a man or a woman, let me tell you" ("Quotation of the Day," 1992).

The previous study also found that the high-scoring states show many signs of anomie—"a state of society in which normative standards of conduct are weak or lacking" (*Webster's New Collegiate Dictionary, 1977*). (See also Durkheim, 1897 [1951]; Merton, 1938; and Pope, 1976.) There are many attributes that make for weakened social ties—conditions likely to produce less connectedness, more fragile relationships, less commitment, and less social support. Critical institutions of social control, the family and the church, are weak. Finally in high-Machismo states there appears to be a tradition of lawlessness, including a history of vigilante justice (Brown, 1969; Frantz, 1969).

Table 2.2
Homicide Rates and Scores on Machismo and Gross Deprivation

Avg. Homicide Rate 1980 - 1984		Machismo		Gross Deprivation	
TX	15.4	AK	4.27	MS	2.73
LA	14.9	NV	2.47	LA	2.14
NV	14.9	WY	2.06	SC	1.74
AK	13.6	HW	1.54	GA	1.64
FL	13.1	CO	1.23	NM	1.59
MS	12.4	NM	1.16	AL	1.53
GA	12.3	AZ	1.03	AZ	1.30
CA	12.0	ID	0.83	FL	1.16
NY	11.5	OR	0.80	AR	0.96
AL	10.9	TX	0.78	AK	0.94
NM	10.8	MT	0.76	NC	0.89
SC	10.3	WA	0.69	TX	0.88
IL	9.7	OK	0.60	TN	0.82
MI	9.7	CA	0.57	NY	0.66
TN	9.5	LA	0.52	KY	0.53
MO	9.3	FL	0.46	VA	0.30
MD	9.2	UT	0.41	IL	0.19
NC	9.1	WV	0.11	CA	0.18
OK	9.0	KS	0.03	MD	0.03
KY	8.7	AL	-0.10	OK	0.00
AR	8.3	AR	-0.13	MO	-0.05

Table 2.2 (Continued)

Avg. Homicide Rate 1980 - 1984		Machismo		Gross Deprivation	
AZ	8.3	GA	-0.13	WV	-0.05
VA	7.9	SD	-0.16	DE	-0.16
IN	6.6	MS	-0.18	MI	-0.19
IA	6.6	ND	-0.28	NJ	-0.20
CO	6.6	IN	-0.29	SD	-0.21
OH	6.5	KY	-0.37	MT	-0.29
NJ	6.3	SC	-0.38	NV	-0.39
WY	6.0	MI	-0.38	IN	-0.40
PA	5.6	MO	-0.42	OH	-0.42
KS	5.6	TN	-0.43	PA	-0.45
WV	5.5	DE	-0.45	ID	-0.47
DE	5.4	NC	-0.45	OR	-0.49
HW	5.1	OH	-0.45	ME	-0.60
WA	4.9	NE	-0.48	MA	-0.64
CT	4.7	MD	-0.48	CT	-0.70
OR	4.7	VA	-0.48	WA	-0.73
MT	3.9	IL	-0.53	WY	-0.75
MA	3.7	PA	-0.71	RI	-0.77
RI	3.7	IA	-0.72	VT	-0.84
ID	3.4	WI	-0.74	CO	-0.85
UT	3.4	MN	-0.75	NE	-0.92

Table 2.2 (Continued)

Avg. Homicide Rate 1980 - 1984		Machismo		Gross Deprivation	
NE	3.1	NJ	-0.99	KS	-0.92
VT	2.9	RI	-1.18	UT	-1.06
WI	2.9	NY	-1.24	WI	-1.08
ME	2.4	ME	-1.31	IA	-1.25
NH	2.1	NH	-1.33	NH	-1.29
MN	2.1	VT	-1.41	ND	-1.32
SD	1.8	CT	-1.67	HW	-1.33
ND	1.7	MA	-1.71	MN	-1.40

As can be seen in Table 2.3, high-Machismo states are above average in crime, especially burglary, rape, and larceny.[6] Internal Revenue Service (IRS) tax audits are exceptionally high. More strikingly, Machismo correlates strongly with many forms of deaths by violence including homicide, accidental deaths, suicide, police deaths in line of duty, white lynchings per million during the years 1882–1927, and black lynchings during that same time period. In addition to such behavioral data, we also have attitudinal evidence for the connection between Machismo and violence. Through a special arrangement with the National Opinion Research Center (NORC), Baron and Straus (1989, pp. 91, 166–68) were able to obtain survey interview data by state for the years 1972–84 from the General Social Survey (GSS) (Davis & Smith, 1985).[7] Using a cumulation of data on approximately 15,000 respondents, the authors constructed a Violence Approval Index based on fourteen questions in the annual survey. Item responses counted in this index include support for the death penalty, opposition to gun controls, support for increased military spending, and approval of hitting another person under a variety of different circumstances. The alpha reliability coefficient of this Violence Approval Index is .68. Table 2.3 shows that state scores on this attitudinal index correlate .66 with Machismo. The

Figure 2.1
Standardized Scores on Machismo

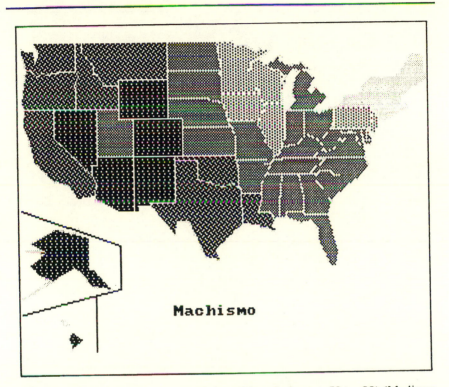

Machismo

Legend: (Darkest shade: +1.0 or higher) (Next darkest: +.50 to .99) (Medium: −.49 to +.49) (Next lightest: −.50 to −.99) (Lightest: −1.0 or lower)

authors also constructed a Violent Behavior Index based on items indicating that the respondent engaged in or was the victim of violent behavior such as beating or being punched, threatened with a gun, or shot at and whether the respondent uses or owns firearms. This index has an alpha reliability coefficient of .85 (Baron & Straus, 1989, p. 91). In Table 2.3 we report a correlation of .62 between the Violence Behavior Index and Machismo.

Although we have demonstrated many strong associations between Factor 3, Machismo, and indicators of crime, violence, and lawlessness, we have yet to establish that the relationship with violence is independent of structural factors such as poverty and race. That is the task of the next section of this chapter, where the focus is on homicide.

Table 2.3
Correlates of Machismo with Various Indicators of Crime,
Violence, and Lawlessness

Variable	r	r with log tranform of variable
Homicide (1980-84 avg.)	.42**	.39**
One-on-one homicide (1980-84 avg.)	.38**	.36**
Family	.43**	.43**
Acquaintance	.38	.34
Stranger	.26	.33
Whites	.61**	.57**
Blacks	.31	.13
Crime rate (1982)	.42**	.37**
Burglary	.74**	.69**
Larceny	.53**	.46**
Rape	.67**	.54**
Homicide	.47**	.40**
Assault	.29	.28
Robbery	.02	.08
Auto theft	.00	.09
IRS tax audits (1984)	.74**	.69**
Machine guns/1,000 (1985)	.59**	.48**

Table 2.3 (Continued)

Variable	r	r with log tranform of variable
Suicide (1980)	.73**	.72**
Accidental deaths (1978)	.68**	.66**
Police deaths/1,000 police (1975-85)	.37**	.44**
Lynchings per million (1882-1927)	.59**	.76**
White lynchings	.73**	.82**
Black lynchings	.54**	.46**
Violence Approval Index	.66**	
Violence Behavior Index	.62**	

Note: Data were available for fewer than 50 states for the following variables: Accidental Deaths (49), Total, White, and Black Lynchings (48), Violence Approval and Violence Behavior Indexes (40).

** $p \leq .01$

HOMICIDE AND THE VARIOUS CONTROL MEASURES

Our measure of homicide for this analysis is the average annual homicide rate for the years 1980–84 based on data published annually by the Federal Bureau of Investigation (FBI) in the *Unified Crime Reports for the U.S.* (See Table 2.2 for state homicide rates.) By covering a five-year period we can minimize data unreliability as well as provide year-to-year transient variations. We also make supplemental use of one-on-one homicide data for 1980–84 compiled by the

State and Regional Indicators Archive at the Family Research Laboratory, University of New Hampshire, NH 03824 (Straus & Williams, 1988). This dataset provides state homicide rates separately for whites and blacks as well as for family homicide, acquaintance homicide, and stranger homicide. Looking at these rates by region, the top chart in Figure 2.2 shows that the South is markedly high in homicide, with the West being a strong second.[8] The lower-left chart shows that for whites, the West and the South have much higher homicide rates than the remaining regions, with the West being highest. The lower-right chart shows comparable data for black homicide, with the West standing out as being much higher than any other region including the South. In other words, the South has the highest overall homicide rate, yet for each race separately the highest region is the West, not the South. The explanation for this is that blacks who generally have much higher homicide rates than whites make up a higher proportion of the population in the South than in other regions. This was first reported by O'Carroll and Mercy (1989), whose findings as well as ours point to the West as a region likely to have a subculture of violence.[9]

The following variables are included as control measures in our more rigorous analysis of the relationship between Machismo and homicide:

Gross Deprivation: This index, designed by us to get at more than just the lack of financial resources, was developed to be a general measure of gross deprivation and impoverished living. In addition to poverty, measures of bad health, poor education, and undesirable family life circumstances are included as index components. The following variables were used to construct the index: percentage of families below the poverty line, gastritis/enteritis deaths per 100,000, male life expectancy, percent age 18 completed high school, median nonwhite/white school years completed, percent households with more than 1.01 persons per room, and percent births to unwed mothers. The alpha reliability of the measure is .91. Table 2.2 gives the scores for each of the states.[10]

Metro Urban Percent: This variable is a measure of the percentage of the state's population living in Standard Metropolitan Statistical Areas (SMSAs) as reported by the 1980 census. We include it as a control because of the many reports of high homicide rates in large metropolitan areas. Possible reasons given for this relationship are the crowding, stress, anonymity, nonconformist lifestyles, and alienation said to characterize big city life.

Percent Black: This variable, also from the 1980 census, allows us to take into account the exceptionally high homicide rates for blacks.

Southernness: This is the six-step measure developed by Gastil (1971) that rates the extent to which a state is under Southern cultural influence. Despite its shortcomings, this variable is, in our opinion, conceptually superior to a crude Confederate/Non-Confederate dummy variable. Also in its favor is the finding by Huff-Corzine et al. (1986, p. 919) that Gastil's Southernness scale is a more consistent predictor of homicides than percent born in the South.

The four control variables described above form the basic set used in the regression analyses to follow. Table 2.4 gives the intercorrelations of Machismo, homicide, and the various control measures used in the analyses.

Figure 2.2
State One-on-One Homicide Rates, 1980–84, by Region

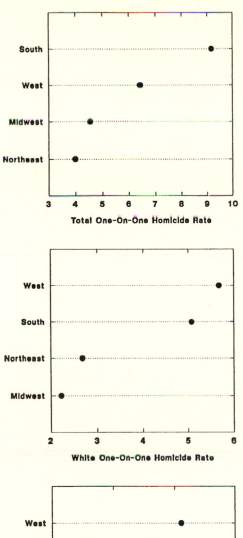

Total One-On-One Homicide Rate

White One-On-One Homicide Rate

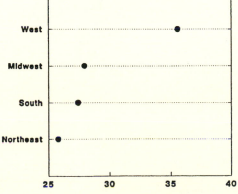

Black One-On-One Homicide Rate

Table 2.4
Correlations among Variables Used in the Regression Analysis

Variable	1	2	3	4	5	6
1. †Homicide 1980-84	1	.766**	.773**	.413**	.749**	.390**
2. Gross Deprivation	.766**	1	.621**	.097	.764**	.183
3. †Percent Black	.773**	.621**	1	.616**	.590**	−.087
4. †Metro Urban Percent	.413**	.097	.616**	1	.152	−.088
5. Southerness	.749**	.764**	.590**	.152	1	.357
6. Machismo	.390**	.183	−.087	−.088	.357	1

Note: Variables marked with a dagger (†) are log transformations.

** $p \leq .01$

CONTROL SET REGRESSION ANALYSIS

As indicated, the main purpose of the regression analysis is to find out whether the relationship we have shown between the cultural variable Machismo and homicide is independent of the control set structural variables: Gross Deprivation, Percent Black, Metro Urban Percent, and Southernness. This analysis makes use of the incremental variance approach developed by Cohen and Cohen and follows their recommendation to use transformed versions of all variables that are proportions, including percentages and rates (Cohen & Cohen, 1983, pp. 265–270).[11]

Table 2.5 shows that the four control variables as a set account for 77.3 percent of the variation in state homicide rates. When Machismo is added to these four variables in the regression equation, 86.8 percent of the homicide variance is accounted for—Machismo uniquely adds a substantial and significant 9.5 percent. This means that the association between the cultural variable Machismo and homicide holds even when the four structural variables are held constant. Southernness adds no significant unique variance.

In addition, we extended this analysis to all the crime, violence, and lawlessness variables listed previously in Table 2.3. The results show that Machismo adds significant additional variance at the .01 level for twenty of the twenty-five dependent variables. It is clear from this analysis that Machismo as a cul-

Table 2.5
Homicide Rate 1980–1984 Regression Analysis: Control Variables and Machismo

Variable	Standardized β weight	T (df=44)
Gross Deprivation	.338	3.532**
†Percent Black	.512	4.686**
†Metro Urban Percent	.091	1.140
Southerness	.045	0.462
Machismo	.364	5.638**

R² Control set + Machismo	.8680
R² Control set only	.7726
Unique variance added by Machismo	.0954

Note: The dependent homicide variable as well as the variables marked with a dagger (†) are log transformations.

** p ≤ .01

tural factor is substantially associated with crime, violence, and lawlessness independently of the structural control variables. Yet the close association between Machismo and violence may still not be independent of other social conditions. As documented in the previous study, high-Machismo states show strong signs of a frontier heritage and anomie—there are many signs of poor social integration and weakened social controls. The high-Machismo states typically have a great influx of newcomers, a high ratio of males to females, a high proportion of males living in households without a female present, high receipts per capita for drinking establishments, a high divorce rate, and a low rate of church membership. In a follow-up study we will test the hypothesis that it is these underlying anomic social conditions more than Machismo itself that account for the high homicide rates and other forms of crime, violence, and lawlessness found in these areas.

NOTES

A monograph version of this chapter has been prepared that includes data sources, more detailed information on the variables, and regression analysis tables for all twenty-five dependent variables studied. This document as well as a copy of the previous study on regional subcultures can be obtained by writing to Dr. Robert S. Lee, Pace University (LSB), One Pace Plaza, New York, NY 10038.

1. For comparative homicide rates for various countries, see the *United Nations 1990 Demographic Yearbook* (1992), Table 21, pp. 454–472.

2. These percentages are based on one-on-one homicides for the average year between 1980 and 1984 as compiled by the *State and Regional Indicators Archive* at the Family Research Laboratory, University of New Hampshire, Durham, NH 03824. (See Straus & Williams, 1988.)

3. See Baron & Straus (1988); Gilles, Brown, Geletta, & Dalecki (1990); Huff-Corzine, Corzine, & Moore (1986); Linsky, Straus, & Bachman-Prehn (1988); Messner (1983); Williams (1984); Parker (1989).

4. One must be careful to avoid stereotypes. Many if not most people in high-Machismo states may not exhibit Machismo values, attitudes, and behavior. The subculture may be carried by only a minority of the population. The same caveat, of course, applies to high-crime states or even the highest-crime neighborhoods of large cities where offenders may be only a small but critical segment of the population.

5. Hawaii does not have some of the frontierlike attributes generally associated with states high on this factor. Although as in other high-scoring states, Hawaii has an influx of newcomers, a young population, and more males than females; the land is not sparsely populated, and the industry pattern and the climate are quite different. Burglary, larceny, and federal tax audits are above average in Hawaii as in other high-Machismo states— but the homicide rate is uncharacteristically low. It is possible that the machismo subculture in Hawaii may be largely a function of the strong military presence there. If so, machismo involvement with violence would be institutionalized rather than expressed in socially proscribed homicidal acts.

6. In addition to standard correlations, Table 2.3 shows correlations with log transformed versions of all listed variables that are percentages or rates. These log transformed variables will be used in the regression analysis to follow.

7. NORC does not normally make GSS data available in this form. The survey is designed to provide a nationally or regional representative sample of the United States rather than projectable samples for each state. Because of this, only the forty states required by the sample design are available in the cumulative GSS file used by Baron and Straus. It should be noted that even though the total number of cases is very large, the number of respondents for the smaller states tends to be low.

8. The datapoints plotted in Figure 2.2 are mean state rates for the region.

9. Kowalski and Petee (1991, p. 76) also question the assertion that the Southern region dominates in homicide rates.

10. The original idea was to use two indicators each from the economic, health, education, and family life domains. The 1980 unemployment measure was dropped, however, as it noticeably lowered reliability. Log transformations were used for the following variables to avoid undue influence of outlier datapoints: gastritis/enteritis deaths, percent households with >1.01 persons per room, and percent births to unwed mothers. All variables were standardized in Z-score form. The signs for male life expectancy and both education measures were then reflected. Following this, a sum was computed and was itself standardized to form the final measure.

11. The authors point out that the unit of measurement for proportions is almost never constant over the scale. Citing an unpublished paper by Tukey, they note that the .04 difference between .01 and .05 is much more important than the .04 difference between .48 and .52 "for almost all purposes except winning elections" (Cohen & Cohen, 1963, p. 263). The use of log transformations in our analysis was strongly recommended by Jacob Cohen in a personal communication on September 17, 1992. We will therefore use log normal versions for all percent and rate variables included in the regression analyses. For those few variables where a state has a zero rate or percentage, as it is not possible to compute a log, the state was assigned a value halfway between zero and the next highest rate before computing the transformation. We consider this preferable to dropping such states from the analysis.

REFERENCES

Bachman-Prehn, Linsky, A. S., & Straus, M. A. (1988). *Homicide of family members, acquaintances, and strangers, and state-to-state differences in social stress, social control and social norms.* Unpublished manuscript, University of New Hampshire, Family Research Laboratory, Durham.

Ball-Rokeach, S. J. (1973). Values and violence: A test of the subculture of violence thesis. *American Sociological Review, 38,* 736–749.

Baron, L., & Straus, M. A. (1988). Cultural and economic sources of homicide in the United States. *Sociological Quarterly, 29*(3), 371–390.

Baron, L., & Straus, M. A. (1989). *Four theories of rape in American society.* New Haven, CT: Yale University Press.

Brown, R. (1969). The American vigilante tradition. In H. D. Graham & T. R. Gurr (Eds.), *Violence in America* (pp. 184–218). New York: Signet.

Cattell, R. B. (1966). The scree test for the number of factors. *Multivariate Behavioral Research, 1,* 140–161.

Cohen, J., & Cohen, P. (1983). *Applied multiple regression/correlation analysis for the behavioral sciences* (2d ed.). Hillsdale, NJ: Erlbaum.

Crutchfield, R. D., Geerken, M. R., & Gove, W. A. (1982). Crime rate and social integration. *Criminology, 20,* 467–478.

Davis, J. A., & Smith, T. (1985). *General Social Surveys, 1972–1984: Cumulative codebook.* National Opinion Research Center, University of Chicago.

Dollard, J. (1937). *Caste and caste in a Southern town.* New Haven, CT: Yale University Press.

Durkheim, E. (1897). *Suicide.* Glencoe, IL: Free Press (1951).

Frantz, J. B. (1969). The frontier tradition: An invitation to violence. In H. D. Graham & T. R., Gurr (Eds.). *Violence in America* (pp. 101–119). New York: Signet.

Gastil, R. D. (1971). Homicide and a regional culture of violence. *American Sociological Review, 36,* 412–427.

Gilles, J. L., Brown, R. B., Geletta, S. B., & Dalecki, M. G. (1990). Legitimate violence or agoraphobia? Re-examining the Legitimate Violence Index. *Sociological Quarterly, 31*(4), 613–618.

Hackney, S. (1969). Southern violence. In H. G. Graham & T. R. Gurr (Eds.), *The history of violence in America* (pp. 387–404). New York: Bantam.

Huff-Corzine, L. Corzine, J., & Moore, D. C. (1986). Southern exposure: Deciphering the South's influence on homicide rates. *Social Forces, 64*(2), 906–924.

Huff-Corzine, L., Corzine, J., & Moore, D. C. (1991). Deadly connections: Culture, poverty, and direction of lethal violence. *Social Forces, 69*(3), 715–732.

Kowalski, G. S., & Petee, T. A. (1991). Sunbelt effects on homicide rates. *Sociology and Social Research,* No. 75, 73–79.

Lee, R. S. (forthcoming). Regional subcultures as revealed by magazine circulation patterns. *Cross-Cultural Research.*

Linsky, A. S., Straus, M. A., & Bachman-Prehn, R. (1988). *Social stress, legitimate violence, and gun availability.* Family Research Laboratory, University of New Hampshire, Durham.

Loftin, C., & Hill, R. H. (1974). Regional subculture and homicide: An examination of the Gastil-Hackney thesis. *American Sociological Review, 39,* 714–724.

Merton, R. K. (1938). Social structure and anomie. *American Sociological Review, 3,* 672–682.

Messner, S. F. (1981). Football and homicide: Searching for the subculture of violence. In S. L. Greendorfer (Ed.), *Sociology of sport: Diverse perspectives* (pp. 53–60). West Point, NY: Leisure Press.

Messner, S. F. (1982). Poverty, inequality, and the urban homicide rate. *Criminology, 20,* 103–114.

Messner, S. F. (1983). Regional and racial effects on the urban homicide rate: The subculture of violence revisited. *American Journal of Sociology, 88*(5), 997–1007.

Nisbett, R. (1993). Violence and U.S. regional culture. *American Psychologist, 48,* 441–449.

O'Carroll, P. W., & Mercy, J. A. (1989). Regional variation in homicide rates: Why is the *West* so violent? *Violence and Victims, 4*(1), 17–25.

Parker, R. N. (1989). Poverty, subculture of violence, and type of homicide. *Social Forces, 67*(4), 983–1007.

Pope, W. (1976). *Durkheim's "Suicide": A classic analyzed.* Chicago: University of Chicago Press.

Quotation of the Day. (1992, June 8). *New York Times,* p. A2.

Redfield, H. V. (1880). *Homicide, North and South.* Philadelphia: Lippincott.

Straus, M. A., & Baron, L. (1990). The strength of weak indicators: A response to Gilles, Brown, Geletta, and Dalecki. *Sociological Quarterly, 31*(4), 619–624.

Straus, M. A., & Williams, K. R. (1988). *Homicide victimization and offense rates by age, gender, race relation of victim to offender, weapon used, and circumstances, for the United States, 1976–79 and 1980–84.* Family Research Laboratory, University of New Hampshire, Durham.

Unified Crime Reports for the U.S. (1981–85). Washington, DC: U.S. Department of Justice.

United Nations 1990 demographic yearbook. (1992). New York: United Nations.

Webster's New Collegiate Dictionary. (1977). Springfield: G. & C. Merriam.

Williams, K. R. (1984). Economic sources of homicide: Reestimating the effects of poverty and inequality. *American Sociological Review, 49,* 283–289.

Wolfgang, M. E., & Ferracuti, F. (1967). *The subculture of violence: Towards an integrated theory in criminology.* London: Tavistock.

3

Assessment of Attitudes toward Terrorism

Harold Takooshian and William M. Verdi

Throughout the 1980s, acts of terrorism were reported almost daily in the media (Jones, 1989). Sadly, this trend continues unabated into the 1990s and crosses all continents—from Bosnia to Rwanda, from Medellin to the World Trade Center. In a one-month period in April 1994 world media reported on the assassination of Mexico's leading presidential candidate, terror campaigns against civilians in Rwanda, car bombings during the elections in South Africa, continued ethnic cleansing in Bosnia, an Israeli physician's massacre of those praying in a West Bank mosque, and the conviction of the bombers of the World Trade Center in 1993.[1]

To the extent that civilian men, women, and children are terrorists' favorite victims, it is natural to expect the civilian public to fear and loathe such terrorists. But is this the case? The in-depth review by Leonard Weinberg and Paul Davis (1989) finds: "If the point of . . . [terrorist violence] is to influence public opinion, the logical question to ask is: What reactions does the public have to the images of terrorist violence to which it has been exposed? Surprisingly, there are few studies that attempt to address this question in a systematic way" (p. 133).

Indeed, among the pollsters and social scientists who write most about public opinion on the problem of rising terrorism, psychologists seem conspicuous by their relative absence (Schmid, 1983). Note, for example, the recent volume of *Measures of personality and social psychological attitudes* (Robinson, Shaver, & Wrightsman, 1991); its 170 scales assess many forms of sociopathy (alienation, authoritarianism, dogmatism, loneliness, machiavellianism, etc.), yet none assesses our attitudes toward violence, including terrorism. One reason for this dearth of research by psychologists is the difficulty in assessing attitudes toward violence in general. One review concluded that psychological measurement difficulties have caused "empirical quantification of hostile feelings, aggressive behaviors, and attitudes toward violence [to lag] behind the development of theory'' on issues involving violence (Velicer, Huckel, & Hansen, 1989, p. 349).

The aim of the present research was threefold: (1) to develop a brief scale to assess one's attitudes toward terrorism (or ''AT''), which might be useful to chart shifts in public attitudes across time and place; (2) to determine the psychometric soundness of this AT scale, using standard indicators of reliability and validity; (3) to suggest further research possibilities in this area.

METHOD

Materials. The authors reviewed several sources to generate a sizable pool of potential items for an AT scale. These sources included writings on the general nature of terrorism, as well as Walter Lang's (1987) encyclopedic overview of the hundreds of specific terrorist groups of the 1980s. This resulted in a pool of some 100 potential items. From these, fifteen items were extracted, to tap three facets of one's attitudes toward terrorism: the concept itself, its effectiveness, and the sort of people who rely on it. These fifteen items were embedded in a larger thirty-six-item survey containing three other brief, five-item scales: authoritarianism, dogmatism, and religiosity. (See Appendix 1.) Each scale item was scored from 0 to 4 points in a Likert-type Agree/Disagree format, so the resulting scale scores could vary from 0 to 60 for AT, and 0 to 20 for authoritarianism, dogmatism, and religiosity.

Respondents. The scale was completed by a sample of convenience of 54 undergraduate students at two universities (Pace and Fordham). It was also completed by 54 law enforcement personnel, including 30 New York Police Department uniformed officers and 24 managers from several federal and local agencies enrolled in a workshop on hostage negotiation techniques. In addition to these student and professional samples, a special effort was made to sample the opinions of three U.S. American nationality groups recently associated with terrorism: Armenians, Iranians, and Irish (Lang, 1987); this attempt yielded a sufficient number of responses from one of these three groups, namely, fifty-five Armenian Americans.[2]

RESULTS

Responses from the 54 professionals and 54 students indeed revealed a strikingly wide range of attitudes on the fifteen terrorism questions. On the 0–60-point AT scale, individuals' scores varied fully from 0 to 55 among the 108 respondents, with near identical means of 24.6 for the students and 25.4 for the law enforcement personnel, as detailed in Table 3.1, which arranges the fifteen AT items in descending order of their correlations with the total AT scores. Among both civilians and law enforcement, there is not a uniform abhorrence of terrorism but, rather, a diversity of opinion that at least occasionally ranges into acceptance or even support of it. Still, we must probe further into these

Table 3.1
Mean Per-item Scores on the Fifteen-Item Terrorism Scale (0–4), Comparing the Responses of 54 Law Enforcement Professionals and 54 Students

	Law enforcement	Students	Corrected item-total correlation
1. It is sometimes understandable if people resort to terrorism as their only way to be heard.	1.2	1.2	.64
2. Terrorists must be considered the enemy of civilized society, regardless of their motives.	0.8	0.8	.60
3. Only a cruel, cowardly group would resort to terrorism to achieve its goals.	1.8	1.7	.59
4. Most terrorists seem like disturbed people who would act violent even in an ideal society.	1.6	1.7	.59
5. Terrorism is sometimes morally justified.	1.1	1.0	.57
Total score on the brief five-item AT-scale:	6.5	6.7	alpha= .79

Table 3.1 (Continued)

6.	I'd say many so-called "terrorists" are courageous people who are ready to die for their cause.	1.6	1.3	.56
7.	Sometimes terrorism is the only effective way for dissenters to resist an unjust system.	1.6	1.5	.56
8.	I'd say the goals of some terrorists have been noble ones, such as freedom.	2.3	1.9	.49
9.	Anyone who resorts to terrorism has to be mentally sick.	2.6	2.2	.47
10.	There is NEVER justification for violence against civilians, no matter how just the cause.	1.0	0.7	.41
11.	Governments should exterminate known terrorists without mercy or due process.	2.1	2.2	.33
12.	At times, innocent people must die to obtain political goals like freedom or equality.	1.6	1.4	.29
13.	Insensitive governments share much of the blame for the acts of terrorism against them.	2.0	2.3	.28
14.	For better or worse, terrorism is effective in gaining publicity and things the terrorists want.	2.5	2.4	.18
15.	I'd say there is really no difference between "terrorism" and "freedom fighting" except the side one is on.	1.7	1.6	.16
	Total score on the full fifteen-item AT-scale:	25.4	24.6	alpha= .82

findings to determine whether this AT scale is psychometrically a sufficently reliable and valid measure of attitudes.

Reliability. To the extent a scale is reliable, it correlates highly with itself, indicating a small "error of measurement" (Anastasi, 1988). Here, reliability of the AT was gauged in three ways. (1) First, the interitem reliability of the fifteen-item scale was measured using Cronbach's alpha (α), revealing a fairly high internal consistency of $\alpha = .82$. (2) It was also possible to assess the test-retest reliability of the scale by retesting, then matching the responses of the same 10 students after a one-week interval; this test-retest reliability was a high $r = .90$. (3) A further item analysis of the five "best" items (see Table 3.1) found it possible to extract a five-item AT scale that correlated $r = .93$ with the full fifteen-item version and had a nearly equal internal validity of $\alpha = .79$ (compared with .82). The brevity and high reliability of this five-item AT makes it especially suitable to embed in larger political or public opinion surveys. Thus, all subsequent analyses of validity below are based on this five-item AT, rather than the fifteen-item version.

Validity. Does the AT measure one's attitudes toward terrorism? A scale is valid to the extent that it correlates with one's other relevant attitudes or behaviors. Clearly, the validation of an AT scale presents special challenges, since it is hardly feasible to sample or candidly question terrorist groups. Three alternative validation methods were used here.

In the first method, concurrent validity was gauged using a twenty-three-item Terrorist Adjective Checklist (TACL), to profile respondents' mental image of the personal features of terrorists. For instance, are typical terrorists immature or highly mature, selfless or selfish, cowardly or strong? This was done in six steps. (1) The writings about terrorism were used to derive a list of twenty-three adjectives often used to describe terrorists. In Table 3.2, note that many of the adjectives seem to go in different, if not opposite, directions. (2) Each adjective was independently rated by four judges from 0 (horrible) to 10 (wonderful) in terms of its favorability, with 5 as the neutral midpoint.[3] (3) Respondents were asked to review this list and mark an adjective N if they feel it never describes those engaging in terrorism and A if they feel it always describes terrorists; respondents leave an adjective unmarked if they feel it is not consistently associated with terrorists. (4) Each response was scored 0 for never, 2 for always, and 1 if unmarked. (5) These frequencies were multiplied by the judges' rating from 0 to 10 for each adjective, and the twenty-three scores for each person were summed, then the sum was divided by 23; this resulted in a total TACL score that could range from 0 to 10, indicating the overall favorability of that respondent's image of the typical terrorist. For the 108 respondents, the mean TACL score was 4.9, with a standard deviation of 0.9. (6) What is important here is that we would expect those most approving of terrorism on the AT scale to have the most favorable view of terrorists' personal features. Indeed, there is a correlation between the 108 respondents' AT and TACL scores of $r = +0.32$ ($p < .001$), indicating the mutually concurrent validity of these two scores.

Table 3.2
Perceptions of the Personal Features of Terrorists: Judges' Ratings of Each Adjective's Positivity (from 0 to 10), and the Percentage of Respondents Who Said the Adjectives "Never" or "Always" Apply to Terrorists

	Judges' rating	Never	Always
Brainwashed	1	2.%	39.%
Calculating	3	5	37
Clever	6	5	20
Cowardly	2	12	36
Cruel	1	1	53
Dedicated	7	5	58
Effective	7	17	10
Fanatic	2	1	59
Idealistic	7	9	33
Immature	3	4	26
Malcontent	3	4	42
Mature	7	36	1
Mentally disturbed	2	2	23
Misguided	3	3	33
Rational	8	43	6
Sadistic	1	3	27
Selfish	2	5	36
Selfless	9	12	16
Self-sacrificing	7	8	29
Sensible	8	46	2
Sincere	9	32	5
Strong	7	12	11
Thrill-seeking	4	6	21

In the second method the factorial validity of the five-item AT scale was gauged with a principal components factor analysis for the 108 respondents. It was found that one single factor emerged with an Eigenvalue exceeding one (3.06), accounting for 61 percent of the AT's variance.

The third method made it possible to assess the construct validity of the scale using a known-groups technique with 55 Armenian-American respondents. These respondents were drawn from two Armenian political factions, 35 of them Dashnags and 20 non-Dashnag Armenians. Since the early 1970s the few acts of Armenian terrorism have typically been credited to a small, secret group called the Armenian Secret Army for the Liberation of Armenia, or ASALA (Corsun, 1982). Dashnags have historically condoned violence to regain their homeland, whereas non-Dashnag Armenians have typically denounced the use of violence by ASALA and others to achieve Armenian political goals. As might be expected, the mean AT score of 13.8 for the 35 Dashnags was significantly higher than non-Dashnag Armenians' mean of 8.2 (p < .0001). Moreover, it was possible to go one step further with some of this Armenian sample by interviewing 15 of these 55 Armenians in greater depth on their specific views of ASALA. These interviews yielded an ASALA rating from 0 (totally denouncing ASALA) to 4 (totally supporting ASALA). When these fifteen "blind" interview ratings were later compared with the computed AT scores, a correlation of r = +.79 further supported the construct validity of the AT scale.[4]

OBSERVATIONS AND CONCLUSIONS

From our analyses so far with some 168 respondents, we can reach at least two clear conclusions about public attitudes toward terrorism. (1) It was possible to develop a brief five-item AT scale that indeed finds that abhorrence is not the only public sentiment regarding terrorism; rather, there is a diversity of views sometimes ranging into acceptance or support. (2) Judging by three indicators of reliability and four indicators of validity, the AT scale seems a psychometrically sound scale that can be embedded within other surveys to chart shifts in popular opinion over time and location.[5]

Still, the assessment of AT continues to face two challenges. For one thing, some respondents appear visibly uneasy answering questions about terrorism. For example, when we asked one professor of Middle East studies for information on terrorism, he declined, saying he preferred to maintain distance from any discussion of terrorism. Similarly, a number of respondents in all groups— students, law enforcement professionals, and ethnic minorities—seemed visibly uneasy in answering the questions; some, like the Iranians and Irish, simply declined. Second, many respondents seemed to maintain "sliding" views about terrorism, depending on which specific group they were considering. A telling media example of this was during the 1991 Middle East peace talks in Madrid; whereas Israeli minister Shamir was one of the Palestinian terrorists' staunchest critics, Arab negotiators displayed a 1947 British poster announcing a reward for the youthful Zionist terrorist Shamir. To the extent that "terrorism is in the eye of the beholder," such cognitive factors may cause a low ceiling to the success of attempts at a single-attitude scale like the AT. This multiple standard of viewing some terrorists as freedom fighters and others as threats to freedom seems to concur with earlier problems described by Simmons and Mitch (1989), Velicer, Huckel, & Hansen (1989), and others, favoring a more complex, less direct cognitive approach toward public attitudes toward terrorism. A future attempt at scale validation may well ask respondents to describe their attitudes toward, say, four specific rival groups (such as Palestinians v. Zionists, or black v. white South Africans) to assess how much the respondent's general attitude is adapted to fit specific terrorist groups.

NOTES

An earlier version of this research was presented to the Conference on Violence and the Prevention of Violence, cosponsored by the International Organization for the Study of Group Tensions and the Institute for Cross-Cultural and Cross-Ethnic Studies, at Molloy College, Rockville Centre, NY, November 9, 1991.

1. Consider the remarkable variety of current groups that have turned to terror to pursue their political goals. These include religious groups such as Christians in Ireland, or Moslems, Jews, and Hindus in the East; national groups such as Latins, Armenians, Basques, and Africans; and ideological groups of both the left and right.

2. The authors warmly thank John Kahvejian, Concepcion Ebrahimi, Charles Bahn, and Brendan Bogert for their valuable cooperation in gathering the views of the Armenian, Iranian, and law enforcement respondents.

3. Each adjective was independently rated by four judges—Robert I. Reynolds, David S. Malcolm, and the two authors—on a scale of 0 (horrible) to 10 (wonderful), with the midpoint of 5 as neutral. These four ratings were averaged to yield the 0–10 mean ratings listed in Table 3.2. The authors thank Drs. Reynolds and Malcolm for their kind cooperation.

4. Due to the sensitivity of this topic and the timing of political events involving Iran, it was not feasible to obtain responses from the Iranian group. However, four Muslim students completed the survey, with a mean AT of 12.8, far higher than the mean of 6.4 for other groups and clearly warranting further inquiry in future research.

5. The findings of the other three scales assessing authoritarianism, dogmatism, and religiosity are reviewed in a separate report by the authors (Verdi & Takooshian, 1993). The AT scale is © 1989 and reprinted here by permission of the authors.

REFERENCES

Anastasi, A. (1988). *Psychological testing* (6th ed.). New York: Macmillan.

Corsun, J. (1982, August). Armenian terrorism: A profile. *U.S. Department of State Bulletin,* 31–35.

Jones, A. P. (1989, June 22). *Testimony on the status of GAO's review of the FBI's International Terrorism Program.* Washington, DC: U.S. General Accounting Office.

Lang, W. (1987). *The world's elite forces.* New York: Military Press.

Robinson, J. R., Shaver, P. R., & Wrightsman, L. S. (Eds.). (1991). *Measures of personality and social psychological attitudes.* New York: Academic Press.

Schmid, A. (1983). *Political terrorism.* New Brunswick, NJ: Transaction Publishers.

Velicer, W. F., Huckel, L. H., & Hansen, C. E. (1989, September). A measurement model for measuring attitudes toward violence. *Personality and Social Psychology Bulletin 15,* 349–364.

Verdi, W. M., & Takooshian, H. (1993). U.S. attitudes toward the terrorism problem. *Journal of Psychology and the Behavioral Sciences 7,* 83–87.

Weinberg, L. B., & Davis, P. B. (1989). *Introduction to political terrorism.* New York: McGraw-Hill.

Appendix 1: Political Opinions Survey

*Please give us your frank opinions on various social issues. Answer each item by circling **A** (Agree strongly), **a** (agree), **d** (disagree), **D** (Disagree stongly). There are no right or wrong answers, only your personal opinions. Save any comments for the end of the survey. This survey is anonymous. THANK YOU.*

1. A a d D   Human nature being what it is, there will always be war and conflict.
2. A a d D   A few strong leaders could make this country better than all the laws and talk.
3. A a d D   People cannot be trusted.
4. A a d D   Most people who don't get ahead just don't have enough will power.
5. A a d D   An insult to your honor should not be forgotten.

6. A a d D   In this complicated world of ours, the only way to know what's going on is to rely on leaders or experts who can be trusted.

7. A a d D   My blood boils whenever a stubborn person refuses to admit he's wrong.
8. A a d D   There are two kinds of people in this world: those for the truth and those against it.
9. A a d D   Most people just don't know what's good for them.
10. A a d D   Of all the different philosophies in this world, there is probably only one which is correct.

11. A a d D   My religious beliefs greatly affect all parts of my life.
12. A a d D   There really is no God up there who judges people's actions.
13. A a d D   People who are religious will be happier in the next life to come.
14. A a d D   Lack of religion is a cause of many of today's social problems.
15. A a d D   Too often, religion creates fanatics.

*In recent history, all sorts of groups have pursued political goals by resorting to violence -- such as bombings and hostage-taking. These include religious **groups**, such as Christians in Ireland, Moslems, Jews and Hindus in the East; national **groups**, such as Latins, Armenians, Africans; and ideological **groups** such as communists and fascists. While some call this terrorism, others call it freedom-fighting. Please answer these questions on the use of political violence:*

16. A a d D   It is sometimes understandable if people resort to terrorism as their only way to be heard.

17. A a d D   Terrorists must be considered the enemy of civilized society, regardless of their motives.

18. A a d D   Only a cruel, cowardly group would resort to terrorism to achieve its goals.

19. A a d D   Most terrorists seem like disturbed people who would act violent even in an ideal society.

20. A a d D   Terrorism is sometimes morally justified.

21. Which words would you use to describe individual terrorists today? Put an **N** beside words you feel are Never true, an **A** beside those you think are Always true of terrorists. Leave blank all the other words you think might apply to some terrorists but not others:

__ Rational	__ Dedicated	__ Cruel	__ Idealistic	__ Strong	__ Clever
__ Fanatic	__ Sensible	__ Calculating	__ Cowardly	__ Misguided	__ Effective
__ Mature	__ Immature	__ Sincere	__ Mentally disturbed	__ Self-sacrificing
__ Malcontent	__ Selfish	__ Selfless	__ Thrill-seeking	__ Sadistic	__ Brainwashed

22. Your age: ____

23. Your gender: __ M __ F.

24. The country where you were raised: _____

25. How many of your four grandparents were born in the USA (Circle one): 0 1 2 3 4

26. Your education:

__ Grammar school __ High school __ Some college __ College grad __ Grad school.

27. If you have further COMMENTS for this survey, please write them on the back...

[7]

43

PART II

Violence Involving the Young

4

Violent Youth: Reflections on Contemporary Child-rearing Practices in the United States as an Antecedent Cause

June F. Chisholm

> If one's early life was unfortunately beset by neglect and abuse, then one is likely to repeat it, and treat one's offspring as one was treated.
>
> Steele (1976)

One of the major problems facing contemporary U.S. American society is the incidence of violence, senseless violence in particular, committed by youth. In an effort to understand the epidemic of adolescent violence in contemporary U.S. American society, this chapter will consider the trend of adolescent violence, briefly review psychological theories on violence, and explore the possible relationship between child-rearing practices and violent behavior. Two examples of intervention strategies aimed at reducing adolescent violence will be presented.

ADOLESCENT VIOLENCE

According to the Federal Bureau of Investigation (FBI) (1992) the rate of violent crime by juveniles, defined as people from 10 to 17 years of age, increased more than 25 percent in the last decade. The rate was up not only among poor youths in urban areas (the rate among black youth is five times that for white youths) but in all races, social classes, and lifestyles. Incidents in the suburbs of Northern Virginia and Maryland involving gang activity among middle-class suburban youth have parents and community leaders concerned about the outbreak of violence there (Davis, 1991); it was reported that one such gang, the YTs (Young Terrorists) severely beat a youth because they did not like his hat or his attitude (Davis, 1991). Officer Granfield, the police chief for that community said, "The youth violence is sort of a reflection of all of society. The tolerance level seems to have gotten to an all-time low" (Davis, 1991, p. B2).

A 1990 national survey found that one high school student in twenty-five carried a gun at least once during a thirty-day period; in New York City, arrests on gun charges increased by 75 percent between 1987 and 1990 for children aged 7 to 15 (*New York Times,* Nov. 1992). In Amarillo, Texas, six adolescents were wounded by gunfire inside their high school when a teenager carrying a handgun began shooting at a fellow student with whom he had been feuding (*New York Times,* Sept. 1992).

These indeed are curious times for adolescents. Aggression and violence in the United States have seemingly become idealized, as evidenced in television programs, films, video, and the media. Our society denounces and glorifies sexual promiscuity, yet Amy Fisher, the New York adolescent who was convicted in 1992 of shooting her alleged boyfriend's wife, has become famously infamous; her signature is purportedly worth as much if not more than that of President Bill Clinton.

Today young people face unprecedented choices and pressures; all too often the parental guidance they need is lacking. At a time when the role of the father in the process of parenting is changing such that many more fathers are assuming more primary-care responsibilities, too many others are reneging on their parental responsibilities by emotionally and financially abandoning their children, particularly if separated or divorced.

THEORETICAL PERSPECTIVES ON VIOLENCE

Theories and research on violence have explored and attempted to understand this phenomenon from different perspectives ranging from the micro level (e.g., the psychology of the offender) to the macro level (e.g., a focus on society itself examining sociopolitical, economic, and cultural factors). According to May (1972) violence is a uniting of the self in action. He writes:

It is an organizing of one's powers to prove one's power, to establish the worth of the self. It is risking all, a committing all, an asserting all. But it unites the different elements in the self, *omitting* rationality. This is why I have said above that the uniting of the self is done on a level that bypasses reason. Whatever its motive or its consequences may be within the violent person, its result is generally destructive to the others in the situation. (p. 188)

Case I

I am reminded of a psychological evaluation of L., a 17-year-old, African-American, single female who was prone to violent outbursts in which she would physically fight against two or more people, males or females, when she felt provoked. She was a street-savvy young woman who prior to this evaluation had not had any psychiatric history or record of misconduct or violence. L. and her boyfriend of ten months were talking about getting married within the next two years. The emergence of the violent outbursts began several months after the sudden death of her beloved mother and the consequent mistreatment by an older sister with whom she was forced to live. Her sister allegedly told L. that since their mother was dead, she was now the mother, and L. had to obey her and live by her rules or else. Her bereavement was complicated by her intentional refusal to feel grief, sadness, and anger over her loss. Moreover, the lack of emotional support by her family and the dire financial circumstances of staving off homelessness by living with a sister whom she despised contributed to her emotional state.

L. had a mercurial quality of becoming hostile and belligerent, at other times displaying a soft-spoken, sensitive, and compassionate concern for others. She understood her fighting in terms of being easily irritated and as a way of ensuring her safety and of protecting her boyfriend, who since her mother's death was the only other person in the world she cared about. What was most significant about her violent behavior was the extent to which she provoked these attacks and her sense of gratification in dealing with them. In relating each incident she became ''alive,'' eager to talk about her moves and countermoves and the harm inflicted on the others. She rarely fought with only one other person; being outnumbered was key to experiencing the ''high.'' She seemed to have little awareness of her provocative behavior or its self-destructiveness. For instance, she described two physical altercations, one in which she deliberately fought back a gang of girls who attacked her because she had ''dissed'' (disrespected) one of them, and the other involving her fighting singlehandedly with a group of boys who had ''dissed'' her boyfriend in her presence.

RESEARCH ON VIOLENT YOUTH

Lefer (1984) discusses why some individuals can restrain themselves from inflicting injury whereas others cannot. Depending on the strength of repression, suppression, inhibition, reaction formation, rationalization, and conscience, a violence-prone individual (VPI) may be categorized as (1) one who uses violence as a means to an end without a need for justification (2) one who uses violence as a means to an end but must justify it to his or her conscience (3) one who is violent only in a dissociated or drugged state or (4) one who becomes symbiotic with another VPI and aids the other in committing violence. Significant differences in dreams were evident among the types of VPIs. The VPIs' dreams often reenacted the violence inflicted upon them and their intimates in childhood and youth.

According to Lefer's classifications, L. exemplifies the Type II VPI, that is, one who uses violence as a means to an end but must justify it to her conscience. An example of a Type I VPI is the sociopath involved in organized crime. In this subculture violent behavior is not only condoned but necessary, and the norm, the sociopath's violent behavior, is ''appropriate.'' The recent controversy surrounding the lack of appropriate treatment for an individual whose crack-induced violent behavior terrorized the upper Westside of New York illustrates Lefer's Type III VPI, namely, one who is violent only in a dissociated or drugged state. The individual in question had been psychiatrically hospitalized forty times for his drug-induced violence, but because of a legal technicality involving the definition of *imminent,* he was always released several hours after the crack was out of his system, when he was no longer in "imminent" danger of harming himself or someone else. As soon as he was discharged from the hospital, he would use more crack and the vicious cycle would continue.

The motives that may generate aggression and violence result from the objective nature of events as well as the way these events are construed. The meaning given to these events is based on past experience, world views, personality, and views handed down by society via parental socialization and family experience (Staub, 1989). Sheldon and Eleanor Glueck's longitudinal research in delinquency found that the quality of the home environment distinguished between delinquent and nondelinquent boys (1950).

Briefly looking back in time, one gets a general sense of how child rearing has changed. In Colonial America it was the duty of parents, priests, and schoolmasters to severely chastise children, even "beat the devil out of them," so that they would grow up as responsible adults (Bakan, 1971). In the early 1600s a Massachusetts law, the "Stubborn Child Act," permitted parents to put a child to death if the child was rebellious and disobedient (Bremner, 1971). By today's standards these practices are considered abusive, if not abhorrent.

Because of the inherent complexities in identifying those implicit rules, and more subtle child-rearing practices in functional families that may nonetheless predispose the adolescent to violence, we will now review the literature on patterns of child rearing among violent youth to establish general parameters for later discussion.

CHILD REARING AMONG VIOLENT YOUTH

The link between a history of child abuse and youth who commit violent acts has not been definitively established (Lewis, Mallouh, & Webb, 1989). In fact, the well-known Schreber case, analyzed by Sigmund Freud, who developed psychoanalytic formulations about the etiology of paranoia, is a classic example of deleterious child-rearing methods, in vogue at that time, that did not result in a child who grew up to became violent (Niedlerland, 1974). On the contrary, the young Schreber was the victim of "soul murder" (Shengold, 1989) and suffered from mental illness.

There is considerable evidence, however, that the effects of maltreatment are severe and longlasting; for example, abused children tend to be more aggressive and have more behavior problems and psychopathology than their peers (Aber & Cicchetti, 1984). The presence or absence of emotional neglect, family criminality, and a support system within and outside of the home; the sex of the abusing parent; and how parents resolve conflicts are all important for understanding the relationship between child abuse and subsequent violent criminal behavior (Kruttschnitt, Ward, & Sheble, 1987).

Green (1985) performed in-depth clinical studies of fifty abused children and their families to identify the characteristics of the abused children and the abusive environment that might facilitate the transmission of violence from generation to generation. He identified the following major factors contributing to this violent behavior: (1) identification with the aggressor or victim embedded in the compulsive reenactment of early traumatic events, (2) paranoid distortion of object relationships, (3) fears of object loss, and (4) central nervous system impairment. Apropos of central nervous system impairment as a factor in the transmission of violence from generation to generation, Youngerman and Canino (1983) reports a case in which the violent behavior of an adolescent was successfully treated with lithium. The adolescent's father, also prone to violent temper outbursts, was impressed with his son's results and sought help; he was also successfully treated with lithium.

Among youth who commit violence against their parents are found strong manifestations of intrafamily violence or aggression between the parents, between parents and children, and between siblings (Kratcoski, (1985). Additionally, low levels of family functioning, characterized by disagreements over money matters, inappropriate disciplining of children, few shared activities, and alcohol abuse, also correlated strongly with youth violence toward parents.

In disturbed or problem families, negative emotions are frequently expressed and directed toward the adolescent with problems; there tend to be fewer negative messages directed toward other children in the family (Doane, 1978).

CURRENT PERSPECTIVES ON PARENTING

Given the ethnic and multicultural diversity as well as social-class differences within contemporary American society, no one model or ideal child-rearing method exists (Fantini & Cardenas, 1980). There must be a recognition of the community values, the dignity inherent in local cultural customs, and the need for tolerance in relating to cultural diversity. Although it is beyond the scope of this chapter to examine the differences in child rearing among these groups, it is worthwhile to acknowledge that differences in child rearing relative to our pluralistic society may affect the issues raised in this discussion.

Recent thinking about family systems and our understanding of unconscious motivations helps to expand our knowledge about the transmission of family patterns across generations. Not only explicit family rules but also powerful implicit rules allow the expression of certain feelings yet inhibit others (Staub, 1989). This is consistent with the object relations theoretical concept of the "unthought known" (Bollas, 1987). As it applies to the present discussion, it refers to the paradigmatic operational processes inherent in family life vis-à-vis parenting.

Within this framework every family, every parent, is implicated in the transmission of violence, not just dysfunctional families or parents known to have neglected and/or abused their children. Practices, not sufficient to be classified as abuse and hence warrant legal sanction, may nonetheless be precursors to maltreatment and/or detrimental to the development of the child. These qualitatively different disturbances in parent-child interaction are likely to be more subtle, more frequent, more continuous, and more detrimental in their long-term effects on the child and family (Lyons-Ruth, Connell, Zoll, & Stahl, 1987).

How can a child grow to adulthood and be emotionally healthy when certain parental attitudes and child-rearing practices stifle the child's expression of anger, hurt, humiliation, frustration, and other negative emotions? This is especially salient when considering the vast range of experiences in ordinary living that may elicit negative emotions in children. How parents respond as well as their role in generating these experiences determines the outcome and subsequent impact on the child's further development.

This is especially pertinent in the area of childhood traumas. The consequences of child rearing, as opposed to child abuse in the case of the traumatized child, can affect the way the child copes and adapts to the circumstances. Terr's (1991) discussion of Type I, Type II, and crossover condition traumas sheds light on these issues.

Type I trauma is the result of one sudden, external blow (psychological). Type II trauma is a series of blows, such as longstanding or repeated ordeals. Crossover conditions involve both Type I and Type II traumas occurring to the young person. These traumatic experiences render the young person temporarily helpless and break past ordinary coping and defensive operations. From Terr's perspective, all traumas originate from external events; that is, none is generated primarily within the child's own mind. There may be biological changes that are stimulated by the external events. However, Terr limits her discussion to the psychological characteristics associated with childhood trauma: visualized or otherwise repeatedly perceived memories of the traumatic event, repetitive behaviors, trauma-specific fears, and changed attitudes about people, life, and the future.

Divorce, for example, although commonplace in our society, often creates the circumstances Terr describes.

Case II

I am reminded of a consultation with a husband and wife who, while in the midst of a contentious divorce, were seeking treatment for their 9-year-old son, who was misbehaving in school. He had become the class bully, having fought several classmates shortly after his father moved out of the house and began living with a girlfriend who had a son about the same age as the patient. Prior to the father's leaving the home, the son's academic work and conduct in school were satisfactory, showing no ill effects of the discord at home. At the time of the consultation however, the boy was angry, hurt, and frightened about his parents' impending divorce, and he told them so in a family session. The parents became overtly distressed at the boy's frank, albeit from their perspective, disrespectful manner. They seemed less concerned about his emotional suffering than his misconduct, which failed to cease despite physical punishment used by both parents that, according to them, had worked in the past.

In gathering information about the family history, it became apparent that this boy's father had been similarly abandoned by his father, the boy's grandfather, when about the same age. Unfortunately, this father had minimal insight into the significance of his history and his son's present difficulties. Having repressed his own emotional pain, the father was immune to his son's suffering and therefore emotionally unavailable to comfort and guide him. The possible connections between his son's aggressive behavior and violent potential to his own repressed suffering and current cruel indifference to his son's emotional distress was beyond either parent's comprehension.

Effective parenting enables parents to encourage and facilitate the development of healthy, well-adjusted children who are prepared to deal with the vicissitudes of life. By definition, effective parenting presupposes that the quality of the parent-child relationship and parenting skills are sound. A child having matured in a family that has facilitated the above has achieved a harmonious balance between the private, inner reality of the self and experience and the public presentation of self in the outer (social) reality. Conversely, ineffective parenting as evidenced in the research on violent youth indicates disturbances in the parent-child relationship that interfere with a child's development, predisposing the child to later difficulties.

Diana Baumrind (1971) has proposed several dimensions for analyzing child-rearing patterns. Although her work focuses on families of preschool children, her findings are consistent with those based on research of family interaction patterns with adolescent populations (Becker, 1964) and are therefore relevant for understanding families with older children and adolescents as well. The dimensions are (1) the degree of warmth and nurturance the parents express toward their children; (2) the extent to which the parents expect the child to be mature and independent; (3) the clarity of rules and the consistency with which those rules are applied; and (4) the amount of communication between parent and child and the extent to which the child's opinion is sought and heeded. Additionally, Baumrind derived three patterns of child rearing: permissive parental style, authoritarian parental style, and authoritative parental style. The permissive parental style is high in nurturance but low in maturity demands, control, and communication; the authoritarian parental style is high in maturity demands and control but low in nurturance and communication; the authoritative parental style is high in all four qualities. Finally, Baumrind describes a subset of parents who are low in control and low in emotional support, whom she labels *neglectful*. In general terms, the authoritative style has been associated with higher self-esteem in young children and with earlier or more complete identity achievement in adolescence (Campbell, Adams, & Dobson, 1984; Rosenberg, 1986).

Elder (1963) believes the most important difference between autocratic and democratic parents of adolescents is the way in which they exercise their *power* in the family. He found that adolescents from democratic families were more self-confident and independent than those from autocratic families. Moreover, the more parents respected adolescents' opinions and sought to involve them in discussions and explanations of decisions, the more the adolescents felt that their parents were people they would ''want to be like'' and the more they chose friends and activities of which their parents would approve.

The adult capable of effective parenting has a keen appreciation of the uniqueness and integrity of the adolescent; the adolescent is not perceived to be, nor treated as, the property or possession of the parent. Moreover, the adolescent is not experienced by the parent as an extension of the adult's self-concept.

THE IMPORTANCE OF TIME

Children and adolescents need time! Parenting children and adolescents takes time! The time involved is a blend of ''real'' or actual time and ''psychological'' time, the latter referring to the child's and adolescent's experience of time, which is more a function of the individual's emotional and cognitive level of development *and* the requisite time frame in which responsive parenting, that is, the active process of engagement and interaction with the child/adolescent, occurs. The adult who successfully navigates between the two time dimensions may be more cognizant of the *process* involved in parenting and function more often than not in the ''being'' mode of existence that Erich Fromm described. What happens in terms of the parents' perspective about the nature of parent-child interactions is that the parent can shift from a future orientation to current events, to a now orientation to the current event. The essential difference is the extent of concentration, attention, and emotional responsiveness to the immediacy of what is occurring, reacting in such a way as to be responsive to short-term as well as long-range goals. For example, a parent who is thinking about the work yet to be done for some important meeting (future event) while simultaneously engaged in a conversation with her adolescent daughter (now event) is not completely invested in the interaction. When this type of interaction becomes a pattern, the adolescent suffers.

I am reminded of a conversation I had with a colleague whose children are now grown. She said that one advantage of being in academia was the flexible schedule. All through her children's childhood and adolescence she prided herself in ''being'' there for them. She was disturbed by a recent conversation with her adult daughter, whose recollection of her mother during those years was quite different; the daughter felt that her mother had always been preoccupied with work and not ''all there.'' Fabe and Wikler (1978) describe four factors that affect how a working mother will adapt to parenting: (1) the demands of her work, (2) her attitudes about her job, (3) her use of child care, and (4) her personal reaction to motherhood. Even with the involvement of the father in child care, the stress and strain of being responsive to the adolescent's needs and fulfilling other, often conflicting responsibilities may affect child rearing vis-à-vis the emotional availability of the parent and the quality of the parent-child interactions.

The concept of quality time may also serve to illustrate the above ideas. In one sense the term *quality time* seems euphemistic in that it serves to assuage the guilt and, in some instances, contradict the common sense of some parents who realize that while they are away from their children, parenting responsibilities must be delegated to others, in many cases to the children themselves (e.g., latchkey children). Alternatively, quality time alludes to a psychological space in which ideas, attitudes, fantasies, expectations, intentionality, parent-child schemes, and skills about parenting determine the characteristics of the actual parenting.

Considerations of the age and stage of development of the child notwithstanding, the parents' experience of not enough time to be with their children and the child's experience of loss, abandonment, or disinterested or tired parents may result in subtle cruelties undermining the efforts of parents to compromise and adapt.

POISONOUS PEDAGOGY

The Harlow studies (1974) confirm Steele's observations presented at the beginning of this chapter and dramatically illuminate the consequences of inadequate models for the young to emulate. Monkeys that had been raised with surrogate terry cloth and wire "mothers" were emotionally and socially deprived and became physically abusive toward their offspring. This research casts doubts on the belief held by many parents that if they do what comes naturally, everything will work out; that their children will be healthy and become well-adjusted adults. This assumption seems valid only for those parents who were not physically or emotionally abused as children. Hoffman (1970) found that when parents use withdrawal of love as punishment, their children come to focus on conventional rules rather than the needs and welfare of others; therefore it is not only physical punitiveness that diminishes children's concern about the welfare of others.

Poisonous pedagogy, a term coined by Miller (1990b), refers to child-rearing practices that are harmful because the intent is to suppress vitality, creativity, and feeling in the child and maintain the "autocratic, godlike position of the parents at all cost" (Miller, 1986, p.18). In general, parents who, primarily through coercive methods, raise children to be obedient, compliant, "well behaved," and deferential to authority figures adhere to a poisonous pedagogy. It is a learning process that teaches power differences when it is difficult for the child to evaluate what is being taught. Miller writes:

No one ever slaps a child out of love but rather because in similar situations, when one was defenseless, one was slapped and then compelled to interpret it as a sign of love. This inner confusion prevailed for thirty or forty years and is passed on to one's own child. That's all. To purvey the confusion to the child as truth leads to new confusions that, although examined in detail by experts, are still confusions. If, on the other hand, one can admit one's errors to the child and apologize for a lack of self-control, no confusions are created. (1990a, p. 35)

Case III

I am reminded of a 4-year-old boy who attended the Head Start program for which I was the psychological consultant. He was in one of the classes I had been visiting on a weekly basis for in-house training for the paraprofessionals. Each week I arrived, this boy would approach me and strike up a brief casual stream-of-consciousness conversation about whatever was on his mind at the moment and then return to the activity to which he had been engaged. This weekly interaction became our ritual greeting. On one occasion he said in a despondent but emphatic tone of voice, "You don't love me!" I was somewhat surprised by this spontaneous, emotionally loaded comment and asked him how he knew this. He replied, "Because you haven't beat the s— out of me yet."

INTERVENTIONS

Lefer (1984) suggests that preventive strategies should address the needs of the younger population in terms of their feelings of alienation, of lack of impact and invisibility when not committing acts of violence, and their feelings of helplessness and depression.

The Conflict Resolution Program in San Francisco focuses on boosting self-esteem and making students more responsible for improving the school's social environment. Teamwork and responsible conduct replace violent behavior through rechanneling the destructive energy into creative learning experiences. Disputes are resolved in a designated room; students in conflict can choose between two peer conflict managers (who have received sixteen hours of training) or an adult to hear the dispute and arrive at a fair, impartial resolution (Carnegie Council, 1989).

An example of a communitywide effort that has been in operation for approximately two years was related by a friend and colleague (Walker, personal communication). She is one of twenty-two members of the Piscataway Turn on Youth Coalition, a group she founded consisting of concerned parents, professionals, the Board of Education, child and adolescent agencies, police department, local government, the business community, adolescents, and other interested community residents of Piscataway, New Jersey. Concerned about the statistics on adolescent crime in the area, the coalition has established a vast social network of community resources aimed at providing primary, secondary, and tertiary intervention strategies for adolescents and their families.

The coalition also recognized that their community lacked sufficient resources and facilities for their adolescents to congregate and engage in educational and recreational activities in a safe, well-supervised environment away from home and school. Adolescents were spending their free time roaming the shopping malls. Professionals and parents sensed a growing apathy and alienation among the youth and felt it was necessary to "turn on" youth who were seemingly "tuning out." The coalition conducted a massive survey involving all but 100 of 1,700 adolescents within the school district to identify what adolescents felt were their needs. As a result of the survey, a teen center will soon be established in Piscataway; its function is multifaceted, involving collaborative efforts of community constituents to meet the needs of Piscataway adolescents and their families.

CONCLUSION

In this chapter we have reviewed theories and research on violence and violent youth. We have explored the possible connection between child-rearing practices and adolescent violence. There is considerable evidence linking harsh and abusive child-rearing practices to later violent behavior. The misatunements and "hidden cruelties" (Miller, 1990b) of child rearing are perhaps more a deprivation of *caring* rather than a deprivation of care, which are also subject to the compulsion to repeat. In other words, the misatunements of everyday life within the family that may give rise to violence in adolescence and adulthood may not solely be a function of aberrant, deviate methods of rearing children or dysfunctional family life. Prothrow-Smith (1991) sums it up this way:

The destructive lessons parents teach when they are physically and psychologically abusive to their children and when they allow their children to be physically and psychologically abusive to others, in conjunction with our society's glorification of violence, the ready availability of guns, and the drug culture are an explosive combination that set our children up to be the perpetrators and the victims of violence. (p. 145)

In order to curtail adolescent violence, public awareness must be increased and a rigorous advocacy campaign for maintaining and improving the provision of services for youth and their families must become a national priority.

REFERENCES

Aber, J. L., & Cicchetti, D. (1984). Socioemotional development in maltreated children: An empirical and theoretical analysis. In H. Fitzgerald, B. Lester, and M. Yogman (Eds.), *Theory and research in behavioral pediatrics* (Vol. 2). New York: Plenum Press.

Bakan, D. (1971). *Slaughter of the innocents: A study of the battered child phenomenon.* San Francisco: Jossey-Bass.

Baumrind, D. (1971). Current parents of parental authority. *Developmental Psychology Monographs, 4* (1), Pt. 2.

Becker, W. (1964). Consequences of different kinds of parental discipline. In M. L. Hoffman & L. W. Hoffman (Eds.), *Review of child development research* (Vol. 1). New York: Russell Sage.

Bollas, C. (1987). *The shadow of the object: Psychoanalysis of the unthought known.* New York: Columbia University Press.

Bremner, R. H. (Ed.). (1971). *Children and youth in America: A documentary history,* (Vol. 2, pp. 1866–1932). Cambridge, MA: Harvard University Press.

Campbell, E., Adams, G., & Dobson, W. (1984). Familial correlates of identity formation in late adolescence: A study of the predictive utility of connectedness and individuality in family relations. *Journal of Youth and Adolescence, 13,* 509–526.

Carnegie Council on Adolescent Development (1989). *Turning points: Preparing American youth for the 21st century.* New York: Carnegie Corp.

Davis, P. (1991, October 22). Violent groups of middle class teens disturb peace of suburbia. *Washington Post, 114,* B1–B2.

Doane, J. (1978). Family interaction and communication deviance in disturbed and normal families: A review of research. *Family Process, 17,* 357–376.

Elder, G. H. (1963). Parental power legitimation and its effect on the adolescent. *Sociometry, 26,* 50–65.

Fabe, M., & Wikler, N. (1978). *Up against the clock.* New York: Random House.

Fantini, M., & Cardenas, R. (1980). *Parenting in a multicultural society.* New York: Longman.

Federal Bureau of Investigation. (1992, August 30). Uniform Crime Reports, violent youth crime is up 25% in decade. *New York Times, 141,* 27 (L).

Glueck, S., & Glueck, E. (1950). *Unraveling juvenile delinquency.* Cambridge, MA: Harvard University Press.

Green, A. (1985). Generational transmission of violence in child abuse. *International Journal of Family Psychiatry, 6* (4), 389–403.

Harlow, H. F. (1974). Syndromes resulting from maternal deprivation: Maternal and peer affectional deprivation in primates. In J. H. Cullen (Ed.), *Experimental behavior: A basis for the study of mental disturbances.* New York: John Wiley.

Hoffman, M. (1970). Conscience, personality, and socialization technique. *Human Development, 13,* 90–126.

Kratcoski, P. (1985). Youth violence directed toward significant others. *Journal of Adolescence, 8* (2), 145–157.

Kruttschnitt, C., Ward, D., & Sheble, M. (1987). Abuse-resistant youth: Some factors that may inhibit violent criminal behavior. *Social Forces, 66* (2), 501–519.

Lefer, L. (1984). The fine edge of violence. *Journal of the American Academy of Psychoanalysis, 12* (2), 253–268.

Lewis, D., Mallouh, C., & Webb, V. (1989). Child abuse, delinquency, and violent criminality. In D. Cicchetti & V. Carlson (Eds.), *Child maltreatment: Theory and research on the causes and consequences of child abuse and neglect.* New York: Cambridge University Press.

Lyons-Ruth, K., Connell, D., Zoll, D., & Stahl, L. (1987). Infants at social risk: Relationships among infant maltreatment, maternal behavior, and infant attachment behavior. *Developmental Psychology, 23* (2), 223–232.

May, R. (1972). *Power and innocence: A search for the sources of violence.* New York: W. W. Norton.

Miller, A. (1990a). *Banished knowledge.* New York: Doubleday.

Miller, A. (1990b). *For your own good: Hidden cruelty in child-rearing and the roots of violence.* New York: Noonday Press.

Miller, A. (1986). *Thou shalt not be aware: Society's betrayal of the child.* New York: New American Library.

New York Times. (1992, September 12). Student wounds six at high school, Vol. 141, p. 8 (L).

New York Times. (1992, November 9). Mowing down our children (Editorial), Vol. 142, p. A16.

Niedlerland, W. (1974). *The Schreber case: Psychoanalytic profile of a paranoid personality.* New York: New York Times Book Company.

Prothrow-Smith, D. (1991). *Deadly consequences.* New York: Harper Perennial.

Rosenberg, M. (1986). Self concept from middle childhood through adolescence. In J. Suls & A. Greenwald (Eds.), *Psychological perspectives on the self* (Vol. 3). Hillsdale, NJ: Laurence Erlbaum.

Shengold, L. (1989). *Soul murder: The effects of childhood abuse and deprivation.* New York: Ballantine Books.

Staub, E. (1989). *The roots of evil: The origins of genocide and other group violence.* Cambridge: Cambridge University Press.

Steele, B. (1976). Violence within the family. In R. Helfer & C. Kempe (Eds.), *Child abuse and neglect.* Cambridge, MA: Ballinger.

Terr, L. (1991). Childhood traumas: An outline and overview. *American Journal of Psychiatry, 148* (1), 10–19.

Thomas, L. (1974). Generational discontinuity in beliefs: An exploration of the generation gap. *Journal of Social Issues, 30,* 1–22.

Walker, R. (1993). Personal communication.

Youngerman, J., & Canino, I. (1983). Violent kids, violent parents: Family pharmacotherapy. *American Journal of Orthopsychiatry. 53* (1), 152–156.

5

Trauma in Children's Lives: Issues and Treatment

Jack L. Herman, Barbara A. Mowder,
Linda Moy, and Linda Sadler

Many things can be traumatic to children. Obviously disquieting events include, for example, loss of parents, abuse, the effects of war and natural disasters, and the observation of violence. But trauma and violence come in many forms and potentially affect children in different ways. The effects are differential depending on children's developmental histories such as at-risk or handicapping conditions, cognitive capacities, relationships with others, social support systems, strength of attachment to the mother and/or father, and temperament/personality features. Thus, in discussing trauma and violence in children's lives as well as the resulting issues and treatment, individual child variables must be kept in mind. What may be severely traumatic and cause dysfunction in one child may not manifest itself as terribly difficult and problematic in another.

With this set of caveats in mind, this chapter focuses on violence and trauma in children's lives. Traumatic and extremely difficult situations concern a substantial portion of the child population (Terr, 1985, 1991). One typical traumatic event children experience is the family dysfunction associated with parental divorce. Less typical, but still strikingly prevalent, is the violence children encounter in child abuse situations. Many other violent and/or traumatic situations exist, such as the loss of one's home during a fire or natural disaster, the violence inflicted on the child or the observation of violence toward family members as observed during conditions of war, and the development of severe child or parent illness. Although the types of trauma and violence children may encounter are broad and range from mild to severe and may represent a single incident or events of a sustained and repeated nature, the resulting impact usually affects children on three levels, the individual, the family, and the community.

When one reflects upon childhood, it is often with pleasant, fond memories. Unfortunately, not every child has a happy set of recollections. On an individual level, trauma can be extremely difficult for the child in terms of intrapsychic coping and interpersonal adaptation. Focusing on individual trauma places emphasis on the individual's coping abilities in dealing with the stressors with which they are faced. These stressors can come from the child in the form of at-risk and handicapping conditions such as hearing, visual, and orthopedic impairments. Additional trauma related to the child's potential handicaps include problems in interactions with parents and others in their surroundings. Indeed, a major potential difficulty with at-risk and handicapped infants and toddlers is the problematic interaction that may develop as a result of parents being unable to read, understand, or respond appropriately to their children's signals and bids for interaction.

Traumatic injuries also can pose physical and psychological barriers for children. Natural illnesses like rubella and meningitis, as well as deleterious accidents such as car accidents and serious falls, can alter children physically and emotionally. The sudden onset of an illness or traumatic injury often demands short- and long-term adaptive resources. If the resources needed are not available, the subsequent effects of an initial injury or disease may develop into related and further complicated difficulties (Haley, Cioffi, Lewin, & Baryza, 1990).

Disabilities, disease, and injury represent, to a great extent, traumas due to accidental causes. There is nothing the individual child nor anyone or anything in the child's environment directly did to cause the child any distress or difficulty. Child abuse, in contrast, represents a quite different set of circumstances. With abuse, someone (typically the parent) is actively inflicting physical, psychological, or sexual abuse on the child. The trauma associated with child abuse is of a different and potentially more alarming nature than that affiliated with accidental traumas. With abuse, a depended-upon and trusted older guardian is actively inflicting pain upon the child. The child not only must cope with the pain and abuse itself but must contend with the fact that the suffering is delivered by someone he or she loves who should be loving and protecting him or her. The prevalence of child abuse is prominent in today's society. Incest trauma (Urbancic, 1987), sexual abuse (Haugaard & Reppucci, 1988), and physical abuse (Van Hasselt, 1988) represent some of the most disturbing and heinous child abuse issues that stem from involvement with dysfunctional individuals, families, and environments.

But children are not only subject to accidental trauma and the application of abuse; they may also be witness to severe violence and traumatic events. For instance, children may observe their mother being beaten, their parents hurt by soldiers, the abuse of a sibling, or the committing of a homicide. Although the physical pain and suffering is not theirs directly, the observation of violent acts can be equally traumatic. Observation of the violent act, if isolated in the child's experience, violates the child's view of the world as a benevolent, ordered, predictable, and safe place. If the observation does not represent an aberrant situation for the child, the continuous vicarious violence creates a world view with aggression, anger, and hurtfulness as the norm. The impact of vicarious violence such as homicide and sexual attacks in terms of trauma in children is well documented (e.g., Pynoos & Eth, 1984, 1986; Pynoos & Nader, 1988a, 1990).

Additional situations also have traumatic potential. In a competitive society excessive and undue social and academic pressures can be deleterious to children if they are not developmentally ready and mature enough to accept the concomitant responsibilities. Expectations beyond children's capabilities to perform create failure and a poor sense of self (Baker, 1987). Consistent unrealistic expectations exaggerate child failures (Chun, 1980), make success unlikely in any circumstance, and may establish interactions marked by disappointment and withdrawal.

Discrimination is likewise potentially traumatic. Discrimination based on such things as gender, race, and sexual preference affect an individual's self-appraisal. Often the self-appraisal is negative, leading to a self-judgment of social failure. Discrimination of any form can undermine a child's self-confidence. In most cases, the basis of discrimination (e.g., race) cannot be changed or "corrected," and unsuccessful efforts in this direction may exacerbate feelings of ineptness and helplessness (Gordon, 1960).

Family trauma can be viewed as a disturbance outside of or within the family structure that upsets the dynamics of the family. Family trauma can involve stressors infringing upon the members of a family, such as family violence and abuse, divorce, loss, and various kinds of uprooting of the family. From the child's perspective, the family retains the status of primary interactional and socialization agent for the bulk of early childhood; thus the child has therefore developed a natural attachment to and familiarity with the interpersonal styles of parents and siblings. Children are continually growing physically, cognitively, and emotionally, and a part of this development process entails the sharpening of awareness and sensitivity at all stages of development. As a result, children are often extremely sensitive to people and events around them, where the problems of parents and siblings may potentially effect positive or negative consequences for a child in the family.

Often abusive, psychotic, and substance-dependent parents, given their conditions, alter their parenting patterns from what would be considered the norm (Kessler, 1988). The sustained trauma of a dysfunctional parent-child relationship distorts the child's self-attitudes and attitudes toward his or her parents, and it inhibits peer relationships. Such dysfunctional and potentially abusive or violent relationships can stem from disrupted ties with parents, addictive parents, and satanic ritual abuse and other cult indoctrinations. All of these circumstances certainly affect individuals and families to varying degrees (Davis, 1990; Forman, 1984; Levin, 1988–89; Putnam, 1991).

Family trauma can be either a rallying or an isolating experience. For a family as a unit to withstand a threatening event necessitates a certain extent of banding together by family members. In cases such as the sudden relocation of the family, divorce of parents, or suicide of a sibling, the interdependence of mother, father, brother, and sister is important in adjusting to the differential stresses of these events. In contrast, for a solitary child to combat family trauma without support creates a rather lonely, isolating experience, and it could seem easier for the child to choose to withdraw when there is not a family support network to help him or her through such trials. The events affecting an individual member can radiate, since families are ideally interdependent. What begins as an individual trauma can develop into a trauma the entire family must confront.

As children mature and their interpersonal network grows, they begin to experience the effects of external interactions in direct and indirect ways. With environmental-community trauma, the effects of events occurring outside the family unit can disturb a family's behaviors, feelings, and thoughts. An incident occurring peripherally or even on the other side of the world does not necessarily have to make direct contact with the individual or the family to bring changes to the family. Resources and services available to community members can be curtailed as a result of the environmental upset, and subsequently social relationships may change, the community's needs may become more demanding, and institutions may instill new policies and procedures in order to respond to the traumatic aftereffects. Events range from tragic accidents such as the shuttle disaster to senseless hate crimes such as an arbitrary sniper attack or the Holocaust. Being a witness to a victim of such events or merely cognizant of the possibility of such happenings can have dramatic and profound effects on children (Gould & Gould, 1991; Pynoos, Nader, Frederick, & Gonda et al., 1987; Pynoos & Nader, 1988b; Mazor, Gampel, Enright, & Orenstein, 1990). Community trauma engages collective resources and compels individuals to seek environmental support.

For the individual, each type of trauma demands something different, something he or she may or may not possess. Despite perceptions of relative intensity, each traumatic incident can be equally devastating. Children of trauma treated under the most supportive conditions may be resilient and responsive to interventions (Masten, Best, & Garmezy, 1990), but the damage that traumas cause can never be completely erased. The promotion of awareness and prevention of trauma and violence may best address these issues.

The following part of this chapter on trauma in children addresses the general issue of psychological treatment. The focus of this discussion is on psychological treatment of abused children in terms of individual, family, and community interventions. The case of abuse as a treatment issue was selected because of the prevalence of abuse as a traumatic issue, the extensive child abuse research base, and the broad literature on treatment of child abuse.

INDIVIDUAL PSYCHOLOGICAL TREATMENT OF ABUSED CHILDREN

Psychological treatment or psychotherapy is conducted in three main formats, individual, family, or group, each of which may be applicable to the maltreated child. Where the abuse has been chronic, there is a high likelihood that this has

resulted in malformation of personality psychological structures, that is, pathological distortions in the child's mental life, sense of self, others, and the world,
with resulting emotional, cognitive, interpersonal, and social malfunctioning. In
such cases, individual psychotherapy may be indicated in the form of play therapy for children between the ages of 4 and 12 or so. Short-term play therapy
may also be applicable as a prophylactic measure when one or two violent
traumatic episodes have occurred. In such cases the therapist can structure the
treatment situation (toys, figures, objects) to recapitulate the traumatic events so
as to promote children's working through of their pathological reactions (Hambridge, 1955; Levy, 1945).

Play therapy enables the inarticulate damaged child to use the child's best
language, the language of play (Erikson 1937; Chethik, 1989), as a form of
metaphoric expression, communication, and coping. The child's symbolic playing out of traumatic experiences and concurrent verbalizations are assimilated
by the therapist and verbally acknowledged, fed back, empathized with, clarified,
and interpreted. This provides an empathic, supportive, and interpersonal medium for children to work through their psychopathology by correcting their
distorted inner perceptions and expectations of self, others, and the world
(Glenn, 1978). Although sexual abuse of children is in most cases a traumatic
violation, it is different from physical assault in terms of cause, intent, occurrence, nature, psychodynamics, and the family dynamics, reporting, and treatment (Walters, 1975). The child therapist must keep this in mind when working
with such children, in contrast to physically violated children, although the same
general principles of treatment may hold. This discussion also assumes that prior
to treatment, there has been adequate identification of abuse, immediate crisis
intervention, and diagnostic determination that psychological treatment is indicated. In addition, while we are concentrating on treatment of the child, coordinated treatment of the parents is essential wherever possible (Wilkes, 1970).

THE THERAPIST

The child therapist who works with violently abused and traumatized children
and abusive parents and adults must be prepared to face and contain a melange
of intense affective reactions. Feelings of horror, repulsion, disgust, and pity for
the child victim, loathing and rage toward the abusive adults, are common.
James (1989) notes that those who become therapists to make themselves feel
good and those who are "faint hearted" are not fitted for such work. She says
that the experience can be quite stressful "emotionally, physically, morally and
spiritually." Intense countertransferential rescue fantasies for the child and murderous wishes for the abuser can compromise the treatment process by creating
overprotection, a failure to set limits when necessary for the child, and alienation
of the parents. This is especially contraindicated because one of the main goals
is to strengthen the parent-child relationship.

Walters (1975) observes that initially professionals should not expect too much from themselves and the child. In the role of the child's savior the therapist may expect an instant positive response from the child, forgetting that the child abuse victim has good reason to be frightened, wary, and distrustful of strange adults. Almost always abused children feel like very bad children, guilty of upsetting and troubling the adult caretakers by their misbehavior. They will tend to be protective of the abuser and shy away from any direct communication of their physically and psychologically painful experiences, all the more so if they sense that the repulsed adult is angry at the abusive adult. Furthermore, by the time the abused child has reached the child therapist, he or she may have been repeatedly interviewed by teachers, principals, and child protective workers and may have been subjected to invasive medical procedures, increasing his or her defensiveness. Simply inviting the child to the playroom and inviting him or her to play may be sufficient to enable most abused children to begin to play out their emotional and psychological reactions to traumatic experiences via the metaphors of their fantasy-directed play.

THE CHILD

Beverly James (1989), expanding on the original work of Finklehor and Browne (1986), describes a phenomenological analysis of nine subjective traumagenic states (emotional conditions originating in traumatic experiences) that enable the development of treatment plans relevant to the profile or pattern of traumagenic states of any particular child. James states that the concept of traumagenic states of childhood provides the therapist with guidelines to the specific dynamics of a child's posttraumatic situation and gives a focus for treatment. Abused and traumatized children evidence one or more of these states:

1. Self-blame
2. Powerlessness
3. Loss and betrayal
4. Fragmentation of bodily experiences
5. Stigmatization
6. Erotization
7. Destructiveness
8. Dissociative/multiple personality disorder
9. Attachment disorder

In discussing physically abused children from a psychoanalytic perspective, Arthur Green (1980) reports that in defense against a sense of utter helplessness and annihilation anxiety, abused children of violent parents identify themselves with the aggressor. In a desperate effort to master such acute feelings, by a reversal of roles they become the aggressive victimizer rather than passive victims, doing unto others what has been done unto them. In this way, they convert a passively experienced painful terror into a grandiose sense of power and control. Green notes that hyperaggressive reactions typically follow incidents of violent abuse. Furthermore, poor superego restraint as a result of previous internalizations of inadequate parental superego models contributes further aggressive-destructive impulsions. There is a subgroup of abused children who have been so terrorized by violent maltreatment as to be reduced to fearful timidity and depression rather than aggressiveness. Such children of violence, feeling that they are very bad, compulsively maintain an illusory hope that by repeating the original sadomasochistic relationship (master-slave, persecutor-victim) the punitive object will finally love them and redeem them, a hope doomed to disappointment.

Green further observes that repeated assaults result in emotionally as well as physically painful feelings linked with primary parental objects. A highly devalued self-concept is formed by such painful self-awareness in which the self-experience is regarded with internalized parental hatred.

Yet ironically, says Green, it is only a potentially hostile facsimile of the violently punishing parent that offers the hope of love and redemption, since only object relations that are painful can recapitulate the original parental object relationship.

Green finds that suicidal attempts, gestures, threats, and self-mutilation commonly appear. These behaviors express masochistic, desperate, if self-destructive efforts to solicit love, forestall abandonment, define oneself through pain, or sadomasochistically punish the loved/hated/feared object via self-punishment. These more blatant forms of pain-inducing actions are accompanied by more subtle forms of pain-dependent and rageful feelings that are alleviated by provocative, belligerent, limit-testing behavior, which elicits punishments and beatings from parents, other adults, and peers; this behavior in turn promotes vicious cycles of masochistic and hostile provocations. Teasing, taunting, provocative behavior may also express the child's desperate efforts to use the punitive adult to suppress emerging, panicking, violent rage. Finally, self-destructiveness provides a medium for the children's unconscious guilt compliance with parental hostility, doing unto themselves what the parent has done to them. In addition, frequent academic failure in school and aggressive behavior result in vicious cycles of parental beatings and increased rage and panic, resulting in further abuse.

As a result of pathogenic parent-child interactions, such children of violence suffer from severe impairments and deficits in ego functions such as impulse control, frustration, anxiety and depression tolerance, reality sensing and testing, body imaging, and maintenance of self- and object representations and object constancy. Coherent, logical, realistic thought processes to modulate affective reactions are not possible. Abused children are prone to use primitive defenses of denial, projection, introjection, and splitting, which severely distort their apprehension of themselves and the world. They seek immediate need gratification, yet are suspicious and distrusting. They need to exploit, manipulate, and control others. They are preoccupied with rageful violent fantasies. They can be pseudo-independent and omnipotent, which thinly covers helplessness, depression, neediness, both dreading and hungry for nurturance. They are hypersensitive to separations, which result in loss of poorly established internal parental object representations, with internal proneness to separation anxieties that may be expressed via hostile, provocative behaviors rather than expressions of need for parental contact.

From the viewpoint of the violent abusive parent, the abused child is scapegoated, perceived as the major cause of parental and family frustrations. The process of scapegoating results from parental projective identifications into the child, often from birth and infancy onward, of unassimilable hostile, painful, toxic parental self-introjects internalized from their parents. These painful, bad images of self in the abusive parent oversensitizes the parent to any difficult, nonconforming, negative, "bad" behavior in the child, even if phase-specific, like two-year negativism, infantile crying, nonresponsiveness to impatient parental efforts at soothing, or childish overactivity. Negative temperamental or congenital factors, the child's appearance or gender, which fail to meet parental idealizing fantasies, may stimulate rageful abusive reactions in already vulnerable, predisposed parents who themselves experienced abusive parenting because of their "badness."

Of particular relevance to the play therapy of children traumatized by violence is the work of Lenore Terr (1981a, 1981b, 1983). She identified eleven characteristics of posttraumatic play:

1. compulsive repetition
2. an unconscious link between the play and the traumatic event
3. literalness of the play with simple defenses only
4. failure to relieve anxiety
5. occurring over a wide age range
6. a varying lag time prior to its development
7. carrying power to nontraumatized youngsters
8. contagion to new generations of children
9. danger
10. the use of doodling, talking, typing, and audio duplication as modes of repeated play
11. the possibility of therapeutically retracing posttraumatic play to an earlier trauma (1981b, p. 308)

Long-term effects of psychic trauma on untreated children observed by Terr included anxiety, fears, and mortification in feeling vulnerable in the traumatic situation. She also found cognitive impairments of a defensive nature, namely avoidance of thoughts about the event, denial, and academic failures, even though the events were available to consciousness. Screen memories, physiological reactions, disturbances in the sense of time, duration, and sequence of traumatic events were present, as well as continued repetitive phenomena, dreams and nightmares, and post-traumatic play and reenactment.

TREATMENT

The treatment of children of violence integrates psychotherapeutic techniques and methods used with troubled children in general (Glenn, 1978; Chethik, 1989) with special knowledge, methods, and sensitivity to the particular psychodynamics and psychopathology of maltreated and traumatized children who are prone to hopelessness, helplessness, and distrust. Therapists must work actively to develop a trusting relationship and involve children in the treatment process to enable them to return to, reexperience in a new way, and work through the painful events that overwhelmed them. James states, "The practitioner needs to work openly, directly, intensely, and playfully, allowing the child to accept his or her past and present feelings and behaviors related to trauma and to change behaviors that are dysfunctional" (1989, p. 19). James's is a wide-ranging, active, directive, structured, eclectic approach in which she intuitively and innovatively uses theoretical ideas and techniques from just about every school of psychotherapy: Rogerian, Rankian, Reichian, Psychoanalytic, Behavioral, Cognitive, Gestalt, Experiential, Family Systems, and so on. She provides multidimensional experiences and teachings to promote cognitive treatment strategies, insight-oriented clarifications and interpretation of emotional conflicts, and enhancement of healthy body experience and functioning. Modalities of treatment besides play and fun include art, music, sand tray play, metaphoric storytelling, body exercises, role playing and psychodrama, as well as direct discussions to enhance the child's self-understanding, promote positive self-feelings, reduce shame and guilt, and relieve cognitive distortions. She structures, encourages, praises, reassures, persuades, explains, and educates.

In the initial exploratory phase with the child she aims to sort out "the child's understanding of what happened, the meaning of the event to the child, the youngster's feelings before, during, and after the traumatic experience, the child's behaviors before, during, and after the event, the child's worries related to self, siblings, and family, in the present and in the future" (1989, p. 51).

In terms of the nine traumagenic states previously described, James works assiduously to (1) reduce self-blame and guilt, (2) empower the child, (3) help the children grieve and cope with loss and betrayal, (4) provide body integration experiences, (5) reduce shame and a sense of stigma, (6) redefine the child's lovability so that erotization of interpersonal relationships is unnecessary, (7) help the child learn self-control and reduce destructiveness, (8) help the child reintegrate and assimilate dissociated aspects of his or her personality, (9) provide corrective experiences to enable the development of a secure attachment.

In contrast to this highly structured, directive, interactive, educational approach, Arthur Green (1980) presents a modified individual psychoanalytically oriented play therapy approach to violently treated physically abused children, this in addition to active therapeutic work with the abusive parents or adults. Because such children often fall into the range of borderline psychopathology, with consequent deficits in psychic structure (ego and superego deficits), their psychological developmental arrest results in severe emotional and cognitive dysfunction and psychosocial deviations. Psychotherapy requires an emphasis on enhancing ego functioning and integration, reality testing, containment of drives and impulses, and the strengthening of higher-level defenses.

Consequently, therapeutic interventions of verbalized therapist observations and interpretations of the structure and content of the child's spontaneous play, include the feelings, cognitions, and repetitive themes and reenactments of abuse. These are expressed in the child's play, especially portrayals of pathological self and object relations, with allusions to highly negative transference reactions in which the therapist is perceived as a dangerous "bad" object.

Green states that "therapeutic interventions must deal with each of the major psychopathological sequelae of child abuse: acute traumatic reactions, poor impulse control, low self-esteem with self-destructive behavior, extreme separation anxiety, and school difficulties associated with learning and behavior disorders" (1980, p. 172).

Alleviating Acute Traumatic Reactions

Acute traumatic reactions as a result of beatings or other maltreatment generate intense annihilation anxieties transferred into the playroom. The therapist needs to reassure children that they are safe and to provide them with appropriate playthings—dolls, family figures, puppets, and drawing and painting materials to master the trauma via repetition and reenactment. The children now have new self-experiences, including a sense of improvement and control over the abusive scenario by either altering outcomes or reversing roles from passive, helplessness abuse to an active, powerful abuser. The child experiences the therapist's empathic reflections, clarifications, and interpretations of feelings and of distorted cognitions.

Strengthening of Ego Functions

By encouraging verbalization and containment of any impulse and action beyond the sphere of symbolic and metaphoric play, the therapist helps the child to abreact painful and uncontrollable affects and to increase frustration and anxiety tolerance and reality testing. Aggression is also sublimated via competitive play and rule-based games rather than violent conflictual action. Simultaneously the child gradually internalizes the ego and superego functioning of the therapist via identification with a positive object in the interactive play. This enables positive developments in ego functions and post–reality-testing defenses.

Improvement of Object Relations

The internal object world of the violently treated child is filled with unbearable introjected images of cruel and malevolent parental figures. The child defends against them by primitive denial, projection, and splitting. Fantasies of the abusing parent as "good" while the "badness" is introjected onto the child itself or projected onto others expresses a desperate effort to preserve a needed positive image of the parent. Excessive splitting of the parental image prevents the child from integrating whatever is positive in the parent-child relationship, which would, even to a small extent, modify the malevolent image. The parent becomes all good and the child or others are all bad.

Green (1980) describes the "fluctuating polarization of the object world" that invades all of the child's interpersonal relations. Initial mistrust and suspicion may be replaced by overidealization in response to therapist's warm acceptance, which inevitably will be disappointed, betrayed, and enraging because of the intensity of the child's wishes for rescue and nurturance and his or her anger when frustrated. He also suggests interpretation of the child's resort to identification with the aggressor as a compensation for helpless feelings, and the child's consequent sense of "badness" and fear of punishment.

Impulse Control

Abused children's hostile aggressive and destructive reactions are major precipitants for referral for treatment. The therapist must strengthen impulse control in the playroom in order to maintain the therapeutic relationship and further normative processes of socialization enabling adaptive social functioning. The therapist must first identify and acknowledge the need to feel strong and powerful, even while he or she may have to limit direct physical assaults on either the therapist or playroom materials. Out-of-control children may need to be held firmly while the therapist continues to engage the violent child in a therapeutic dialogue aimed to help him or her regain self-control. Additionally, the therapist's firm but nonhostile manner obviates the child's tendency to identify with the aggressor, enabling gradual neutralization of aggression.

Improvement of Self-esteem

Improvement of self-esteem is enhanced in the playroom climate of warm acceptance and respect for the child while furthering the child's sense of mastery through play. The message that his or her maltreatment results from parental inadequacies and problems rather than his or her "bad" behavior also promotes a more positive sense of self.

Strengthening Object Constancy and the Capacity to Tolerate Separation

Green observes that abused children, equating maltreatment with a concerned parental effort to make them "good," become puzzled when their provocative behavior does not elicit punishment. They interpret this lack of interest as abandonment, as they do if the therapist is late or must cancel a session or is seen with another child. This needs to be interpreted, along with active reassurance. The child may be allowed to take home small tokens as reassurance of the therapist's caring and to promote internalization of the therapist's positive mental object representation. Therapist absences should be worked through before and after the absence.

Improvement of School Performance

The frequent presence of learning dysfunctions and disabilities in maltreated children necessitates the therapist's maintaining communication with the child's school and endorsing proper educational remediation. The child's tendency to act out displaced aggression against classmates and teachers needs to be interpreted to school personnel, who must be guided in managing the child's provocative behavior in terms of nonpunitive setting of limits.

Family Interventions

Working with the entire family is often a necessary and critical component of the treatment of a child who is a victim of violence. The pathology that gives rise to child abuse is located within the family as a whole and most often cannot be solely attributable to an individual family member. Dysfunctional patterns of interactions become ingrained in the disturbed family system and perpetuate a manner of relating and communicating that leads to the violence present in these families. Change in the family depends on the cooperation of the group. This becomes a struggle for the entire family because it may be that the violence within the family has been successful in diverting the attention away from the underlying problems existent in the family and/or marital relationship. There is often a strong resistant pull made by all family members to maintain the familiar control and balance in their lives, despite the pathological outcome of violent trauma.

To work most effectively with a family where violence against children is occurring or is a high risk, there must be either strong internal motivation for help and a degree of loyalty and attachment among the members or external controls such as a statutory mandate for treatment. There is a growing consensus that treatment of family violence cannot be successful without the interagency involvement of the community. When severe victimization is going on in a family, authoritative intervention of the courts or other community agencies is often vital to the treatment process and to the protection of the child. When parents lack normal conscience and behavioral control, "the dangerous and repetitive acting out of these adults, the unreliability of their promises all make authoritative intervention imperative for the protection of children" (Anderson & Shafer, 1979, p. 439). Because child abuse is the result of the interaction of personal, family, and societal variables, treatment must incorporate a variety of treatment modalities as well as the involvement of various resources in the community. It has been seen that the treatment of abusive or neglectful families cannot be successful without measures to address the concrete and practical problems of their lives. Successful treatment in the long term must also include the provision of community services such as help with housing, day care, and employment assistance (Coulborn Faller, Ziefert, & Okell Jones, 1981).

The eclectic approach to family treatment used by most therapists is in response to the diverse and serious nature of child abuse. Generally, no one therapeutic modality or fixed treatment plan can meet the overall needs of a family where abuse has taken place (Bentovim, 1981). Models of family treatment with abuse cases tend to incorporate principles from a variety of theoretical orientations. Klavans Simring and Mishne (1989) recommend a model incorporating the principles from systems, psychoanalytic, structural, and strategic theories of the family. Attention focuses on interactions and relationships, environmental concerns, specific presenting problems, and communication patterns. Once the therapist has "engaged the family and learned something about how the family lives, their reality problems and their difficulty in getting along with each other, he or she is ready to pinpoint the specific interactions between family members that give rise to abuse" (p. 72).

Integrative family approaches to the treatment of child abuse most often incorporate techniques of systems or strategic based models. These models offer the therapist with the influential power to help promote an adaptive, need-fulfilling balance between the family and surrounding community (Pardeck, 1988). To engage an abusing family in treatment and to keep it involved in supportive community services requires working through great resistances (Dale, Morrison, Davies, Noyes, & Roberts, 1983). Helping that family overcome its resistance to treatment is a crucial factor requiring an eclectic approach with active strategies.

In many cases of child maltreatment or of violence against children, family treatment provides many advantages over other modalities. Initially, it provides the opportunity for the therapist to assess the interaction among family members. A family assessment is almost always essential whether or not family therapy is ultimately used in the treatment plan. The assessment involves the evaluation of the family's habitual process of interaction to determine how the behavior of all the members influences and is influenced by the behavior of the rest of the family. Family therapy is almost always indicated when there is dysfunction in a parent-child subsystem, or when cross-generational patterns are reinforcing symptomatic behavior (Clarkin, Frances, & Moodie, 1979). If it is seen that family dysfunction is primarily a product of problems between the couple in the household, the most parsimonious intervention may be deemed to be treatment of the couple. If this relationship can become more cooperative and harmonious, or if the couple can agree to leave the child out of their conflicts, abuse and neglect may be alleviated. However, in situations where child maltreatment is more deeply entrenched in the family dynamics, then family work is a preferential treatment modality (Coulborn Faller et al., 1981). The assessment of family functioning may indicate that the family treatment may not be appropriate if parents are found to be severely psychotic, mentally retarded, substance abusers, sociopathic, or cruel, or if they have a history of inflicting severe physical trauma. There are those clinicians who believe family treatment is suitable only when child maltreatment is mild and/or when the abuse can clearly be linked to specific family interactions. Even when the family is chaotic and severely dysfunctional, therapy with the entire family can be effective when treatment remains focused on specific familial interactions (Klavans Simring & Mishne, 1989).

Working together as a family enables the abusing family to benefit from the experience of having all members simultaneously receive treatment. In this way, they have the added advantage of reducing the tendency for therapeutic gains to be sabotaged by family members who are not involved in therapy (Coulborn Faller et al., 1981). The experience also provides members with the opportunity to learn to communicate more directly, to problem solve, to learn more effective child management techniques, and to learn to empathize with one another (Klavans Simring & Mishne, 1989).

The family therapy arena provides the opportunity for the development of empathy among family members, which is an essential element of the treatment process in abusing families (Pardeck, 1988). Encouraging family members to share their feelings and experiences in the treatment setting enables them to bring their pain and struggle out in the open. By doing so, parents, particularly those who themselves were maltreated as children, may develop a new perspective about their children's behavior and may begin to better understand their own reactions to it. The children may in turn begin to understand their parents better, contributing to the development of a healthier mutual identification between parents and children (Klavans Simring & Mishne, 1989). Treatment approaches that specifically encourage the development of empathy within the abusing family strive to create an empathic therapeutic environment for the family. The empathic responses of the therapist are seen to provide a "reparenting" experience for the parents and a secure hold for the family that allows for individual development. The abused child benefits not only from the empathic responses of the therapist but also from the empathy the parents acquire from the experience of therapy itself (Cornett, 1985).

Parents who abuse their children have often experienced childhood violence and rejection, and they have unmet needs for dependency, nurturance, and esteem. For this reason, a therapist cannot take for granted the need to establish a professional relationship at the outset of treatment. According to a program developed by Bentovim (1981), the therapist must initially work to gain the parent's trust, which may be promoted by offering practical help, support and guidance. The therapist must be available to provide a parenting experience to the parent and to display uncritical acceptance, nonpossessive warmth, and empathy. The next step in Bentovim's plan is concerned with the maturation of parents by identifying with therapists. It is during this phase of treatment that the therapist begins to confront and interpret the behaviors of family members. Treatment then continues to become more psychotherapeutic in nature, incorporating the treatment orientation and modality to best suit the particular case.

The essential element of an effective program to treat abusing families, as outlined by Bentovim (1981), is a flexible team approach. "When the overall aim is the development and emotional maturity of all members of the family, then a therapeutic modality which merely focuses on one aspect of the problem cannot be sufficient" (p. 170). Therefore, although providing a reparenting experience is a necessary element in the process of promoting maturation, it is thought that it may not in itself change the pattern of relationships between the parent and the abused child. The program calls for a team of professionals whose services to the family would include treatment of the parents, the family, dyads within the family, individuals, and groups.

Offering a variety of therapeutic modalities to the abusing family is considered to be the most effective means of treatment. The special and complex needs of maltreated children and their families often require the incorporation of different approaches, including group and individual treatment. Group treatment for both children and parents can provide various benefits to the family system. Family members can experience a sense of relief in meeting others who can relate to their pain, anxieties, and frustrations. Activity groups can provide younger children with the cathartic experience of playing and expressing themselves freely. These groups also aim to help to develop effective limits (Lynn, 1989). Furthermore, activity groups provide the children with a safe arena where they will naturally play out familial patterns of abuse and then learn to develop new, positive ways of interacting with others. Group leaders need to be able to provide corrective experiences through the development of relationships demonstrating concern, support, and protection. Interventions in groups of abused children need to be implemented slowly and, at first, consist only of empathic and understanding comments made in response to actions. The vulnerability of abused children makes the verbalizing or sharing of feelings too premature and threatening at the beginning phases of treatment. As the group progresses, the leader begins to identify patterns of behavior occurring in the group and helps the children to become aware of their interactions and to learn to trust each other. As trust develops, the children lessen their mutually abusive or defensive interactions and begin to share their experiences and promote a mutual aid process (Lynn, 1989). Although children's groups have focused on care and stimulation, there is a need to help children deal with the emotional consequences of the atmosphere of violence and rejection in which they have grown up. It is thought that groups need to help children with the consequent pattern of poor self-esteem and the pseudo-mature, obsessive, and difficult behaviors that lead to the rejection by peers, parents, and teachers (Bentovim, 1981).

Groups for parents encompass a wide variety of approaches. They can focus on education, caretaking, peer support, behavior modification, group process, or the development of insight. Most often, abusing parent groups aim to educate and to help parents acquire more effective parenting and communication skills (Lynn, 1989). Psychotherapy groups are more appropriate for mildly abusive parents who are capable of insight. Abusive parents often come from deprived backgrounds and can benefit from the mutual identification, support, and nurturance of the therapy group. However, it has been pointed out by Phillips and Gonzalez-Ramos (1989) that extremely socially and emotionally deprived mothers, particularly those who are of ethnic minorities, will require the more intense nurturance of an individual relationship with a therapist. It is recommended that initial work with these mothers consist of individual treatment until they begin to develop a sense of trust and security. Initially group situations may be too threatening if parents fear they will be judged or exposed. Once in a group situation, parents need to feel nurtured and supported by group members and the leader, so that the group as a whole provides an atmosphere of security and caring. Members may be so needy that they may not be able to provide nurturance to others, requiring the leader to be active in modeling and in providing direct expressions of emotional support. In addition, groups of abusing parents may require other modifications to more traditional treatment, such as being provided with transportation, child care, or refreshment (Lynn, 1989). A goal of treatment groups involving members of abused families is often to provide a network of support in the community. Unlike traditional groups where outside contact is often discouraged, these groups can serve as a resource between meetings and can help to enlarge the extended family and community network for isolated families (Bentovim, 1981).

Pardeck (1988) states that it is necessary for all family members to be in individual treatment before the therapist can begin working with the family as a whole. In other words, the family must be ready to pull together. This implies that the parents are ready to accept responsibility for their actions and that the victimized child has had enough individual treatment to be ready to come together with his or her family.

However, often the abusing family is not highly amenable to treatment. To engage the family in treatment of any kind requires the therapist to work through tremendous resistance. Dale et al. (1983) explain resistance in family treatment as being comprised of the intrapsychic resistance in each family member as well as the collective resistance of the family based on the perceived threat to its maladaptive equilibrium. The initial job of the therapist is to work with the abusing family's resistance by rechanneling it toward more positive purposes. The force of resistance is seen as potentially promoting more positive family dynamics with respect to the establishment of adaptive functioning and interpersonal equilibrium within the family system.

The techniques Dale et al. (1983) recommend to rechannel resistance and to engage a family in treatment are influenced by a variety of factors, including the reason for the referral, the presenting problem, the type of legal mandate for treatment, the quality of the resistance, and the current level of risk to the child. Initially, the orienting approach to treatment is either a *linear approach* or a *systems approach*. A linear approach involves a detailed description of the immediate family and the history of the families of origin. This process enables the therapist to gain important information about the family and also provides the family with a cathartic experience. A systems approach focuses on the here and now and is more task oriented. It is often initially used with families at high risk for violence, but its successful implementation is dependent on a relatively low level of resistance. If much resistance is encountered, the therapist has the option of shifting to the linear approach, where the focus is off the immediate problem, thereby providing the family with relief from mounting tensions. To reduce the level of threat to family members, history taking is defined as "non therapy," and it is made clear that there is no change expected at this initial stage of the process. Another approach, offered by Klavans Simring and Mishne (1989) involves the technique of "joining" to initially engage the family in treatment. When seeing the family for the first time, it is recommended that the therapist try to put family members at ease by spending a few minutes speaking to each family member individually about nonthreatening, casual subjects.

If the family remains resistant to becoming engaged in the treatment process after the use of initial approaches, Dale et al. (1983) suggests a range of strategies can be used to increase the control of the therapist and to combat resistance and induce change. The authors recognize that their model of treatment is in marked opposition to others that advocate a long-term nurturing style of intervention. They take an active, authoritative stance in treating child abuse within the family system and contend that it is imperative that resistance be tackled in an assertive manner. The therapist has a wide range of strategy options to choose from in response to the type of resistance encountered. For example, if the family's resistance is of the hostile type, the therapist can establish control of the situation by remaining aloof and nonresponsive to the family's angry arguments. In this way, the family must make a clear decision about whether or not to stay in treatment. The use of humor is recommended to counter the family's attempts to sabotage the sessions with the manipulative use of anger to avoid issues. With a family who is resisting treatment in a passive-hopeless manner, the therapist might use paradoxical injunctions and prescribe the need for the problem to stay the same or to get worse. In using paradoxical injunctions, the aim is for the therapist to gain more control of the problem at hand, but implementation must be done with considerable caution when the presenting problem is a direct threat to a child. This strategy is also recommended to be used with a challenging family who is resisting the therapist's instructions, so that the prescription to increase the threatening behavior may actually serve to provoke its decrease. When working with a passive-aggressive family, the therapist might simply remain silent. It is seen that many families may use silence to manipulate the therapist into being more active and more verbal, enabling the family to continue resisting change. By remaining silent, the therapist demonstrates that it is the family who is responsible for the work in treatment.

Once the family is engaged, Bentovim (1981) recommends that the treatment focus on the interactive patterns among family members and that interventions attempt to change patterns seen within the therapeutic situation. The therapist must support and encourage the use of more positive responses and interactions. Particularly with abusing families, it is necessary for the therapist to "encourage warmth and praise instead of coldness and rejection, point out the way parents and children are sharing and experiencing the same feeling, and help both parents and children to find unused aspects of themselves in their relationships with each other" (p. 176). Reframing is a technique that the therapist can use to help change the family's perception of a behavior so that it can be seen in a more positive light (Klavins Simring & Mishne, 1989). For example, a child's constant demands upon a parent can be reframed to be seen as a reflection of his or her wish to share more time and to be closer with the parent. A more dramatic and confrontive technique is offered by Bentovim (1981), who suggests that videotaping the family can help members become more aware of aspects of their interactions and become more attuned to the precipitants of violence toward the children.

Community Intervention

Although it is important to choose and to use the techniques appropriate for a family to make changes, the growing consensus is that organized and efficient community involvement is the most important element in the treatment of violent, abusing, and neglectful families. Particularly if the child is removed from the home and a child protection services agency and/or court system becomes involved in the case, the therapeutic portion of the treatment program must be fully integrated with the interagency system.

In child abuse cases, service providers can extend throughout a large network of community agencies. Therefore treatment must be coordinated among the therapists on the therapeutic treatment team, as well as among the various agencies involved in the case. Those involved must be representative of the disciplines with the professional expertise to determine if abuse and/or neglect has occurred and if so, how to help alleviate the problem (Ziefert & Coulborn Faller, 1981). Baglow (1990) recommends a community-based model of treating child abuse where the connection between the therapy and containment aspects helps to unify the treatment. It is crucial to coordinate efforts and work together, with the clinical team handling the treatment and the agency with the statutory powers helping the family to follow through with treatment plans. Ziefert and Coulborn Faller (1981) recommended that child protective services be in a pivotal position in the organizational setup of community treatment teams. Coordination requires clear, thorough communication among all the service providers involved in a case. Plans, responsibilities, and goals must be agreed upon and understood by all. It is necessary that all involved parties have a unified definition of what constitutes child abuse and what the parameters of the family's responsibilities are while in treatment. Baglow (1990) firmly states that it is essential that any change in the agreed-upon plan be discussed with other participating agencies. Organized consistency, firm boundaries, and limitations help to keep a family contained within the system and in treatment. Furthermore, clear communication and coordination among service providers, within the team and interagency, allow the family to experience unity and support so lacking in their own family system.

Abusing families have strong influence on the treatment teams and the agencies with which they become involved. The effects of powerful pathological family dynamics can stimulate the destructive forces in the groups working with them, bringing out existing conflicts and tensions among the professionals (Dale, Walters, Davies, Roberts, & Morrison, 1986). Dynamics within treatment teams or within the interagency system may begin to mirror the family dynamics resulting in polarization or the splitting into factions. This phenomenon may be compared to an extension of a countertransference reaction going "beyond the therapist-family system, through the team, to the entire inter-agency systems" (p. 7).

When families have a multitude of problems, they need the combined efforts of a variety of specialized services to address as many needs as possible. Especially important to address are the concrete problems responsible for much of the stress that becomes a centrally contributing factor to child abuse and neglect. The family may need help dealing with public assistance or legal systems, arranging for transportation, shelter, or educational services. Many professionals working together can facilitate monitoring the status of child abuse in a family, as well as distribute some of the overwhelming responsibility of the totality of the family's situation (Coulborn Faller et al., 1981). The constant pressures inherent in child abuse cases may also be alleviated to some degree using a cotherapy model of family intervention, providing the opportunity for anxiety to be shared and dispelled (Dale et al., 1983). However, it must be kept in mind that many maltreating families lack the ability to form primary relationships, which is an issue of particular therapeutic importance (Coulborn Faller et al., 1981). Therefore, the goal of helping family members develop a healthy, primary relationship within their own family may be undermined by the involvement of too many professionals in their case. Coulborn Faller et al. (1981) recommend the use of a primary therapist who concentrates on the relationship aspect of functioning, with secondary service providers having a less intimate relationship with the family.

Treating child trauma with a family approach is a challenging endeavor. It often can be a highly effective means of treatment because it enables reduction of the dysfunctional patterns of interactions within the family system that give rise to and perpetuate child abuse and neglect. However, families in which severe trauma has occurred need to be treated from a variety of different approaches, in light of the highly complex and sensitive issues typically involved in such cases. Successful treatment of child trauma often depends on the commitment of the entire family as well as of the community and the interagency system that comprises a critical component of the treatment plan.

SUMMARY

The subject of trauma in children raises a broad range of issues. Certainly children's developmental and social status places them in a difficult position to comprehend and cope with violence and traumatic situations. To the extent children come from a warm, supportive family characterized by a network of caring relationships, children are in a good position to develop and utilize short- and long-term coping strategies. However, not all trauma and violence represent an idiosyncratic circumstance in the child's life. Frequently, the violence is directed at the child or the child is a direct witness to ongoing violence within the family. In such circumstances, the need for treatment and intervention is immense. Fortunately, research reveals that treatment is effective for many children who experience difficult situations; unfortunately, such treatment is not available or utilized by all who could benefit.

REFERENCES

Anderson, L. M., & Shafer, G. (1979). The character-disordered family: A community treatment model for family sexual abuse. *American Journal of Orthopsychiatry, 49*(3), 436–445.

Baglow, L. J. (1990). A multidimensional model for treatment of child abuse: A framework for cooperation. *Child Abuse & Neglect, 14,* 387–395.

Baker, H. S. (1987). Underachievement and failure in college: The interaction between intrapsychic and interpersonal factors from the perspective of self psychology. *Adolescent Psychiatry, 14,* 441–460.

Bentovim, A. (1981). Setting up the treatment programme. In Neil Frunde (Ed.), *Psychological approaches to child abuse* (pp. 163–180). New Jersey: Rowman & Littlefield.

Chethik, M. (1989). *Techniques of child therapy: Psychodynamic strategies.* New York: Guilford Press.

Chun, K. (1980). The myth of Asian American success and its educational ramifications. *IRCD Bulletin, 15,* 1–12.

Clarkin, J., Frances, A., & Moodie, J. (1979). Selection criteria for family therapy. *Family Processes, 18,* 391–403.

Cornett, C. (1985). The cyclical pattern of child physical abuse from a psychoanalytic self-psychology perspective. *Child and Adolescent Social Work, 2*(2), 83–92.

Coulborn Faller, K., Ziefert, M., & Okell Jones, C. (1981). Treatment planning, process, and progress. In K. Coulborn Faller (Ed.), *Social work with abused and neglected children.* New York: Free Press.

Dale, P., Morrison, T., Davies, M., Noyes, P., & Roberts, W. (1983). A family-therapy approach to child abuse: Countering resistance. *Journal of Family Therapy, 5,* 117–143.

Dale, P., Walters, J., Davies, M., Roberts, W., & Morrison, T. (1986). The towers of silence: Creative and destructive issues for therapeutic teams dealing with sexual abuse. *Journal of Family Therapy, 8,* 1–25.

Davis, S. K. (1990). Chemical dependency in women: A description of its effects and outcome on adequate parenting. *Journal of Substance Abuse Treatment, 7*(4), 225–232.

Erikson, E. (1937). Configurations in play. *Psychoanalytic Quarterly, 6,* 139–214.

Finkelhor, D., & Browne, A. (1986). The traumatic impact of child sexual abuse. *American Journal of Orthopsychiatry, 55*(4), 530–541.

Forman, M. (1984). A trauma theory of character neuroses and traumatic transferences. Chicago Psychoanalytic Study and the Chicago Institute for Psychoanalysis Conference: Psychoanalysis: The vital issues (1981, Chicago, IL). *Emotions and Behavior Monographs, No. 3,* 321–345.

Glenn, J. (1978). *Child analysis and therapy.* New York: Jason Aronson.

Gordon, M. (1960). Assimilation in America: Theory and reality. *Daedalus, Journal of American Academy of Arts and Sciences, 90,* 263–285.

Gould, B. B., & Gould, J. B. (1991). Young people's perception of the space shuttle disaster: Case study. *Adolescence, 26*(102), 295–303.

Green, A. (1980). *Child maltreatment.* New York: Jason Aronson.

Haley, S. M., Cioffi, M. I., Lewin, J. E., & Baryza, M. J. (1990). Motor dysfunction in children and adolescents after traumatic brain injury. *Journal of Head Trauma Rehabilitation, 5*(4), 77–90.

Hambridge, G. (1955). Structured play therapy. *American Journal of Orthopsychiatry, 24,* 601–617.

Haugaard, J. J., & Reppucci, N. D. (1988). *The sexual abuse of children.* San Francisco: Jossey-Bass.

James, B. (1989). *Treating traumatized children.* Lexington, MA: Lexington Books.

Jones, D. P. (1986). Individual psychotherapy for the sexually abused child. *International Journal of Child Abuse and Neglect, 10,* 377–385.

Kessler, J. (1988). *Psychopathology of childhood.* Englewood Cliffs, NJ: Prentice Hall.

Klavans Simring, S., & Mishne, J. M. (1989). Family treatment. In S. M. Ehrenkranz, E. G. Goldstein, L. Goodman, & J. Seinfeld (Eds.), *Clinical social work with maltreated children and their families.* New York: New York University Press.

Kramer, E. (1974). *Art as therapy with children.* New York: Shocken Books.

Levin, M. L. (1988–89). Sequelae to marital disruption in children. Special Issue: Children of divorce: Developmental and clinical issues. *Journal of Divorce, 12*(2–3), 25–80.

Levy, D. (1945). Psychic trauma of operations in children and a note on combat neurosis. *American Journal of the Disabled Child, 69,* 7–25.

Lynn, M. (1989). Group treatment. In S. M. Ehrenkranz, E. G. Goldstein, L. Goodman,

& J. Seinfield (Eds.), *Clinical social work with maltreated children and their families.* New York: New York University Press.

Masten, A. S., Best, K. M., & Garmezy, N. (1990). Resilience and development: Contributions from the study of children who overcome adversity. *Development and Psychopathology, 2*(4), 425–444.

Mazor, A., Gampel, Y., Enright, R. D., & Orenstein, R. (1990). Holocaust survivors: Coping with post-traumatic memories in childhood and 40 years later. *Journal of Traumatic Stress, 3*(1), 1–14.

Pardeck, J. T. (1988). Family therapy as a treatment approach to child abuse. *Child Psychiatric Quarterly, 21*(4), 191–198.

Phillips, L. J., & Gonzalez-Ramos, G. (1989). Clinical social work practice with minority families. In S. M. Ehrenkranz, E. G. Goldstein, L. Goodman, & J. Seinfeld (Eds.), *Clinical social work with maltreated children and their families.* New York: New York University Press.

Putnam, F. W. (1991). The satanic ritual abuse controversy. *Child Abuse and Neglect, 15*(3), 175–179.

Pynoos, R. S., & Eth, S. (1984). The child as witness to homicide. *Journal of Social Issues. 40*(2), 87–108.

Pynoos, R. S., & Eth, S. (1986). Witness to violence: The child interview. *Journal of the American Academy of Child Psychiatry, 25*(3), 306–319.

Pynoos, R. S., & Nader, K. (1988a). Children who witness the sexual assaults of their mothers. *Journal of the American Academy of Child and Adolescent Psychiatry, 27*(5), 567–572.

Pynoos, R. S., & Nader, K. (1988b). Psychological first aid treatment approach to children exposed to community violence: Research implications. *Journal of Traumatic Stress, 1*(4), 445–473.

Pynoos, R. S., & Nader, K. (1990). Children's exposure to violence and traumatic death. *Psychiatric Annals, 20*(6), 334–344.

Pynoos, R. S., Nader, K., Frederick, C., Gonda, L., & Arroyo, W. (1987). Grief reactions in school age children following a sniper attack at school. Special Issue: Grief and bereavement. *Israel Journal of Psychiatry and Related Sciences, 24*(1–2), 53–63.

Schaefer, C. (Ed.). (1981). *Therapeutic use of child's play.* New York: Jason Aronson.

Terr, L. (1981a). Psychic trauma in children. *American Journal of Psychiatry, 138,* 14–19.

Terr, L. (1981b). Forbidden games: Post-traumatic child's play. *Journal of the American Academy of Child Psychiatry, 20,* 741–760.

Terr, L. (1983). Life attitudes, dreams, and psychic trauma in a group of "normal" children. *Journal of the American Academy of Child Psychiatry, 22,* 221–230.

Terr, L. C. (1985). Psychic trauma in children and adolescents. *Psychiatric Clinics of North America, 8*(4), 815–835.

Terr, L. C. (1991). Childhood traumas: An outline and overview. 140th Annual meeting of the American Psychiatric Association (1987, Chicago, IL). *American Journal of Psychiatry, 148*(1), 10–20.

Urbancic, J. C. (1987). Incest trauma. *Journal of Psychosocial Nursing and Mental Health Services, 25*(7), 33–35.

Van Hasselt, V. B. (1988). *Handbook of family violence.* New York: Plenum Press.

Walters, D. (1975). *Physical and sexual abuse of children: Causes and treatment.* Bloomington: Indiana University Press.

Wilkes, J. R. (1970). Involving parents in children's treatment. *Canadian Mental Health, 18,* 10–14.

Zeifert, M., & Coulborn Faller, K. (1981). The interdisciplinary team and the community. In K. Coulborn Faller (Ed.), *Social work with abused and neglected children.* New York: Free Press.

6

Incest: The Most Personal Violence

Dan Meyer

In his melancholic meditation upon civilization, Sigmund Freud (1930 [1961]) wondered about the value of diagnosing society's neurosis. He believed that such an exercise would be futile, as no one possessed the authority to impose the treatment. He recognized, nonetheless, that in spite of this difficulty it would not be long before someone would "embark upon a pathology of cultural communities" (p. 91). The events of the last thirty years seem to confirm his prediction. The social revolutions occasioned by the women's movement and the march toward equality have created a climate that has promoted the questioning of the status quo. The "social neurosis" that supported and tolerated the sexual and physical abuse of children, spousal abuse, and the abuse of the elderly, through secrecy and denial, has not only been diagnosed but has been deemed in need of treatment and dramatic change. Survivors speak out, press for legislative and judicial change, and litigate for damages. Radio and television talk shows, books and articles in popular magazines, movies, and dramas have revealed the scope and consequences of abuse in a way unthinkable just a few decades ago.

The issue of incest, believed by Freud to be at the heart of psychopathology in his early writings (see Freud, 1896 [1953], Masson, 1984) came to be minimized by him and by the clinical community as a direct factor in the development of madness. Experience was replaced by fantasy as a central causative factor of psychological distress; the harm caused by the other was replaced by unfulfilled wishes of the self. The Oedipal myth, shaped by Freud to suit his own purposes, led two generations of therapists away from the reality of reports of abuse. The victim became the initiator, the offender an innocent party. Bender and Blau (1937) argued that victims as young as four years of age were seductive and the instigators of incest; they went on to claim that the event resulted in little or no damage to the children! This assertion was to be echoed in papers by Landis (1956) and Yorukoglu and Kemph (1966). Thus, accusations were interpreted as wishes, memories as imagined events. Two generations of abused children/adult survivors did not receive support, validation, or effective treatment; two generations of offenders avoided prosecution and remained hidden from scrutiny.

The focus of this chapter is on the adult offender, the incidence of incest, its consequences to the victims, identification and treatment of offenders and victims, and some thoughts on current and future solutions to this problem. Case material is presented to illustrate relevant concerns.

Since the landmark paper by Kempe, Silverman, Steele, Droegenmuller, and Silver (1962) on the abuse of children, it has been increasingly more difficult to deny the scope of the problem of incest. During the past thirty years clinicians have become more sensitized to the presence of this problem in their patients. As an actual experience, incest is less likely to be misinterpreted or invalidated by therapists (Rush, 1977). Denial on the societal and personal levels has diminished. Mandatory reporting legislation, with concomitant training requirements for licensure acquisition or renewal, have compelled treatment providers to be exposed to the breadth of this most personal of violations. A host of books written for and about survivors (Armstrong, 1979; Brady, 1979; Vale Allen, 1980) have alerted the public to alternatives to silence about the trauma of incest. Television and radio talk shows, as well as popular movies, have served to educate and train the general population about prevention and/or treatment. Even the psychoanalytic community has been provoked, if not necessarily converted, by the controversial works of Masson (1984, 1990).

It is clear that there have been profound changes within the legal community, within the professional community, and within the public at large in regard to perceiving the seriousness and scope of incest and its consequences. Awareness seems to be heightened as never before. In spite of these changes, and the constructive consequences they have inspired, incest remains a grave problem. Although some have argued, perhaps with some justice, that the problem of incest will never be changed until the societal issue of patriarchy is fundamentally altered, interim solutions that can minimize or prevent further harm are required.

INCIDENCE AND OFFENDERS

The question of frequency of incestuous behavior has always been a thorny one. Due to the secrecy surrounding incest, at least until very recently, estimates were extremely low. In a 1955 text Weinberg reported that the number of prosecuted cases amounted to one or two cases per million, an amount that underrepresented the problem by at least a factor of 10,000. More recent findings point to a prevalence of one in a hundred (Finklehor, 1979), while overall estimates of childhood sexual abuse range from 3 percent to 31 percent for boys and 6 percent to 62 percent for girls (Peters, Wyatt, & Finklehor, 1986). Variations in frequency are due to the different definitions of abuse, sampling variations, and methodological dissimilarities. Blume (1990) has claimed that as many as 25 percent of women have been abused by someone they knew and trusted as children. As Breines and Gordon (1983) suggest, incest occurring this frequently is hardly a taboo in this society.

Perpetrators of adult-to-child incest are almost universally believed to be males (Breines & Gordon, 1983; Landis, 1956; Lester, 1972; Weinberg, 1955). Breines and Gordon (1983) and Mayer (1983) regard this to be a reflection of a patriarchal society in which men are socialized to regard women as objects, and women are trained to be passive. More recent investigators (McCarty, 1986; Travin, Cullin, & Protter, 1990; Wakefield & Underwager, 1989) have begun to look at the involvement of women and incestuous behavior. The underreporting of female perpetrators may reflect the reluctance of boys/men to report sexual experiences as abusive; the disguised nature of contact between mothers and children; and, simply, the belief that this kind of behavior is rare. The latter factor, consistent with the idea that incest is a consequence of a patriarchal society, is similar to other cultural myths about sexual abuse and sexual violence. That is, it was commonly believed that incest was a rare problem (Weinberg, 1955), that it was relatively harmless (Bender & Blau, 1937; Landis, 1956), and that it afflicted only the undereducated and lower classes (Peters, Wyatt, & Finklehor, 1986). As the polemics subside, it becomes possible to look at this problem in a more objective and fair way. Feminists were right in their insistence that attention be paid to the issue of incest; their work made it impossible to continue to deny the reality of sexually abused children. It is now time to give permission to those who do not fit the stereotype of victim and offender to come forward and be treated. This can happen only if we are able to acknowledge that adult incestuous behavior, while dominated by men, is nonetheless a human problem that finds expression in men and women. This awareness is not an instance of blaming the victim; it is, rather, a nonaccusatory stance based on research findings and experience.

Banmen (1982) has suggested that although father-daughter incest is the most commonly reported, it is likely that sibling incest occurs most frequently. Kaplan and Becker (1992) pointed out a variety of reasons why inappropriate sexual contact between siblings remained underreported. Families may prevent disclosure for fear of exposing the family to outsiders; threats may frighten the victim away from reporting; and parents may not believe their children. It should be noted that these reasons are similar to those that prevent reporting adult-child abuse. De Jong (1989) has developed a list of criteria that can be used to distinguish between experimental and exploitative sexual contact between related children. An age difference of five years or more, the use or the threat of the use of force, penile penetration or attempted penetration, and injury to the victim were identified as indicators of abuse.

EFFECTS OF INCESTUOUS CONTACT

The effects of incest are varied and idiosyncratic, and they are related to the age of the victim, relationship of the offender, use of force, and extent of the behavior. Mayer (1983) has developed a continuum of consequences that are tied to these variables. Although the taboo indicates that all incestuous behavior is to be avoided, it is necessary to distinguish among offending actions. An inappropriate kiss or caress committed while intoxicated and then not repeated is very different than sexual contact such as fellatio or intercourse occurring frequently. Finkelhor (1979), de Young (1982), and Abel, Becker, and Cunningham-Rathner (1984) have addressed the issues of the role of the child and have argued that contrary to some common arguments, informed consent for child-adult sexual behavior is simply not realistic and that the adults who support this behavior are the victims of distorted cognitions.

Whereas Landis (1956) and Bender and Blau (1937) minimized the consequences and DiPietro (1987) found no differences in comparing female adolescent victims with nonabused sisters or matched nonvictim sisters, other researchers and clinicians have found both long- and short-term harmful sequelae. The experience of incest has been found to be associated with self-injurious behavior (de Young, 1982), chemical dependency (Yeary, 1982; Edwall, Hoffman, & Harrison, 1989), relapse to addictive behaviors (Young, 1990), eating disorders (Tice, Hall, Beresford, Quinones, & Hall, 1989), antisocial behavior (Benward & Densen-Gerber, 1975), hysterical seizures (Goodwin, Simms, & Bergman, 1979), childhood eroticization (Yates, 1982), and hospitalized psychiatric patients (Rosenfeld, 1979; Emslie & Rosenfeld, 1983). Whereas Rosenfeld and Emslie and Rosenfeld did not posit that the psychopathology stemmed from incest, Breggin (1991), in a scathing criticism of biological psychiatry, has argued that both the child and adult survivors of sexual abuse are routinely misdiagnosed as schizophrenics, learning disabled, or otherwise impaired. He criticized psychiatry for looking to genetics and/or neurological factors to the exclusion of experiential and environmental issues; in a subtle way, this emphasis on biological factors has contributed to the structure of denial and secrecy. Breggin urged his readers to interview carefully all alleged cases of childhood psychopathology for instances of abuse; this caveat also applies to adult cases as well.

Although is it patently dangerous to generalize from an N of one, the following case lends credence to Breggin's report.

Florence, a white female of 32, had been hospitalized for eleven years in a psychiatric setting. During that time she had received at least ten different major psychiatric diagnoses and had been treated with a wide variety of psychotropic medications. In fairness to the facility, it should be noted that she did present a range of symptoms, including episodes of catatonia, withdrawal, and poor socialization. In spite of this, she was well regarded by the staff and had been working in a limited capacity with the physical therapy department. Prior to being seen for treatment by me, she had been in therapy with a therapist who had difficulty maintaining appropriate boundaries. Although there had not been any physical contact between the patient and therapist, it was clear that the therapist had been acting in a seductive manner. The focus of the treatment was the obviously repressed/suppressed anger and the gap between her potential and her status as a patient. During the course of treatment she was able to reveal, for the first time, that she had been a victim of prolonged sexual abuse by a paternal uncle who lived in her parents' house. She had been seduced through trust and then threatened with harm if she disclosed the abuse. A failed sexual relationship as an adult led to her pronounced withdrawal and hospitalization; she was never questioned about the abuse. As she worked through the trauma and its effects, she became less dependent upon the institution and eventually sought placement in a halfway house. Some time later she returned to her original career and severed all ties with the hospital. Follow up over several years found her to be functioning well, married, and relatively free of symptoms. She never returned to psychotropics.

This case is not unusual; nor is it necessarily unrepresentative of hidden traumas in hospitalized patients or among those in outpatient settings. As Breggin indicated, there is a need to shift, at least in the interview stage, to nonbiological considerations while considering diagnoses. Pribor and Dinwiddie (1992) have looked at psychiatric illnesses associated with childhood incest in an outpatient setting. They found a higher prevalence of disorders among the victims than they found among a matched group of nonvictimized women. They advised that women looking for treatment for depression, anxiety disorders, and substance abuse difficulties should be interviewed about the possibility of abuse histories. As Herman and Herschman (1981) reminded us, large numbers of adult women entering treatment for the usual range of mental health problems are survivors of incest, a fact often missed by therapists.

IDENTIFICATION AND TREATMENT OF OFFENDERS AND VICTIMS

It is rare that an offender voluntarily comes forward and identifies himself or herself as a perpetrator. Incest is a criminal offense, and as such the offender places himself or herself in jeopardy upon reporting. In addition to a potential criminal investigation, the volunteer will face investigations from Child Protective or Social Service agencies; petitions to have him or her removed from the home; Family Court appearances; loss of contact with the victimized child, as well as with other children in the home; attorney contacts and fees; and worst of all, the possibility of the case being reported in the press. The family may be put on public assistance, and foster care may come into play. Tyler and Brassard (1984) have suggested that the press be barred from printing information about convictions/indictments, that the legal process be streamlined and made more consistent across families, and that communities develop diversion programs as an alternative to incarceration. The thinking here is to lessen the probability of further trauma to the family and to enhance the probability of a successful treatment for the offender, the victim, and the family.

Most offenders come to the attention of the community because there has been a disclosure by the child to the nonabusing parent or to a trusted adult; other avenues, such as physical evidence during a health examination or sexually inappropriate behavior may also lead to an investigation. Once notified, the local child protective agency will conduct an evaluation as soon as possible; if sufficient evidence exists to proceed, the agency will ensure the safety of the child victim, and other children if necessary, and an order of protection will be filed, ordering the abusing caregiver to stay away from the child. A criminal investigation may follow.

The management of the child-victim immediately after the report is of paramount importance. Support from the nonabusing caregiver is the most critical issue here; sensitive, empathic, and well-trained interviewers conducting the examination are the next essential step (Sgroi, 1982). Damon, Card, and Todd (1992) have recommended familiarization with the protocol developed by the American Professional Society on Abused Children for all those conducting evaluations. Sgroi (1982) has emphasized that the initial interview be viewed as the opportunity to engage the child, as the first therapeutic contact for the child, as a chance to validate or negate the allegation of abuse, and as the time to determine whether or not the child needs protection. Sgroi's chapter (1982) should be read by all those who may need to interview a child for sexual abuse or who may have to review such an interview. A follow-up interview with the nonoffending caregiver is also of value both in establishing credibility of the child-victim and in setting a foundation for treatment (Damon et al., 1992). Although the estimates of false reporting of sexual abuse of children are low (Everson, & Boat 1990), Wakefield and Underwager (1989) have found that false reporting of sexual abuse has become a strategy in divorce and custody suits, and hence they advise caution when conducting an investigation. They were especially concerned that the interviewers not use leading questions, or techniques which point the child in a particular direction.

A word needs to be said about the use of anatomically correct dolls. Children who report sexual abuse are often evaluated with these dolls; the children can point to, or manipulate, the dolls to demonstrate what has happened to them. Although this is an extremely popular technique, it is important to keep the limitations in mind. Conte, Sorenson, Fogarty, and Dalla Rosa (1991) discovered that over 90 percent of their sample of 212 respondents acknowledged using the dolls in assessing children for sexual abuse. However, this same group ranked the dolls ninth in order of importance in determining whether or not the abuse had occurred. These authors went on to point out that this technique has not yet met the standards for reliability and validity that are expected of psychological tests. Thus, although they may be a good tool, the dolls should not be the sole source of information in making a determination or presenting a report to a court or agency.

Assessment of the offender is a very difficult endeavor. As Becker and Kaplan (1990) have noted, there is no assessment instrument that can attest to guilt or innocence of the alleged offender. Levin and Stava (1987), in a review of Minnesota Multiphasic Personality Inventory (MMPI) findings, concluded that positive findings were outweighed by negative or inconclusive outcomes. In an excellent text that looks at the issue of retraining sexual offenders, Knopp (1984) has concluded that deciding whether or not an offender is suitable for a community-based program cannot be based on objective criteria. She stated that the evaluator can take into account a wide range of material, including clinical interviews, police reports, the results of psychological tests, the statement made by the victim, and the influence of the legal questions and consequences. In the end, she claimed, the clinician will rest upon his or her experience and training. This obviously points to the need for extensive training and education in the area of sexual abuse and assessment. It is only recently that this issue has been addressed by graduate programs in a systematic fashion (Pope & Feldman-Summers, 1992; Jackson, Long, & Skinner, 1991). Thus, the identification process of the offender, unless he or she admits guilt, is one filled with obstacles and difficulties.

Treatment of the offender has occurred in a variety of settings and modalities. Outcome studies have been in short supply (Becker & Kaplan, 1990), whereas reports on treatment approaches have been expanding at a geometric rate. (A recent examination of the Silver Platter computer search in psychology listed eighteen outcome studies and several hundred reports on victim and offender treatment.) While psychodynamic approaches are still being attempted (see, for example, Ganzarain & Buchele, 1990), the prevailing model for treatment is the cognitive-behavioral one. The program originally developed by Abel, Becker, Rathner, Kaplan, and Reich (1984) has been adapted for use with the incestuous offender. Covert sensitization, assertiveness and social skills training, cognitive restructuring, and sex education and values clarification are provided in group settings, during twelve to forty-eight sessions. Offenders are expected to diminish their deviant fantasies by associating an unpleasant outcome, such as incarceration, just as the thought of performing an inappropriate act emerges. Characteristally but not universally, the social skills deficit found with the incest offender is moderated by the assertiveness training. The justifications and rationalizations used by the offender to support his or her behavior—this is really good for the child; I am just teaching her (him) about sexuality—are challenged as cognitive distortions of reality. The offender is then provided with accurate information that theoretically replaces the distortions. Finally, the sex education and values clarification seek to point the offender in the right direction with respect to satisfying sexual needs and to come to respect the right of the child to be left alone. Some programs also use the technique of satiation, in which the offender masturbates to orgasm using a suitable fantasy; the client then continues to masturbate to an inappropriate fantasy for a prolonged period of time. The idea, clear to all, is to associate pleasurable sexual feelings with appropriate sexual fantasies and activities, and to associate unpleasant feelings to deviant or inappropriate sexual fantasies. The client verbalizes his thoughts into a tape recorder during the satiation work; the tape is then reviewed by the therapist. This approach, in combination with family therapy and psychopharmacotherapy, has been found to be effective with incest offenders over a ten-year period (Dwyer & Myers, 1990). Although this is a promising result, the small sample size diminishes its strength.

A program predicated upon family reunion that has had success in treating the offender, the victim, and the family as well is the community-based program developed by Henry Giarretto (1989). Based in California, this approach involves the criminal justice system, attorneys, probation officers, treatment providers, and the entire family. Therapy is provided to the offender, the victim, and the family by professionals and by peers (adults as well as children). The objective is the reconstruction of the family and its dynamics, with an aim of avoiding the isolation and family disintegration that frequently accompanies the disclosure of incest. The peer support is provided by Parents United and by Sons and Daughters United, groups bound together by common experience and by common hope. Chapters of Parents United now exist around the country.

Treatment for the offender is essential. Pithers, Kashima, Cumming, Beal, and Buell (1988) have found, however, that the combination of treatment and intensive supervision is the most effective strategy for preventing relapse among released offenders. This approach, with slight modifications, can be a cost-effective one in communities seeking to divert the incest offender from incarceration. A jailed offender is not working and supporting his or her family; a diverted offender, monitored carefully by the probation department, can remain an asset to the family while in treatment. The use of weekend sentencing, another type of diversion, achieves the same goals and communicates to the victim that the offender is being punished for the wrongdoing. Both strategies depend upon the offender's being able to admit guilt and own responsibility for the actions. Neither strategy is a satisfactory solution for the violent offender or the one who stays in denial.

Treatment of the child victim has received much attention over the last twenty years. There seems to be consensus about the basic structure of the treatment process, but as Conte (1990) has pointed out, there are no treatment outcome studies. Thus, although there are a number of effective interventions, the clinician must be careful to individualize the treatment to the age and sex of the child, severity and duration of the abuse, and method of disclosure.

Ney (1987) has suggested that there is a natural sequence in the issues that a victimized child undergoes in treatment. He lists seven stages, all of which, in his estimation, must be completed. They are as follows: (1) Abused children must come to realize that they are victims. (2) They need to protest against their maltreatment. (3) They should deal with whatever guilt feelings they have about their involvement. (4) They must recognize the losses in their lives and then mourn them. (5) They must look at present relationships and evaluate them in the light of new knowledge. (6) When possible, they should reconcile with their abusers. (7) Finally, they must create a new life and make use of what they have experienced and learned in their work and dealings with others. This list would seem to apply to adult survivors as well.

Sgroi (1982), on the other hand, has identified ten issues that should be addressed in the therapy. Among them are the "damaged goods" syndrome; the guilt, fear, and depression that follow the disclosure; the impaired self-esteem and capacity to trust; the repressed anger and hostility along with the pseudo-maturity; the role confusion and the issue of self-mastery and control. Ney's stages and Sgroi's issues can be handled in individual, group, and family modalities.

As treatment proceeds, individually or in group with the victim, it is essential that the child be firmly linked with the nonabusing caregiver. The support provided by this adult, and by other supportive siblings, makes the progress of the child possible. The child needs to know that he or she is still accepted, that the disclosure has been acknowledged and validated, and that life will be okay at some point in the future (Conte, 1990). Boatman, Borkan, and Schetky (1981) compared the effects of individual, group, and family therapy modalities with a small sample (N = 40) of child incest victims. They regarded individual psychotherapy as the treatment of choice for very young children, for whom play therapy would be natural, and as the treatment for those whose diagnosis was severe enough to warrant a one-to-one setting. Group was valuable for the older child or adolescent and provided a setting in which peer support and the sharing of experiences helped to reduce the feeling of abnormality or uniqueness. Family therapy was used as an adjunct to individual and family interventions. The program developed by Giarretto (1989) and alluded to earlier seeks to reintegrate the family whenever possible. At some point in the treatment, when the child is strong enough and feels the support of the nonabusing family members, a confrontation between the abusing parent and the child is afforded. The child can then express his or her anger, frustrations, hurt, and sadness; the caregiver can display remorse and ownership of the abuse. The parent absolves the child of any responsibility for the incestuous behavior, agrees to respect boundaries in the future, and contracts to continue with the required treatments. Some children will not reach this point; the abuse may have been too severe, or its impact too damaging. The child needs to be in control of this encounter, a final stepping stone on the way toward reintegrating the family.

The following two cases reveal the harm that incest caused and continues to cause the victims and the perpetrators. In addition, these cases challenge the black-and-white positions usually taken and insist instead that we look at incest in a dynamic, interactional fashion.

Seventy years ago in a rural area of western New York, a father sexually violated his three daughters. The middle girl became pregnant and delivered a child. Concerned about the evidence of his misbehavior, the father murdered the infant at birth. The third daughter eventually married and left the father's violence. She and her husband had five children, one of whom was a girl. During this child's early years, the father would often engage in a form of play that she later came to understand as sexual in nature. As a teenager she had to endure caresses and visits to her bedroom at night, which were disturbing. If the mother knew, she did not do anything to interfere or to protect the child. These experiences were forgotten as her life progressed. A good student for whom college was accessible, she married a man of whom her parents disapproved. Shortly after the birth of a female child, the husband, long unfaithful, left her. Some time after the divorce, she married a man whose wife had betrayed him sexually. After they began living together, he asked his stepdaughter, now about seven, to touch his genitals; she refused. For the next eight years or so he acted in a provocative and inappropriate manner with the child. He found opportunities to expose himself to her, or to rub her back and fondle the sides of her breasts as he did so; this behavior was remarkably similar to the abuse the mother had suffered at the hands of her father. At night while watching television the stepfather would sit on the couch in a nightshirt without underwear as the stepdaughter sat across from him. The girl's mother was lying on the couch with her head on his lap; she would later say that she was unaware of his behavior. During this period of time the marriage was rocked with frequent arguments and occasional violence. Alcohol was abused by both parents. In her late adolescence, the girl avoided the stepfather, but shortly after she turned 18, he kissed her on the lips. At this point she reported this as well as the other incidents to her mother and insisted that she do something. The mother left the house with her daughter and sought treatment for her, for herself, and for her husband.

During her treatment the mother was able to come to terms with her own victimization; memories of the events with her father returned. Discussions with one of her brothers, who recalled more clearly some of the earlier events, filled in the missing gaps. She was able to confront her father, as well as her mother, after considerable therapeutic work had been accomplished; the revelation of the infanticide did not emerge until nearly the end of treatment. The husband made significant progress in his therapy. He came to see his hostility toward his stepdaughter and toward his wife as stemming from the wounds of an exceptionally harsh and neglectful childhood, as well as from his anger toward his first wife. He was able to acknowledge his responsibility for his actions, expressed remorse to the stepdaughter by letters, and confessed to his sons, from his first marriage, what he had done. The daughter, also in treatment, remained angry and unforgiving toward the stepfather. She was noted to be pleased by the new living arrangement; for once again, she had her mother to herself. She would not accept his apologies; she felt that her mother was aligning herself with him and resented her for it. When the mother chose to move back with her husband after two years of separation and treatment, the daughter became furious. She terminated her therapy long before the provider thought she was ready. She established her own household but continued to see the mother. Less angry over time, she became more accepting of the mother's decision. They are now trying to achieve a reconciliation, an event the mother feels is no longer far away. The daughter has completed a professional training program and is actively dating. Apart from the self-imposed separation from the mother's household, her life is apparently satisfactory. The mother believes that the cycle of violence begun by her grandfather more than seventy years ago has been brought to an end.

The second case demonstrates the tenacity of denial and the price people will pay to maintain their innocence.

A woman about to be divorced agreed to allow her husband to have custody of the two children, a boy and a girl. Some time later, after the divorce, she met another man and remarried. The children spent time with the natural mother and the stepfather on weekends. After one visit, the children complained to the natural father of unusual experiences while with the natural mother. An investigation by the local social service agency resulted in accusations of cultlike sexual abuse of both children by the woman, her new husband, and their friends. The mother lost visitation rights; both she and the stepfather were criminally indicted but not tried on the charges. She became pregnant, had a son, and moved to another state with her husband. One of the original investigating workers filed a report with the family court in the new state. A new investigation was initiated by that state's social service agency, and the child was removed and placed in foster care. The parents were directed to participate in a treatment program for incestuous families. While in treatment, each in a separate group, they maintained their innocence and denied any wrongdoing, accusing the natural father of inventing the whole story. In spite of evidence to the contrary, they refused to budge from their position. She became pregnant again and had another son. Following his birth, the agency removed him as well. A petition to terminate their parental rights was initiated; experts were called to testify in family court. The judge ruled that the preponderance of evidence pointed to their culpability and ordered their rights terminated. An appeal of the court's decision was found to be without merit. The parents continued to maintain their innocence; both children were placed for adoption.

These cases reveal, in very different ways, the pain and suffering encountered by incestuous families. It is of some interest that both families came to rely upon religion to help them through their plight. The mother in the first case sought counsel from her pastor, who directed her to participate in treatment, to work at saving the marriage, and to do all that she could to assist her daughter. The second couple were also deeply involved in the practice of their religious beliefs. It appeared to others that the religion shielded them from facing their problems head on. They also turned to VOCAL, an organization of people who believe that they have been violated by child abuse laws. While their court hearings were pending, they maintained supervised visitation with their children; it was clear that they loved them both. However, in spite of clear warnings from the agency involved, they could not bring themselves to admit to any kind of abuse and lost their children as a consequence.

CURRENT AND FUTURE SOLUTIONS

As this brief survey suggests, we have a long way to go in the treatment and management of incest. Outcome studies, which control for demographic variables, type and extent of the abuse, age and relatedness of the child and the adult, and types of modalities, are needed in the area of treatment of both the offender and the victim. Training of professionals in the area of mental health, criminal justice, and the social service systems needs to continue and expand. Treatment providers need to enhance their skills, to support one another in this difficult and often unrewarding work.

Many populations are still not identified or cared for in a systematic fashion. Sibling sexual abuse rarely comes to the attention of public agencies. The reported instances of incest are just a fraction of the actual incidence. An entire group of survivors have received little or no attention: the elderly. As one of my cases makes clear, there are those, who may now be in nursing homes or in retirement, who have not had a chance to tell their story or to receive treatment. An outreach toward this forgotten group seems to be indicated.

Abuse of all kinds is out of control in this country. The data about homicide rates, violent crimes, and aggression in the home point to a virtual epidemic (Straus & Gelles, 1990). Violence in the daily lives of citizens has numbed many to its bite. Although a host of causes have been hypothesized, not many effective solutions have been proposed. As a nation we are more careful about licensing drivers than we are about teaching couples and parents how to be nonviolent. The sexual abuse of children is embedded in this culture of tolerance for violence. Although there have been changes for the better, the issue of unnecessary violence toward children and others remains a pressing problem. It is not enough to punish the offender or provide treatment for the victim, or to educate professionals about their responsibility for reporting. Passing tougher legislation or adding judges to the family courts will not stop the pain. We must, as a nation and a society, demand prevention programs and training for our young people and for those about to marry or bear children. Government at the national and state levels must establish an attitude of nontolerance of violence in its citizens and support universal education in the grammar schools and high schools on nonviolent solutions to dispute and conflict. By example and legislation and support, the government needs to provide the right of safety to children and other victims of abuse. We have brought the problem of abuse to consciousness; now is the time to learn other responses to anger and frustration.

REFERENCES

Abel, G., Becker, J., and Cunningham-Rathner, J. (1984). Complications, consent, and cognitions in sex between children and adults. *International Journal of Law and Psychiatry, 7,* 89–103.

Armstrong, L. (Ed.). (1979). *Kiss Daddy goodnight: A speak out on incest.* New York: Simon & Schuster.

Banmen, J. (1982). The incidence, treatment and counseling of incest. *International Journal for the Advancement of Counselling, 5,* 206–210.

Becker, J., and Kaplan, M. (1990). Perpetrators of child sexual abuse. In R. T. Ammerman and M. Hersen (Eds.), *Treatment of family violence: A Sourcebook* (pp. 266–279). New York: John Wiley.

Bender, L., & Blau, A. (1937). The reactions of children to sexual problems with adults. *American Journal of Orthopsychiatry, 8,* 500–518.

Benward, J., & Densen-Gerber, J. (1975). Incest as a causative factor in antisocial behavior: An exploratory study. *Contemporary Drug Problems, 4,* 323–340.

Blume, E. S. (1990). *Secret survivors: Uncovering incest and its aftereffects in women.* New York: John Wiley and Sons.

Boatman, B., Borkan, E. L., & Schetky, D. H. (1981). Treatment of child victims of incest. *American Journal of Family Therapy, 9,* 43–51.

Brady, K. (1979). *Father's days: A true story of incest.* New York: Dell.

Breggin, P. (1991). *Toxic Psychiatry: Why therapy, empathy, and love must replace the drugs, electroshock, and biochemical theories of the "new psychiatry."* New York: St. Martin's Press.

Breines, W., & Gordon, L. (1983). The new scholarship on family violence. *Signs, 8,* 490–531.

Conte, J. R. (1990). Victims of child sexual abuse. In R. T. Ammerman & M. Hersen (Eds.), *Treatment of family violence: A sourcebook* (pp. 50–76). New York: John Wiley.

Conte, J. R., Sorenson, E., Fogarty, L., & Dalla Rosa, J. (1991). Evaluating children's reports of sexual abuse: Results from a survey of professionals. *American Journal of Orthopsychiatry, 6,* 428–437.

Damon, L. L., Card, J. A., & Todd, J. (1992). Incest in young children. In R. T. Ammerman & M. Hersen (Eds.), *Assessment of family violence: A clinical and legal sourcebook* (pp. 148–172). New York: John Wiley.

de Jong, Allan (1989). Sexual interactions among siblings and cousins: Experimentation or exploitation? *Child Abuse and Neglect, 13,* 271–279.

de Young, M. (1982). Self-injurious behavior in incest victims: A research note. *Child Welfare, 61,* 577–584.

DiPietro, S. B. (1987). The effects of intrafamilial child sexual abuse on the adjustment and attitudes of adolescents. *Violence and Victims, 2,* 59–78.

Dwyer, S. M., & Myers, S. (1990). Sex offender treatment: A six-month to ten-year follow-up study. *Annals of Sex Research, 3,* 305–318.

Edwall, G. E., Hoffman, N. G., & Harrison, P. A. (1989). Psychological correlates of sexual abuse in adolescent girls in chemical dependency treatment. *Adolescence, 24,* 279–288.

Emslie, G., & Rosenfeld, A. (1983). Incest reported by children and adolescents hospitalized for severe psychiatric problems. *American Journal of Psychiatry, 140,* 708–711.

Everson, M. D., & Boat, B. W. (1990). Sexualized doll play among young children: Implications for the use of anatomical dolls in sexual abuse evaluations. *American Academy of Child and Adolescent Psychiatry, 29,* 736–742.

Finkelhor, D. (1979). *Sexually victimized children.* New York: Free Press.

Freud, S. (1896). The etiology of hysteria. *In Collected Papers* (Vol. 1, pp. 183–219). Translated by Joan Riviere. London: Hogarth Press (1953).

Freud, S. (1930). *Civilization and its discontents.* Translated and edited by James Strachey. New York: W. W. Norton (1961).

Ganzarain, R., & Buchele, B. J. (1990). Incest perpetrators in group therapy: A psychodynamic perspective. *Bulletin of Menninger Clinic, 54,* 295–310.

Giarretto, H. (1989). Community-based treatment of the incest family. *Psychiatric Clinics of North America, 12,* 351–361.

Goodwin, J., Simms, M., & Bergman, R. (1979). Hysterical seizures: A sequel to incest. *American Journal of Orthopsychiatry, 49,* 698–703.

Groth, A. N. (1982). The incest offender. In S. M. Sgroi (Ed.), *Handbook of clinical intervention in child sexual abuse* (pp. 215–240). Lexington, MA: Lexington Books.

Herman, J., & Herschman, L. (1981). *Father-daughter incest.* Cambridge, MA: Harvard University Press.

Jackson, T. L., Long, B., & Skinner, L. J. (1991). Sexual assault training: Prevalence in clinical psychology doctoral programs. *Professional psychology: Research and Practice, 22,* 333–335.

Kaplan, M. S., & Becker, J. V. (1992). Adolescent perpetrators of incest. In R. T. Ammerman & M. Herson (Eds.), *Assessment of family violence: A clinical and legal sourcebook* (pp. 332–347). New York: John Wiley.

Kempe, C. H., Silverman, F., Steele, B., Droegenmuller, W., & Silver, H. (1962). The battered child syndrome. *Journal of the American Medical Association, 181,* 17–24.

Knopp, Fay. (1984). *Retraining adult sex offenders: Models and methods.* Syracuse: Safer Society Press.

Landis, J. (1956). Experiences of 500 children with adult sexual deviants. *Psychiatric Quarterly Supplement, 30,* 91–109.

Lester, D. (1972). Incest. *Journal of sex research, 8,* 268–285.

Levin, S. M., & Stava, L. (1987). Personality characteristics of sex offenders: A review. *Archives of sexual behavior, 16,* 1–6.

Masson, J. (1984). *The assault on truth: Freud's suppression of the seduction theory.* Toronto: Collins Publishers.

Masson, J. (1990). *Final analysis: The making and unmaking of a psychoanalyst.* Reading, MA: Addison-Wesley.

Mayer, A. (1983). *Incest: A treatment manual for therapy with victims, spouses and offenders.* Florida: Learning Publications.

McCarty, L. M. (1986). Mother-child incest: Characteristics of the offender. *Child Welfare, 65,* 447–458.

Ney, P. G. (1987). The treatment of child abuse children: The natural sequence of events. *American Journal of Psychotherapy, 41,* 391–401.

Peters, S. D., Wyatt, G. E., & Finklehor, D. (1986). Prevalence. In D. Finklehor (Ed.), *A sourcebook on child sexual abuse* (pp. 15–59). Beverly Hills, CA: Sage.

Pithers, W., Kashima, K., Cumming, G., Beal, L., and Buell, M. (1988). Relapse prevention of sexual aggression. *Annals of the New York Academy of Sciences.* New York: New York Academy of Sciences.

Pope, K. S., & Feldman-Summers, S. (1992). National survey of psychologists' sexual and physical abuse history and their evaluation of training and competence in these areas. *Professional psychology: Research and practice, 23,* 353–361.

Pribor, E. F., & Dinwiddie, S. H. (1992). Psychiatric correlates of incest in childhood. *American Journal of Psychiatry, 149,* 52–56.

Rosenfeld, A. (1979). Incidence of a history of incest among 18 female psychiatric patients. *American Journal of Psychiatry, 136,* 791–796.

Rush, F. (1977). Freud and the sexual abuse of children. *Chrysalis, 1,* 31–45.

Sgroi, S. (1982). *Handbook of clinical intervention in child sexual abuse.* Lexington, Mass.: Lexington Books.

Strauss, M., and Gelles, R. (1990). *Physical violence in American families.* New Brunswick, NJ: Transaction Press.

Tice, L., Hall, R. C., Beresford, T. P., Quinones, J., & Hall, A. K. (1989). Sexual abuse in patients with eating disorders. *Psychiatric Medicine, 7,* 257–267.

Travin, S., Cullen, K., and Protter, B. (1990). Female sex offenders: Severe victims and victimizers. *Journal of Forensic Sciences, 35,* 140–150.

Tyler, A. H., & Brassard, M. R. (1984). Abuse in the investigation and treatment of intrafamilial child sexual abuse. *Child Abuse and Neglect, 8,* 47–53.

Vale Allen, C. (1980). *Daddy's girl.* Toronto: McClelland & Stewart.

Wakefield, H., & Underwager, R. (1989). Evaluating the child witness in sexual abuse cases: Interview or inquisition? *American Journal of Forensic Psychology, 7,* 43–69.

Weinberg, S. K. (1955). *Incest behavior.* New York: Citadel.

Yates, A. (1982). Children eroticized by incest. *American Journal of Psychiatry, 139,* 482–485.

Yeary, J. (1982). Incest and chemical dependency. *Journal of Psychoactive Drugs, 14,* 133–135.

Yorukoglu, A., & Kemph, J. (1966). Children not severely damaged by incest. *Journal of the Academy of Child Psychiatry, 5,* 111–124.

Young, E. B. (1990). The role of incest is sure in relapse. *Journal of Psychoactive Drugs, 22,* 249–258.

7

Violence in the Schools

Joseph O'Donoghue

Throughout the 1980s it was customary to regard violence in the schools, whether student versus student or student versus teacher, as a phenomenon confined to the nation's troubled inner-city schools (Baskin & Thomas, 1986; Evans & Evans, 1985). Whenever violent assaults were reported in suburban schools, the tendency was to interpret the attacks as atypical events that were not part of a pattern of violence (Feder, 1985; Feschbach & Feschback, 1982).

The interpretation of school violence as basically an inner-city phenomenon has been challenged in the 1990s. Recent reviews of national media reports of acts of school violence, resulting in serious injury or death of students and teachers, suggest (1) that the number of such events has dramatically increased in the 1990s and (2) that acts of school violence are now distributed across the entire spectrum of U.S. American schools (Cooper, 1990; *Newsweek,* 1992; Stephens, 1991).

The reported emergence of broadly distributed acts of school violence has been associated with a parallel increase in reports regarding the possession of guns and other weapons of violence by students inside the nation's schools. One in five U.S. American high school students, and almost one in three U.S. American boys, now routinely carries a gun, knife, or some other weapon, and this pattern of weapon carrying by students has become a national phenomenon applicable to schools in all regions (National, 1991).

These developments are occurring in a context of widespread reluctance on the part of school boards and school administrators to acknowledge the extent and the consequences of violent behavior in schools (Berger, 1989; Stower, 1988). This reluctance to report injuries to students and teachers as the result of violent attacks has been linked to concerns that the reporting of such events would erode local support for schools perceived as violence prone and thereby increase the overall damage sustained by the schools (Kennedy, 1991; Martin, 1990).

Administrative reluctance to disseminate information on acts of violence within schools has been cited as a major factor responsible for the appearance of annual reports, prepared by teacher unions, comprehensively reviewing the pattern of school violence within their areas of employment. These reports may be regarded as early steps in providing the type of data necessary (1) to recognize the dimensions of the problem and (2) to determine the framework of analysis most likely to provide insights in the development of alternatives to school violence. This chapter suggests the adoption of that type of cross-cultural perspective that has been found to be effective in investigating complex phenomena occurring in highly diverse settings (Adler, 1989). A review of reports of school violence in the United States, and the preliminary analysis of these events, is followed by a review of analysis of school violence now being conducted in other nations. A concluding section suggests a number of research considerations that can be derived on the basis of the review.

SCHOOL VIOLENCE: THE U.S. PATTERN

As indicated above, an explosion of media accounts indicates that violent behavior, resulting in injury or death, has become a pervasive feature in U.S. American schools. Efforts to block the introduction of weapons into school property through the use of metal detectors and mandatory body searches are recognized as having only limited effectiveness (Cohn & Thomas, 1989; Kopetman, 1989). The 33 percent of male high school students who now carry guns, knives, or razors into U.S. American schools report little difficulty in escaping detection (National, 1991).

The introduction of armed security personnel has not had a meaningful impact in reducing acts of violence. In March 1992 a student shot and killed two other students in a school hallway at a time when two police officers were less than twenty feet from the location of the murder of the two students (*Newsday,* 1992). A recent annual report on school violence, prepared by a teachers' union in a metropolitan area, cited 1,131 incidents of serious assaults (i.e, robberies, rapes, and murders) as occuring within the school system over a twelve-month period. Comparable reports prepared by school administrators in other areas throughout the United States indicate a similar pattern of large-scale violence in the nation's schools (Los Angeles, 1989).

The reluctance of school officials to report and then assist in prosecuting criminal acts of violence in school settings has understandably impeded research into the factors associated with school violence. An early effort in this regard was initiated by Feschbach and Feschbach (1982), who reported that empathy training provided very early in the school experience of children and then systematically expanded in each subsequent year of schooling can lead to lower levels of aggressive behavior of students toward students, and students toward teachers. A key component of an effective pattern of violence reduction, as proposed by Feschbach and Feschbach, is the early introduction of positive self-evaluation into the thought patterns of students.

The impact of introducing topics related to violence into the early stages of elementary school curriculum has been analyzed in regard to a sample of New York City public schools (Commanday, 1984). Programs designed to cover topics dealing with counterviolence strategies, such as effective intervention tactics in violent confrontations, have been reported as lowering the levels of violent acts in participating schools (Greenbaum, 1987). One technique found to be highly effective is the advance rehearsal, by teachers and students in a classroom setting, of the respective roles to be played upon the appearance of a sudden burst of anger, or violent behavior, in a school setting (McEvoy, 1990).

Pynoos and Nader (1990) report that classroom-conducted therapy in the wake of violent behavior in the school can be an effective response to the posttraumatic stress experienced by children directly exposed to school violence. Dyston (1990) found that the death of a close family member as the result of violence was a factor linked to violent behavior toward teachers by certain students. Related research by Haran (1988) has examined the effect of one student's sudden, violent death upon the behavior of classmates, using a model that links class and community in a pattern of violence prevention.

A somewhat broader framework of investigation examines the impact of gang membership upon violent behavior within schools. Analysis by Evans and Evans (1985) indicates that a significant component of violent acts occurring in school contexts can be traced either to direct membership in neighborhood groups inclined toward violence or to indirect involvement in a violent subculture outside the school. Violent behavior is perceived as linked to status benefits acquired by the perpetrator; violence toward the teacher is an assertion of the group's repudiation of the educational system. Support for this type of suggested linkage has been found in reviews of the experience of teachers attacked by students (Feder, 1985).

Various teacher associations have charged that school boards and other administrative bodies with responsibility for school administration have not vigorously pushed for criminal prosecution of students charged with attacks upon teachers. An association of teachers in Milwaukee has played a major role in securing court-imposed penalties upon students who have assaulted teachers in class, thereby reversing a pattern in which the local school boards routinely opted for administrative sanctions, for example, suspension from school, rather than criminal prosecution (Hager, 1989). The United Federation of Teachers, New York City, now provides legal counsel to member teachers who choose to participate in court action against students who have attacked teachers.

Data on classroom attacks upon teachers, which would be essential in developing an understanding of overall violence in the schools, have not been gathered in a systematic pattern that would (1) identify the background factors most closely associated with student attacks upon teachers and (2) provide a broad framework for the understanding and development of effective interventions.

Attacks of student upon student, as reported in the nation's media, appear to mirror the pattern of violence among school-age individuals in the larger society (Plummer, 1989). Attacks upon teachers, as both symbols and maintainers of education as an institution, would seem to warrant a special focus in the analysis of school violence.

SCHOOL VIOLENCE: THE GLOBAL PATTERN

On an international basis Japan, Australia, and Canada have become the early leaders in providing a still limited, but expanding, database in regard to acts of school violence. The increasing availability of data on school violence in Japan, including student violence against teachers, can be perceived as linked to the heavily centralized aspects of Japanese education. Unlike the United States, where responsibility for the control of school violence is widely diffused among locally elected, and frequently status conscious, school boards, in Japan a single administrative system is ultimately responsible for the overall control of elementary and secondary schools (O'Donoghue, 1992). Comprehensive reports on all aspects of school administration, including acts of violence as well as exam scores, are routinely submitted to education officials in Tokyo, thereby providing the nation's analysts with access to data on violent behavior in the schools.

Kikkawa's (1987) analysis of violence within Japanese schools suggests that many minor acts of student violence upon student are not immediately recognized as violent acts by teachers and school administrators, which often leads to a slow buildup of eventually explosive force in major acts of school violence. One possible alternative to this scenario, as suggested by Kikkawa, is the systematic strengthening of reporting techniques among teachers in regard to the early signs of violence, with a constant monitoring of information regarding minor acts of violence directed toward students or toward teachers. An essential component of this process is the development of long-term reporting on the impact of acts of school violence upon victims.

The data classification patterns established by Japanese educators in regard to the full range of possible acts of violence would seem to be of particular value in the cross-cultural study of school violence, because of their inclusion of a broad spectrum of variables (Kobayashi & Takahashi, 1988). This broadly based analysis represents a response to a nationwide increase in reported acts of school violence in the late 1980s (Kikkawa, 1987). Japanese researchers are now analyzing (1) the characteristics of perpetrators of school violence and (2) the characteristics of those teachers and students most likely to be victimized in school assaults (O'Donoghue, 1992).

Another insight into the benefits of a cross-cultural approach to school violence is provided by the Australian Institute of Criminology, which has assigned a high priority to the investigation and analysis of assaults and related crimes occurring in that nation's educational system (Challinger, 1987). Containment of violence, in the framework of analysis suggested by the Australian investigators, is more likely to occur as the result of a research focus on value changes in the larger society; behavior changes in the school-age population in regard to violence containment require an early altering of values acquired outside the school system.

The possibility of reducing acts of school violence through the early recognition of likely offenders and victims, in a manner similar to the Japanese focus mentioned above, has been investigated in the United Kingdom. Winkley (1986) has reviewed five distinctive patterns of achieving control over violent behavior in schools through the use of value analysis. A checklist of attitudinal characteristics administered to school personnel and students has been found to be an effective administrative tool in an early identification of violence-prone situations. Related research conducted at a number of diverse educational settings in the United Kingdom has had some success in reducing acts of violence through the use of behavior-anticipating models developed by teachers (Kniveton, 1986).

Research in Sweden into the sources of school violence can provide additional insights regarding the value of early identification of violence-related factors. An investigation into the preschool values and attitudes of children subsequently engaged in acts of school violence found that factors associated with the mass media, rather than factors linked to the school system, were sources of explanation for violent behavior within schools (Jonsson, Falk, Hultman, & Landin, 1988). In a somewhat related research effort, a Canadian investigation into school violence has raised similar questions regarding the source of violence. Cusson (1990) reports that in certain contexts an experience-based code of expectations derived from an analysis of events occurring in the environment outside the school can serve as an effective guide in lowering rates of school violence. This Canadian study, with its focus on the total life experience of children participating in school violence, would appear to be an expansion of the type of value investigation cited earlier with regard to Japanese analysts (Kikkawa, 1987; Kobayashi & Takahashi, 1988).

CONSIDERATIONS IN FUTURE RESEARCH

A number of considerations, applicable to future research into school violence, can be provided on the basis of the above review of national and international patterns of investigation and analysis.

1. The explosion of reported incidents of school violence in recent years appears to be part of a recognizable trend in the case of nations in the most advanced stages of industrialization. Reports of school violence are now routinely distributed across the full range of schools in these nations, with an obvious acceleration of the rate and the negative consequences. Analysis of school violence, however, is in the early stages of development; in some nations, for example, the United States, investigations into school violence are impeded by the reluctance of local administrators to accept an external review of their effectiveness in the control of violence. This obstacle, however, can be circum-

vented through the use of data now being systematically acquired by groups outside the formal administrative system of the schools, for example, by the teacher unions in the United States, or the institutes of criminal investigation in Australia and other nations. Use of these groups and institutions by researchers can serve as a preliminary source of data until such time as uniform patterns of national reporting are adopted.

2. Research into school violence is likely to be most effective if it is conducted on a cross-cultural basis. Violent behavior in school settings is clearly an international phenomenon undergoing a spectacular rate of increase within industrialized nations. Research conducted in a broad range of national settings, and in highly diverse contexts within those settings, is more likely to include the extensive array of factors that can be linked to a comprehensive understanding of a global phenomenon. Analysis of school violence in nations other than the United States has generally tended to be more broadly based and to introduce factors that appear to have considerable research value, for example, the focus of Japanese analysts on changes in the larger society, the role of media reporting as reviewed by researchers in Sweden. A cross-cultural approach, with a focus on diverse patterns of socialization and value changes between generations, can be expected to bring additional insights for research whose complexity requires cooperation among international analysts.

3. The above approach would appear to be especially helpful to U.S. American-based research regarding school violence. The existence of a long-established gun culture in the United States, with a value and attitude cluster that accepts the negative consequences of widespread gun possession, is a phenomenon that requires investigation in terms of its relationship to gun-linked violence in schools. Societies that do not have as extensive a gun culture, for example, the United Kingdom and Canada, have experienced dramatic increases in school violence in patterns similar to that of the United States. But the substantial drop in price of hand guns in the United States, which in recent years reduced the street price of a hand gun to less than $25, and the price of bullets to less than twenty-five cents each, represent a dimension of school violence requiring comparison to other societies. The administrative response to the March 1992 assassination of two students in a New York City public school included the allocation of $21 million to improved security, with an emphasis on the use of metal detectors at school entrances. This expenditure occurred despite the absence of any research that links metal detectors to reduction in rates of school violence. The impact of various security methods in reducing acts of violence in schools has obvious research value. But such research should occur in a context where the impact of gun availability, in a culture that accepts gun possession as a legally established right, becomes an aspect of comparative research involving educational systems located in diverse cultures.

4. Future research into school violence would seem to require a systematic analysis of the impact of school violence on a nation's teachers, current and future. The production of annual reports by teacher unions, with a comprehen-

sive listing of assaults upon teachers, can be partially attributed to a failure by school administrators to respond adequately to injuries sustained by teachers. Media reports of school violence indicate that following the death or serious injury of a teacher in their school, many teachers reaffirm their intention to remain in the school system despite the increasing risk of personal injury, or death, inflicted unexpectedly by a student objecting to an educational directive. However, teachers also report a dramatic change in their personal satisfaction level when the school system repeatedly fails to control violence directed toward their students and toward themselves. It would appear essential that research into school violence examine the impact of violence on teacher effectiveness, teacher recruitment, and teacher retention. The immediate focus in today's analysis of school violence is understandably upon the victims and the context in which they undergo violence. The long-term consequences, however, may be even more devastating in terms of the educational outcomes for an entire generation of U.S. Americans whose schools were characterized by unprecedented amounts of violence.

REFERENCES

Adler, L. L. (1989). *Cross-cultural research in human development: Life span perspectives.* New York: Praeger.

Baskin, M. G., & Thomas, L. M. (1986). School metal detector searches. *University of Michigan Journal of Law Reform, 19,* 1037–1106.

Berger, J. (1989, November 11). Ferocity of youth violence is up. *New York Times,* p. 31, col. 5.

Burke, D. (1989). A study on fear: Violence in Montreal's schools. *Maclean's 102,* 42–43.

Challinger, D. (1987). *Proceedings of the annual conference.* Canberra: Australian Institute of Criminology.

Cohn, D., & Thomas, P. (1989, February 14). Student shot at school. *Washington Post,* p. 1, col. 6.

Commanday, P. M. (1984). Peacemaking: The management of confrontation. *Emotional First Aid: A Journal of Crisis Intervention, 1,* 39–47.

Cooper, S. (1990). *Correlates of violence among weapon carrying adolescents.* Boston: Boston University Press.

Cusson, M. (1990). School violence: The problem and the solution. *Apprentissage et Socialisation, 13,* 213–221.

Diglio, A., & Sanchez, R. (1989, February 17). Fairfax schools to use metal detectors and dogs. *Washington Post,* p. 1, col. 5.

Dyston, J. (1990). Effects of violence on children's academic performance. *Journal of the National Medical Association, 82,* 17–22.

Evans, W. H., & Evans, S. S. (1985). The assessment of school violence. *Pointer, 29,* 18–21.

Feder, J. (1985). *An investigation of the perceived effects of assault on classroom teachers.* New York: New York University Press.

Feschbach, N. D., & Feschbach, S. (1982). Empathy training and the regulation of aggression. *Academic Psychology Bulletin, 4,* 393–413.

Greenbaum, S. (1987). What can we do about school bullying? *Principal, 67,* 21–24.

Hager, P. (1989, June 1). School districts not liable for campus violence. *Los Angeles Times,* p. 3, col. 4.

Haran, J. (1988). Use of group work to help children cope with the violent death of a classmate. *Social Work with Groups, 11,* 79–82.

Jonsson, A., Falk, B., Hultman, J., & Landin, I. (1988). We have it like this: A study of violence among people. *Pedagogisk Psykologiska Sweden, 502,* 1–179.

Kennedy, J. M. (1991, October 10). Students: Armed and dangerous. *Los Angeles Times,* p. 1, col. 1.

Kikkawa, M. (1987). Teacher opinions and treatments for bully/victim problems among students. *Journal of Human Development, 23,* 25–30.

Kniveton, B. H. (1986). Peer models and classroom violence. *Educational Research, 28,* 111–116.

Kobayashi, J., & Takahashi, Y. (1988). A study of student attitudes toward violence. *Report of the Japanese National Research Institute of Police Science, 29,* 131–136.

Kopetman, R. (1989, April 16). School erecting 10 foot high wall to deflect bullets. *Los Angeles Times,* p. 1, col. 3.

Los Angeles Board of Education. (1989). *School and security task force report.* Los Angeles.

McEvoy, A. (1990). Combating gang activities in schools. *Education Digest, 56,* 31–34.

Martin, D. (1990, December 5). Violence drives teacher from where he belongs. *New York Times,* p. 32, col. 2.

National Center for Disease Control. (1991). *National Survey of High School Behavior.* Atlanta: Author.

Newsday. (1992, February 27). Slain at school, p. 5, col. 1.

Newsweek. (1992, March 9). It's not just New York, pp. 25–27.

O'Donoghue, J. (1992). *The world of the Japanese worker.* New York: International University Press.

Plummer, W. (1989). A Kentucky boy's wild cry for help. *People's Weekly, 32,* 44.

Pynoos, R. S., & Nader, K. (1990). Children's exposure to violence and traumatic death. *Psychiatric Annals, 20,* 334–344.

Stephens, R. D. (1991). Bullies and victims: Protecting our schoolchildren. *U.S.A. Today, 120,* 72–74.

Stower, D. (1988). School violence is rising and your staff is the target. *Executive Educator, 10,* 15–21.

Winkley, D. (1986). The angry child in the ordinary school. *Maladjustment and Therapeutic Education, 4,* 33–42.

8

Juvenile Violence and the Death Penalty

Joan M. Reidy Merlo

In 1988 the Supreme Court ruled in *Thompson v. Oklahoma* that Thompson, who was 15 years old at the time that he committed murder, was too young to be executed.[1] Thus, the court prohibited the execution of persons below the age of 16 but did not rule, at that time, on whether it was constitutional to inflict the death penalty on juveniles who were 16 or 17 when they committed their crime. That question was answered on June 26, 1989, when the Court decided in the cases of *Wilkins v. Missouri* and *Stanford v. Kentucky* that age 16 would be the constitutional lower age limit for the death penalty in the United States.[2]

In addition to the Wilkins and Stanford cases, the justices heard the case of Johnny Penry, "a retarded Texas man who suffered brain damage at birth and had an I.Q. of about sixty with the mental functioning of a seven year old" (*New York Times,* 1989, June 27, p. 1). In the Penry case, the Court ruled that the execution of the mentally retarded was not "categorically prohibited" by the Constitution.

With the Wilkins, Stanford, and Penry decisions the United States joined a small group of countries in the world that have passed legislation allowing children and the mentally retarded to suffer the death penalty. Such legislation, in fact, is in violation of a United Nations resolution adopted in 1976.

The Wilkins and Stanford decisions did not, of course, occur in a vacuum. For decades prior to 1989 the attitudes surrounding the death penalty in general, and the death penalty regarding juveniles in particular, had been changing. Perhaps the most important example of these changing attitudes occurred with *Furman v. Georgia,* which was deliberated in 1972.[3]

In the Furman case the Supreme Court decided that state death penalty statutes were "freakishly" and randomly applied and ruled that the death penalty be halted. By 1976 the concerns raised in the Furman case had been settled, and in that year the Court ruled again and reversed its former decision. In effect, in *Gregg v. Georgia* (1976) the Supreme Court decided that given the right of juries to hear aggravating or mitigating circumstances, new state death penalty statutes did not violate Eighth Amendment guaranties (Territo, Halsted, & Bromley, 1992, pp. 397–398).[4]

An almost immediate result of the Gregg ruling was the reinstatement of the death penalty regarding adults and juveniles. Decisions about limitations on the death penalty because of age were still several years away. Meanwhile both the Court and the individual states would undergo many changes in attitude.

These attitudinal changes, both before and after Furman, can best be understood by reviewing the history of the juvenile justice system in the United States. Three stages or eras delineate this history, namely, (1) the era of the child savers (Platt, 1969), (2) the era of juvenile rights, and (3) the era of juvenile accountability.

THE ERA OF THE CHILD SAVERS

The focus of the era of the child savers in juvenile justice was the desire of early-twentieth-century reformers to decriminalize juvenile crime. One of the first steps toward decriminalization was the establishment of separate facilities for the incarceration of juveniles and adults who until that time were jailed together. New York State, for example, responded to this need for separate facilities for juveniles and adults in 1824 when it established the Society for the Reformation of Juvenile Delinquents in the City of New York. New York courts could then place juveniles with the society instead of imprisoning them in an adult facility (Sobie, 1981, p. 678). The idea of separate facilities for children under the age of 16 spread rapidly to other states as well.

Separate juvenile facilities led to the need for a separate court, and in 1899 the first juvenile court was established. Sobie, in 1981, explained the necessity of establishing a "Children's Court" as follows:

At the turn of the century, the concept of a separate juvenile court also began to emerge. By then, the routine placement of children in rehabilitative programs and the practice of charging many juvenile offenders with misdemeanors regardless of the actual crime committed inevitably raised questions concerning the continued practice of hearing delinquency cases in courts devoted to adult felony matters. (p. 680)

Besides separating children from adults during judicial processes, the newly established court also affirmed *parens patriae,* a principle established in the chancery courts of fifteenth-century England. Originally *parens patriae* had little to do with children's judicial rights; it was intended instead to protect children's property rights. By the time the principle of *parens patriae* was introduced into the United States, "the concept was broadened considerably to include personal injury and the *protective* powers of the court became its primary justification" (Short, 1990, p. 22). The concept of *parens patriae* was meant to be the guiding principle concerning the deliberations of the juvenile court. In practice it meant that whatever the court did was supposedly for the child's own welfare.

The entire court process, in fact, was intended to be nonthreatening and non-adversarial. In 1945 Schramm described a juvenile court proceeding. He said:

The child before him (the judge) is not a defendant. There is no conviction, no sentence. There is no life-long stigma of a criminal record. In a juvenile court . . . the child . . . is the recipient of consideration, of guidance and of correction. The stake is no less than the saving of a human being, at a time more favorable than any in an uncertain future. (p. 194)

Similarly, Platt (1969) described the reformers' idea of a courtroom as follows: "The courtroom should not be a courtroom at all; just a room, with a table and two chairs, . . . and where in a more or less informal way the whole may be talked over" (p. 194).

Reforms in incarceration facilities and court procedures were followed by reforms in the standards of evidence required in the juvenile court. Now the procedure in the juvenile court would be similar to the practice in the civil court. In other words, in both courts charges need to be proven only by "a preponderance of the evidence" rather than the criminal court's standard of "proof beyond a reasonable doubt" (Sobie, 1981, p. 684).

Against this backdrop of reform, solicitude, and protection, problems within the court system itself began to mount. For example, probation officers, who were expected to act as social workers as well as officers of the court, were given impossibly large caseloads and were therefore unable to maintain the personal contact with the juveniles in their charge as was required by the re-habilitative mandate of the court. In addition, preventive measures were practically nonexistent and treatment programs were often not therapeutic at all but were punitive instead (Polier, 1964; Haller, 1970; Short, 1990).

Murphy (1929) commented on the abuses that existed then in the juvenile court. He wrote, "How many of these courts are anything other than criminal courts in which the ordinary punitive justice is, at the whim or pleasure of the presiding judge, tempered with mercy?" (p. 81). Platt (1969) summed up the problems that existed in the court when he noted the shift in emphasis from rehabilitation and protection to abuse and arbitrary justice. He wrote, "What seemingly began as a movement to humanize the lives of adolescents soon developed into a program of moral absolutism." (p. 116).

Criticism of the court mounted and provided the groundwork for the second phase in juvenile justice: the era of juvenile rights. This era spanned the decades of the 1960s and 1970s and focused, almost exclusively, on due process reform.

THE ERA OF JUVENILE RIGHTS

The era of due process reforms and changes in the juvenile system was, again, preceded by similar reforms in the adult system. For example, a defendant's right against self-incrimination was established in *Miranda v. Arizona*.[5] Similarly, in *Gideon v. Wainwright* the right of a defendant to have counsel present during criminal proceedings was introduced for adult criminal offenders.[6]

Such due process reforms in the adult court were followed by similar reforms in the juvenile court. In general, the juvenile reforms would test the limits of *parens patriae,* which, as stated above, is the principle that suggests that whatever the court does is for the child's own welfare.

In 1966 *Kent v. United States* established procedures concerning waiver to the adult court.[7] The Kent case is regarded as the first major case involving a juvenile heard before the Supreme Court. In 1961 Kent admitted to offenses involving housebreaking, robbery, and rape. Because he was 16 at the time the crimes were committed, the juvenile court had complete jurisdiction over him and recommended that his case be waived to the adult court for trial. The waiver to the adult court occurred although Kent's attorney filed a motion requesting that the case remain with the juvenile court. No hearing was held in the juvenile court before the waiver and the judge failed to rule on any of the motions filed by Kent's attorney. At the trial in the adult court, Kent was found "not guilty by reason of insanity" concerning the charge of rape; he was, however, found guilty of the housebreaking and robbery charges and was subsequently sentenced to thirty to ninety years on three counts of each. Had he remained under the jurisdiction of the juvenile court, he would have received a maximum stay in a juvenile facility of five years. The case was finally heard before the Supreme Court in 1966.

The Justices concluded in a five-to-four vote that Kent should not have been waived to the adult court without a formal hearing. In addition, it held that Kent's right to due process was violated when he was denied effective assistance of counsel. Justice Fortas, writing for the majority, said, "There is evidence, in fact, that there may be grounds for concern that the child received the worst of both worlds; that he gets neither the protection accorded to adults nor the solicitous care and regenerative treatment postulated for children" (*Kent v. United States,* p. 556).

The Kent decision was important for several reasons, including the fact that it paved the way for *In re Gault,* which contributed sweeping reforms to the juvenile court.[8] Gerald Gault was 15 years old when he was taken into custody on suspicion of making a lurid phone call. Gault was given a hearing in juvenile court during which he was never confronted by the person making the complaint, was given no aid in his own defense, and was not protected against self-incrimination. In addition, no record or transcript of his hearing was ever made; after a second hearing, Gault was found to be delinquent and was committed to the Arizona State Industrial School for an indefinite length of time. Ordinary juvenile court policy at that time stipulated that the child be held for "the remainder of his minority"; in other words, Gault could be held for almost six years, until he was 21 years old. Had Gault been an adult at the time, Arizona state law would have prescribed a small fine or a *maximum* sentence of two months in jail. The Arizona Supreme Court upheld the decision of the lower court, saying that the lower court acted properly and that it had fulfilled its obligation under *parens patriae.*

In 1976 the final appeal of Gault's case was heard before the Supreme Court, and on May 15 a decision was reached. The decision provided the following rights to juveniles: the right to have a written notice of charges, the right to counsel, protection against self-incrimination, and the right to confront and cross-examine witnesses. Again, Justice Fortas wrote on behalf of the court. He said that ''neither the Fourteenth Amendment nor the Bill of Rights is for adults only'' (*In re Gault*, p. 3). Further, he said that ''under our constitution, the condition of being a boy does not justify a kangaroo court'' (*In re Gault*, p. 28).

The Gault case became a criterion in that it acted as a prologue for other sweeping changes in the juvenile system. More important, however, is that while extending the rights of due process to juveniles, this case would also act as a harbinger of the next era in juvenile justice, the era of juvenile accountability. In effect, the Gault decision would usher in a process of recriminalizing juvenile crime, thus changing the original, protective nature of the juvenile justice system in general, and the juvenile court in particular.

Two additional cases delineate the rest of the juvenile rights era. The first, *In re Winship,* involved the level of proof required in the adjudicatory phase of juvenile court hearings.[9] In 1967 Winship, who was 12 years old, was charged with stealing $112. Proof of guilt for the crime was established through ''a preponderance of evidence,'' and subsequently Winship was placed for eighteen months in a state training school. In addition, the court provided for possible subsequent annual extensions that could, if applied, entail six years of incarceration.

In 1970 the Supreme Court heard the case and decided that the level of proof required to establish defendant guilt in criminal cases be ''proof beyond a reasonable doubt,'' not ''a preponderance of evidence,'' thereby reversing the standard that had been in effect since the establishment of the juvenile court.

The last clear case of the extension of due process rights occurred in 1975 with *Breed v. Jones.*[10] This case raised a significant constitutional question regarding double jeopardy. In effect, a petition of delinquency was granted for Jones in the juvenile court. Simply put, Jones was found guilty of armed robbery. However, at the disposition (sentencing) stage of the hearing, it was decided that Jones was not responsive to the programs available to him through the juvenile court. Jones was then transferred (waived) to the California criminal court, tried as an adult, and found guilty again. He was then committed to the California Youth Authority for an indeterminate period.

In 1975 the Supreme Court ruled that Jones's prosecution ''in Superior Court, after an adjudicatory proceeding in juvenile court, violated the Double Jeopardy Clause of the Fifth Amendment.'' Thus, a juvenile cannot be waived to the adult court for trial after the adjudicatory process has been initiated in the juvenile court, thereby avoiding the possibility of being found guilty twice.

The era of due process was about to end as the decade of the 1970s closed. Demands for juvenile accountability grew as the nature of juvenile crime became more aggressive and more violent.

THE ERA OF JUVENILE ACCOUNTABILITY

The demand for juvenile accountability had its origin in the 1970s even as broad due process reforms were being established. As early as 1971 the Supreme Court denied due process when it determined in *McKeiver v. Pennsylvania* that juveniles are not guaranteed the right to a trial by jury.[11]

By the late 1970s various other demands for accountability were being enacted at the state level. Most of these reforms provided guidelines for the transfer of juveniles to the adult court when a serious crime was committed. In 1978 New York State enacted a unique transfer procedure that took the right of initial determination of some felony cases out of the hands of the juvenile court. In effect, New York's Juvenile Offender Act did not provide the defendant with the protection of the juvenile system in the early stages of the justice process, thereby reversing a procedure found in every other state. The act was considered a radical step away from separate court systems for juveniles and adults and a step that reversed the decriminalization of juvenile crime enacted in the early part of the century (Sobie, 1981; Singer & McDowall, 1988).

In 1984 the Supreme Court again denied an element of due process to juveniles when it ruled in *Schall v. Martin* that juveniles could be held without bail for their own protection or for the protection of the community.[12] The demands for accountability culminated when the Supreme Court rendered its decisions regarding the death penalty.

In the first of these cases, which was *Eddings v. Oklahoma,* the court agreed to rule on the issue of the constitutionality of the death penalty.[13] When Eddings was 16 years old he was found guilty of killing a highway patrol officer and was sentenced to death. However, when the case was completed, the Court skirted the constitutional issue and did not decide on the death penalty itself. Rather, it concluded that "great weight" must be given to mitigating circumstances, one of which would be the offender's age. By neglecting to hand down a ruling the court gave tacit approval to the death penalty for juveniles. In fact, in the dissenting opinion the justices said that "The Court stops far short of suggesting that there is any constitutional proscription against imposition of the death penalty on a person under the age of eighteen" (Regoli & Hewitt, 1991, pp. 426–427; *Eddings v. Oklahoma,* p. 104).

The Supreme Court's hesitancy to grapple with constitutional issues involving the death penalty was again noted, two years later, when it refused to hear the case of James Terry Roach. Roach, a 17-year-old with an I.Q. of seventy, was sentenced to death for his participation in the murder of two teenagers. Despite pleas from former president Jimmy Carter, the secretary general of the United Nations, and Mother Teresa, Roach was put to death in South Carolina's electric chair in January 1986. He became the third juvenile to be executed within a twelve-month period (Seligson, 1986).

Perhaps the most notorious of the death penalty cases concerned Paula Cooper, who in 1985 along with three others entered the house of Ruth Pelke and robbed and stabbed the 78-year-old woman thirty-three times. Cooper, who was 15 years old on the day of the murder, was found guilty and was sentenced to die in the electric chair in the state of Indiana. Her case coalesced the opinions of people on both sides of the death penalty issue. On the one hand, Cooper had committed an appalling, brutal act, and those who favor the death penalty saw this case as a justification for such a sentence. On the other hand, the case aroused international controversy because of the willingness of the United States to put its children to death. The case never reached the U.S. Supreme Court because the Indiana Supreme Court, in 1989, set aside the death penalty citing a 1987 change in state law that raised the minimum age for that sentence from 10 to 16 years. Cooper was sentenced to sixty years in prison (Regoli & Hewitt, 1991, p. 422; *New York Times,* July 14, 1989, p. 8).

In June 1989 the court deliberated the question of the death penalty for juveniles for the last time when it ruled, in separate cases (Wilkins; Stanford; and Penry), that the constitution does not bar the execution of persons who are retarded or who were juveniles when they committed their crime. As discussed earlier, the result of these deliberations was that the Court set the minimum age for the death penalty at 16. The first test of the decisions came within five months of the ruling. On November 30 Dalton Prejean, who was Louisiana's longest-serving death row inmate, was to be executed for the murder of a state trooper. Prejean, who was retarded, was 17 years old when he committed his crime. In a strange twist, on November 29 the Supreme Court granted an emergency stay of execution until the justices decided whether they would hear his formal appeal requesting a permanent stay of execution. On May 18, 1990, just a few hours after the Court denied his plea for a stay of execution, Prejean was put to death in the electric chair. As of this writing he is the last person to be executed for a crime committed when the offender was a juvenile. (*New York Times,* November 29, 1989, p. 22; *New York Times,* November 30, 1989, p. 23; *New York Times,* May 19, 1990, p. 9.)

In summary, it appears that the fate of juvenile offenders in our country has come full circle; from a time before the era of the child savers when age was nearly irrelevant, through a time of being "saved" and of having rights guaranteed, to a time when age, again, is nearly irrelevant. Many experts on the subject of juvenile justice see the future as a time of compromise. On the one hand, they expect better rehabilitative treatment for those involved in less serious, less violent crime; on the other, harsher treatment for more violent offenders (Gelber, 1990). One thing seems certain, at least for the immediate future: The

United States will stand alone when compared to almost every other country in the world because of its willingness to kill its children and its mentally retarded.

NOTES

1. *Thompson v. Oklahoma,* 108 S. Ct. 2687 (1988).
2. *Wilkins v. Missouri* and *Stanford v. Kentucky,* 109 S. Ct. 2969 (1989). The Wilkins and Stanford cases were deliberated together. Wilkins was found guilty of killing a woman during the commission of a robbery; Stanford was found guilty of rape and murder.
3. *Furman v. Georgia,* 408 U.S. 238 (1972).
4. *Gregg v. Georgia,* 428 U.S. 153 (1976).
5. *Miranda v. Arizona,* 384 U.S. 436 (1966).
6. *Gideon v. Wainwright,* 372 U.S. 335 (1963).
7. *Kent v. United States of America,* 383 U.S. 541 (1966).
8. *In re Gault,* 387 U.S. 1 (1967).
9. *In re Winship,* 397 U.S. 358 (1970).
10. *Breed v. Jones,* 421 U.S. 519 (1975).
11. *McKeiver v. Pennsylvania,* 402 U.S. 528 (1971). In 1968 McKeiver, then age 16, was charged with robbery, larceny, and possession of stolen goods.
12. *Schall v. Martin,* 104 U.S. 207 (1984). In 1977 Martin allegedly hit a youth in the head with a loaded gun and stole his property. He was 14 years old at the time and was detained overnight in a juvenile facility.
13. *Eddings v. Oklahoma,* 455 U.S. 104 (1982).

REFERENCES

Gelber, S. (1990). The juvenile justice system: Vision for the future. *Juvenile and Family Court Journal, 41,* 5–18.
Haller, M. (1970). Urban crime and criminal justice: The Chicago case. *Journal of American History, 57,* 619–635.
Murphy, J. (1929). The juvenile court at the bar. *Annuals of the American Academy of Political and Social Science, 145,* 80–97.
New York Times (1989, June 27). Court says young and retarded can be executed, p. 1.
New York Times (1989, July 14). Woman's execution for murder at 15 is barred, p. 8.
New York Times (1989, November 29). Retarded slayer faces execution for killing at 17, p. 22.
New York Times (1989, November 30). Court blocks execution of slayer who killed at 17, p. 23.
New York Times (1990, May 19). Louisiana executes man who killed at age 17, p. 9.
Platt, A. (1969). *The child savers.* Chicago: University of Chicago Press.
Polier, W. (1964). *A view from the bench: The juvenile court.* New York National Council on Crime and Delinquency.
Regoli, R., & Hewitt, J. (1991). *Delinquency in society: A child-centered approach.* New York: McGraw-Hill.
Schramm, G. (1945). The judge meets the boy and his family. *National Probation Association 1945 Yearbook,* pp. 182–194.

Seligson, T. (1986, October). Are they too young to die? *Parade*, pp. 4–7.

Short, J. (1990). *Delinquency and society*. Englewood Cliffs, NJ: Prentice Hall.

Singer, S., & McDowall, D. (1988). Criminalizing delinquency: Deterrent effects of New York Juvenile Offender Law. *Law & Society Review, 22*, 522–535.

Sobie, M. (1981). The juvenile offender act: Effectiveness and impact on the New York juvenile justice system. *New York Law School Law Review, 26*, 677–722.

Territo, L., Halsted, J., & Bromley, M. (1992). *Crime and justice in America: A human perspective*. New York: West.

PART III

VIOLENCE IN ADULTHOOD

9

Male Violence against Women: A Global Health and Development Issue

Nancy Felipe Russo, Mary P. Koss,
and Lisa Goodman

> In all countries and cultures, women have frequently been the victims of abuse by their intimates. They have been battered, sexually abused and psychologically injured by persons with whom they should enjoy the closest trust. This maltreatment has gone largely unpunished, unremarked, and has even been tacitly, if not explicitly condoned.
>
> —United Nations
> (1989, p. 11)

> We cannot hope to respond effectively to violence against women unless we confront the attitudes that nurture the violence and then condone it.
>
> —Senator Joseph Biden
> (1993)

As the U.N. report *Violence against Women in the Family* states, the problem of male violence against women "has been recognized internationally and seen as a serious obstacle to development and peace." Violence and the threat of violence are ubiquitous sources of death, injury, and stress in the lives of women that cross lines of culture, age, ethnicity, economic status, and national boundary.[1] As the U.S. Center for Disease Control has pointed out, there is "increasing awareness in the public health community that this violence is a serious public health problem, and that nonfatal interpersonal violence has far-reaching consequences in terms of morbidity and quality of life." Such consequences involve both physical and mental health, and have implications for the health and economic development of society as well as for the woman and her family.[2]

VIOLENCE AGAINST WOMEN: MULTIPLE FORMS, COMMON CHARACTER

Violence against women and female children takes many forms around the globe, including physical and sexual abuse of children; gender-based murder, including infanticide and bride murder; sexual harassment; intimate violence, including physical and sexual assualt; stranger rape, forced prostitution and female slavery; suttee (self-cremation by widows who in order to be "good and virtuous wives" must throw themselves alive on their husband's funereal pyre); genital mutilation; state-sponsored torture, abuse, and harassment; attacks and murder of women leaders; rape by security forces; and systematic rape in wartime. *Immediate steps must be taken to condemn violence internationally and to recognize that violence against women is a violation of basic human rights.* In addition, more needs to be known about the forms that violence takes in women's lives cross-culturally, and how its effects merge and interact with other aspects of women's situations, including women's responsibilities, rights, protections, and options within their family, social, economic, political, and religious contexts. The discussion of violence in this chapter reflects the literature on violence from the United States and Great Britain. Some of the concepts, methods, and insights from that literature may be helpful in filling out the portrait of the violence that women experience around the world. This is clearly but one small piece of the global picture, however.

Although there are many ways to conceptualize and define violent acts men use against women, Liz Kelly has pointed to their common character: the *abuse, intimidation, coercion, intrusion, threat and force men use to control women.*[3] Whether such acts be physical, visual, verbal, or sexual, they are experienced by a woman or girl, at the time or later, as a threat, invasion, or assault, have the effect of hurting her or degrading her, and/or taking away her ability to control contact (intimate and otherwise) with that individual.[4] An important feature of this perspective on violence is that it attempts to include the elements of violence that have been reported as important by its victims.

NEEDED: CULTURALLY SENSITIVE PORTRAITS OF VIOLENCE FROM THE POINT OF VIEW OF ITS VICTIMS

Developing culturally sensitive portraits of violence, including its linkages and effects, is critical, for how violence is conceptualized has implications for both research and intervention. Feminist contributions to understanding violence include the development of concepts and the attendant vocabulary to describe and analyze women's experiences of violence, a vocabulary that is being expanded to incorporate women's experiences cross-culturally. Feminists from many disciplines have been involved in this process of "naming" violence in ways that give voice to women's experiences rather than make them invisible.[5] Terms such as *sexual terrorism, battered women, marital rape, date rape, female slavery, sexual exploitation,* and *sexual coercion* have been developed in the past two decades to classify experiences and empower women to talk about their experiences. International collaboration is needed to develop new models and methods that can further help women articulate their subjective experience of violence. Work such as that of anthropologist Nancy Scheper-Hughes, who so powerfully articulates the interconnections between violence, poverty, and motherhood in the favelas of Brazil, is an example of how women's phenomenological experiences can be used to inform theoretical understanding of how violence can pervade and shape women's daily existence.[6]

Analyzing causes and consequences of diverse forms of violence separately from one another may obscure the realities of women's experiences, realities that can vary widely across cultures. For example, in the United States, separating violent behaviors such as battering and rape into discrete categories imposes distinctions that are more convenient than real. Many women who are raped are also viciously physically assaulted; battered women are frequently sexually assaulted by their male partners; and victims of sexual harassment are physically threatened, brutally assaulted, and raped.[7]

The ways in which a phenomenon is named and defined can affect such things as incidence rates, models of causal dynamics, and assessment of effects—all of which are used to assess the urgency, pervasiveness, and scope of a problem and to shape the interventions designed to ameliorate it. For example, in the United States, by focusing on "domestic violence" or "spousal violence," lumping together attempts at self-defense with acts aimed at domination and control, focusing on tactics to settle disputes rather than enquiring about attacks "out of the blue," and failing to distinguish between slapping a face and breaking a rib, some researchers have been able to construct a conclusion that husbands and wives are "equally" violent.[8]

By not including the victim's perspective in conceptualizing acts of violence, legal definitions of violence have trivialized the effects of acts that are in fact experienced by women as threatening and terrorizing. For example, "flashing" is considered a "minor" crime yet is reported as being a terrorizing experience by flasher victims.[9] Until recently stalking was not considered an offense requiring legal action in the United States; a perpetrator had to threaten or harm before legal authorities could intervene. Reports from victims make clear that understanding the dynamics and impact of violence requires conceptualizations that include threats (verbal and nonverbal) as well as direct physical acts.[10] We do not, by any means, seek to equate murder, torture, and mutilation with verbal threats but, rather, to emphasize the importance of conceptualizing and understanding violence from the perspective of the woman experiencing it.

FOCUS ON INTIMATE VIOLENCE

One of the most widespread, legitimized, invisible, and neglected forms of violence against women around the world is *intimate violence.*[11] Intimate violence may be defined as violence between individuals who are known to each other.[12] Such violence includes acts labeled female infanticide, child abuse; child sexual abuse and incest; bride and other gender-related murder by fathers, husbands, and other family members; and elder abuse; as well as acquaintance rape, date rape, marital rape, courtship violence, dating violence, and partner violence (which includes wife beating or battering). Whatever women's developmental stage across the life span, in the United States women are consistently more likely than men to experience intimate violence.

Although public awareness of intimate violence against women is increasing, the pervasiveness and impact of such violence has yet to be fully comprehended. For example, in the United States, women are more likely to be assaulted, killed, or raped by a current or former male partner than by all other categories of assailants combined. Women are most likely to be sexually assaulted by people they know and often love and trust. Nearly half of the aggravated assault and completed rapes identified in a recent criminal victimization survey were perpetrated by men with whom the victims were romantically involved.[13] This is a sizable number of women: In 1990, 102,555 rapes of women were reported to the police. A woman reports a rape to the police every five to six minutes. A recent national study estimates that 14 percent of women have been forcibly raped.[14]

An estimated one in four wives is physically battered. It is also estimated that some form of violence will occur at least once in over half of all marriages, with 3 to 4 million American women battered each year by their partners. The prevalence of physical abuse among dating college students on some campuses has been found to reach the rate for married couples. Levels of severe intimate violence in cohabiting or dating partners in the United States also appear to be increasing.

Marital violence, which has been most thoroughly studied around the world, has at least three manifestations: physical, sexual, and psychological. Regardless of whether intimate violence has physical, sexual, or psychological dimensions, it need not be constant or severe to create an environment of unremitting terror. The effects of the threat of violence must not be trivialized, for they can be psychologically and socially devastating. Even if incidents of partner abuse are infrequent, they can be debilitating because their unpredictability makes victims less able to organize ways of protecting themselves and their children.

Violence against women and children are linked. One hospital-based study of child abuse victims found that records of 59 percent of the mothers of such victims had evidence of victimization histories themselves. Further, the rate of violence against single mothers was four times the rate against married mothers.[15] Although some studies have reported that men and women commit acts of partner violence in roughly equal numbers, the form, severity, and consequences of violence differ for the sexes. Women's violence is nearly always in self-defense and is much less severe in consequences than men's violence.

LINKAGES BETWEEN MALE VIOLENCE AGAINST WOMEN AND OTHER SOCIAL PROBLEMS

Violence compounds stress and drains coping resources of women, their families, and society. The social and economic costs of the physical effects of male violence against women around the world are unknown, but data from the United States suggest that they can be staggering. For example, wife battering is the single most common cause of injuries to women requiring medical intervention in the United States. In addition, women are at highest risk for battering in their childbearing years, and violence in pregnancy has been linked to severe and negative pregnancy outcomes. More than one out of three rape victims sustains serious physical injury; experiences of rape and battering have been linked with increased self-reported symptomatology across nearly all body systems, higher levels of injurious health behaviors (e.g., smoking), and greater use of medical services. Women who are victimized become heavier users of the medical system; one study found that victimization severity was the single, most powerful predictor of total yearly physician visits and outpatient costs. Although women of diverse circumstances experience violence, those who live under high stress with few coping resources are already at higher risk for physical and psychological problems, particularly women living in poverty, homeless women, and women who experience marital problems or disruption.

Male violence against women is used to maintain women's disadvantaged social and political status, directly and indirectly. Sexual victimization in childhood has been linked to adolescent pregnancy in the United States. In one study of 535 teenage mothers, 55 percent had been molested and 44 percent had been raped.[16] Further, many adult married women do not have full control over the circumstances under which they have sexual intercourse. Among the estimated one in four wives who are physically assaulted by their partners,[17] approximately 33–46 percent are sexually assaulted as well.[18] In severely abusive relationships, forcible rape can occur several times a month.[19] In one study of 221 married abortion patients, nearly one out of four reported they had been afraid of their husbands, and more than one in six had been forced by their husbands to have sexual intercourse against their will (the legal definition of rape).[20] These are not conditions that promote consistent contraceptive practice.

Such research findings suggest that health, social, and economic problems of women that result from unintended pregnancy, including unwanted childbearing, teenage motherhood, shorter birth intervals, and large family sizes, will not be ameliorated by family planning programs as long as the effects of male violence on women's reproductive choices is ignored.[21] Such programs must recognize that there are real differences in physical and social power and status between men and women that contribute to the risk of unintended and unwanted pregnancy, and these differences are manifested in the pervasiveness of violence and the threat of violence against women. The goal of eliminating unintended pregnancy will not be achieved as long as society continues to tolerate marital rape and other forms of physical and sexual abuse of females of all ages. Women's right to say no to unwanted and unprotected sexual intercourse—even if the person desiring intercourse is her husband—is a necessary condition for achieving that goal. Such things must be kept in mind in the development of laws, policies, and programs to prevent unintended pregnancy around the world.

SOME NEEDED ACTIONS

Women's status and male violence against women are inextricably linked; advances in one cannot occur without addressing issues raised by the other. Immediate steps must be taken to affirm U.N. and governmental commitments to women's political and social equality, condemn violence internationally, and recognize that violence against women is a violation of women's basic human rights. Global efforts to identify and prevent the myriad forms of male violence, as well as to provide assistance to its victims, must be sensitive to the sociocultural context. These efforts should include the development of new understandings of how violence against women manifests itself cross-culturally, identification of the kinds of research tools and methods that are needed to study violence from the point of view of its victims, and the development of a portrait of the physical, mental, social, and economic effects of male violence. There is a particularly urgent need to train health care workers to screen for and treat the victims of violence, and to develop programs for prevention. Until the hidden forms, effects, and costs of male violence against women are understood and prevented, such violence will continue to undermine the health and well-being of women, children, and societies around the world and prevent women from fully participating in economic development activities.

NOTES

1. Heise, L., Pitanguy, J., & Germain, A. (1993). *World Bank background paper on violence against women as a health issue.* Unpublished manuscript.

2. For an expanded review of this literature, see Goodman, L., Koss, M. P., & Russo, N. F. (1993). Violence against women: Physical and mental health effects. Part I: Research findings. *Applied & Preventive Psychology: Current Scientific Perspectives, 2,* 79–89; Goodman, L. A., Koss, M. P., & Russo, N. F. (1993). Violence against women, Physical and mental health effects, Part II: Conceptualizing post-traumatic stress. *Applied & Preventive Psychology: Current Scientific Perspectives, 2*(3), 123–130; and Koss, M. P., Goodman, L. A., Browne, A., Fitzgerald, L., Keita, G. P., & Russo, N. F. (1994). *No safe haven: Violence against women at home, at work, and in the community.* Washington, DC: American Psychological Association. This work extends the work of the Task Force on Male Violence against Women of the American Psychological Association. Members of the task force are Mary P. Koss and Lisa Goodman, Co-Chairs; Angela Browne, Louise Fitzgerald, Gwendolyn Purycar Keita, and Nancy Felipe Russo. An earlier draft by Nancy Felipe Russo was used as a background paper for a workshop on violence against women at Arizona State University.

3. Kelly, L. (1988). *Surviving sexual violence.* Minneapolis: University of Minnesota Press, p. 78.

4. Ibid. p. 41.

5. McHugh, M. C., Frieze, I. H., & Browne, A. (1993). Research on battered women and their assailants. In M. Paludi & F. L. Denmark (Eds.), *Handbook on the psychology of women* (pp. 513–552). Westport, CT: Greenwood Press.

6. Scheper-Hughes, N. (1992). *Death without weeping: The violence in everyday life in Brazil.* Berkeley: University of California Press.

7. Koss, et al., 1994.

8. Ibid.

9. MacNeill, S. (1987). Flashing: its effect on women (pp. 93–109). In J. Hanmer M. Maynard (Ed.), *Women, Violence, and Social Control.* Atlantic Highlands, NJ: Humanities Press International.

10. Koss et al., 1994.

11. See Goodman, Koss, & Russo, 1993. Full citations to the literature can be found in that report, which is available upon request from N. F. Russo, Psychology, ASU, Tempe, AZ 85287-1104. See also Koss et al., 1994; and Koss, M. P., Goodman, L. A., Fitzgerald, L., Keita, G. P. & Russo, N. F. (1993). Male violence against women: Overview. *American Psychologist,18,* 1054–1058.

12. Koss, M. P. (1988). Women's mental health research agenda: Violence against women. *Women's Mental Health Occasional Paper Series.* Washington, DC: National Institute of Mental Health.

13. Kilpatrick, D. G., Saunders, B. E., Veronen, L. J., Best, C. L., & Von, J. M. (1987). Criminal victimization: Lifetime prevalence, reporting to police, and psychological impact. *Crime and Delinquency, 33,* 478–489.

14. National Victims Center, (1993, April 19). *Rapes in America: A report to the nation.* Arlington, VA: National Victims Center.

15. McKibben, L., DeVoss, E., & Newberger, E. H. (1989). Victimization of mothers and abused children: A controlled study. *Pediatrics, 84,* 531–35.

16. Royer, D. & Fine, D. (1992). Sexual abuse as a factor in adolescent pregnancy and child maltreatment. *Family Planning Perspectives, 24* (1), 4–11, 15.

17. Straus, M. A., Gelles, R. S., & Steinmetz, J. K. (1980). *Behind closed doors: Violence in the American family.* Garden City, NJ: Anchor/Doubleday.

18. Frieze, I. H., & Browne, A. (1989). Violence in marriage. In L. Ohlin & M. H. Tonrey (Eds.), *Crime and justice—An annual review of research: Family violence.* Chicago. University of Chicago Press; Straus, M. A., Gelles, R. S., Steinmetz, J. K. (1980). *Behind closed doors: Violence in the American family.* Garden City, NJ: Anchor/Doubleday.

19. Browne, A. (1991). *Violence against women.* Manuscript prepared for the American Medical Association.

20. N. F. Russo & L. Pope (1993). Unpublished tables.

21. Russo, N. F. (1993). Psychological aspects of unwanted pregnancy and its resolution. In J. D. Butler & D. F. Walbert (Eds.), *Abortion, medicine and the law* (4th ed., pp. 593–626). New York: Facts on File.

10

Domestic Violence and Its Prevention

Herbert H. Krauss and Beatrice J. Krauss

Domestic violence may occur between any of a family's constituent elements (Gelles, 1990). In the United States, despite methodological difficulties in reporting and surveying, it is estimated to be most common between husbands and wives (Straus, 1991; Thorne-Finch, 1992), and parents and children (Gelles, 1990; Straus, 1991). Most often, victims are women or children (Straus, 1991).

An enormous number of individuals are affected as aggressors, victims, or witnesses. In 1985 a nationwide random sample survey indicated that 10.7 percent of children during the previous year "had been the victim of a severe violent act" (Biglan, Lewin, & Hops, 1990, p. 107; Straus & Gelles, 1986). A 1993 national survey found that 34 percent of "adults in the United States . . . witnessed a man beating his wife or girlfriend and . . . 14 percent of women report that a husband or boyfriend has been violent with them . . . [and] as many as 30 percent of women treated in emergency departments (EDs) have injuries or symptoms related to physical abuse" (McLoughlin, Lee, Letellier, & Salber 1993).

In the family setting, incidents of violence often reoccur, escalate, spread to include other family members, and have transgenerational effects. In an analysis of crisis calls from battered women in Atlanta, Georgia, for example, 80 percent of first-time callers reported battery prior to the current incident that prompted the call (Murty & Roebuck, 1992); 97 percent reported verbal abuse immediately before the physical attack. Although in only 16 percent of the 9,919 calls received during two years of the Atlanta study were the victim's children reported present at the time of assault, in 80 percent of those cases the children were also mildly or moderately battered (Murty & Roebuck, 1992). Although not all persons who have been battered or witnessed battering as children become batterers or victims of battery as adults (Carroll, 1980; Gelles, 1990; Ney, 1992), numerous authors have cited these two conditions as a significant risk factor for adult domestic aggression and victimization (e.g., Pepler & Rubin, 1991; Telch & Lindquist, 1984).

Multiple factors may influence adoption of both the "aggressor" and "victim" role. Studies of nonhuman animal models and humans suggest that mediating biological factors include physical differences that promote a positive outcome for the aggressor (e.g., size); disinhibitors such as alcohol or head injury (Denno, 1990); conditions that promote irritability such as withdrawal from sedative-hypnotics or chronic pain; and intoxication with phencyclidine (PCP) (Miller & Potter-Efron, 1989). Evidence for genetic influences on aggression are weak (Elliot, 1988). Although the male hormone testosterone has been implicated in promoting aggression, researchers suggest in humans its influence is indirect and strongly influenced by setting (Burrowes, Hales, & Arrington, 1988). Alcohol, associated with over 30 percent of cases of intrafamilial violence in numerous studies (Murty & Roebuck, 1992), is likewise seen to have an auxiliary, rather than causal, role. Only PCP is cited by multiple researchers as having biological effects that seem direct and independent of social setting (Elliot, 1988; Miller & Potter-Efron, 1990).

Physical characteristics of "victims" may not only enhance perception of them as targets, unlikely to retaliate effectively—women, for example, may be more severely beaten if they do choose to retaliate (Murty & Roebuck, 1992)—but may also place them "out-of-role" for eliciting more prosocial family behavior. Elders with cognitive deficits and premature infants, for instance, are overrepresented among victims of abuse (Brenton, 1977; Soeffing, 1975).

Intra- and interpersonal catalysts to violence include difficulties in labeling emotions, difficulties in labeling others' actions (Dodge & Frame, 1982), restricted problem-solving competencies, unrealistic family role expectations, and biographically engendered routinization of violence. For example, researchers on aggressive or hostile adults and children have noted an overuse of "aversive" interpersonal management techniques—nagging, complaining, sarcasm, insults, and punishment (Biglan, Lewin, & Hops, 1990)—to the exclusion of praise, reward, and a problem-solving orientation. These tactics elicit behaviors—escape, retaliation, for example—that then "justify" aggression.

Some adult batterers witnessed or were victims of violence as children. Clinicians (e.g., Ney, 1992) posit various reasons for this: As adults, batterers are then able to extract revenge; adult battery is an act of denial for what they had borne or witnessed as children; batterers are frustrated as adults that their neediness is not met and that their spouses and children do not adequately nurture them; batterers learned aggression as a problem-solving device from parental models (Patterson, Capaldi, & Bank, 1991); and batterers possess an inadequate repertoire of other problem-solving techniques (Rubin, Bream, & Rose-Krasnor, 1991). Most children, however, have exposure to both violent and nonviolent models; recent theorizing, therefore, has looked at why the "aggressive" model might be chosen to be imitated. Carroll (1980), for example, in an empirical study of problem families, found that transgenerational transmission of violent behavior to children was associated with a lack of warmth in *both* parents and with being the same sex as the aggressive parent.

Different ages and different societies create and maintain distinct forms and targets of violence. The anthropologist Raoul Naroll (1983) notes systematic cross-cultural variation in the incidence of wife beating as a function of other societal characteristics that also threaten or weaken interpersonal ties, for example, drunken brawling and men's divorce freedom. The historian of family life Paul Veyne (1987) suggests that easy adoption rules and inheritance laws allowing capricious assignment of benefits made patricide epidemic in ancient Rome.

Societies differ in their expectations of and sanctions for hostile or injurious behavior; they also create forms or places in which violence is ignored, promoted, or decried. In their cross-cultural summaries of wife beating, Counts, Brown, and Campbell (1992) differentiate between physical reprimands of wives, the intention of which is discipline, and wife battering, where the intent or result is injury. Reprimands directed toward wives are common in societies where women make a major contribution to subsistence. Appropriate forms for expression of angry emotions and behavior have also varied over time in the United States. In the colonial United States, angry displays were considered passionate. "[O]ur founding fathers felt relatively free to storm and rage when the mood seized them and even took temper to be a sign of manliness" (Stearns & Stearns, 1986, p. 2). Family behavior was often regulated by business norms, since home and business were rarely separate, as in the family shop or farm (Gadlin, 1977). Only with the advent of the Industrial Revolution did the spheres of public and private, work and home life become relatively detached in the United States. Home was the province of the woman and children; its purpose was to provide the man with a haven from the rigors of the work world (Gadlin, 1977). From then to the present, wives and children were viewed ideally as a source of emotional satisfaction, and the children realistically more and more as an economic liability.

A FRAMEWORK FOR UNDERSTANDING FAMILY VIOLENCE

Numerous explanatory schemas have been advanced to account for violence in general and family violence in particular (Viano, 1992): exchange theory (e.g., Gelles, 1983), culture of violence theory (e.g., Wolfgang & Ferracuti, 1967), resource theory (e.g., Blood & Wolfe, 1960), patriarchal theory (e.g., Dobash & Dobash, 1979; Martin, 1976), ecological theory (e.g., Garbarino, 1977), social learning theory (e.g., Bandura, 1973; O'Leary, 1988), evolutionary theory (e.g., Levinson, 1989), sociobiological theory (e.g., Gray, 1985), social conflict theory (e.g., Retzinger, 1991), and general systems theory (e.g., Straus, 1978). Although each of these has made contributions at a particular level of analysis, no convincing, integrated, comprehensive theory has yet been put forward. For example, sociobiologists have suggested agonistic acts ("any activity related to fighting, whether aggression or conciliation and retreat," Wilson, 1975) are aimed at maintaining the "inclusive fitness" of group members through selective preservation of those with the greatest reproductive potential. The individual's own genes are likewise perpetuated through a "calculus of genetic relatedness," that is, agonistic and prosocial behaviors aimed at kin selection. Nurturing of family members is seen as one aspect of kin selection; rejection of deviant offspring is a way of maintaining inclusive fitness. Sociobiology does not give an adequate explanation for why so much violence occurs within rather than outside the family. Culture of violence theory suggests that complex societies develop subgroups within which violent actions are normative; it does not explain why wife beating is so widespread (Counts, Brown, & Campbell, 1992).

There is a need for higher-order theory that integrates and synthesizes results generated at multiple levels. Acknowledgment is increasing in science generally that causation is bidirectional, operating from the lowest levels of material organization up, and from the highest levels of social and cognitive organization down (e.g., Sperry, 1993). This multiple-level, bidirectional approach has been accepted as a difficult, but necessary, strategy for understanding and mediating family violence. Earls (1991, p. 161), director of a recently founded program on human development and criminal behavior at the Harvard School of Public Health, enumerates the difficulties of the multilevel research required:

We know from separate studies that genetic factors, sex differences, biomedical insults, individual differences in personality, family influences, social and community characteristics, cultural and ethnic differences, and cross-national differences all contribute in some way to violence . . . and we have little understanding about how they might be operating in combination.

DRAMATURGICAL ANALYSIS

Duke Senior. Thou seest we are not all alone unhappy.
This wide and universal theater
Presents more woeful pageants than the scene
Wherein we play in.
Jacques. All the world's a stage
and all the men and women merely players.
They have their exits and their entrances,
And one man in his time plays many parts.
(Shakespeare, *As You Like It,* Act II, Scene 7, Lines 137–143)

Modern dramaturgical analysis—influential in sociology, social psychology, and personality theory—can be traced to the seminal essays of Kenneth Burke (e.g., 1989). His work, supplemented by the insights of the currently underappreciated American personality theorist George Kelly (e.g., 1955, 1963, 1969), provides the guiding analogy, or in Burke's coinage "anecdote," namely, life as theater, by means of which family violence may be better understood.

Kelly (1963) argues that to survive an individual must learn to anticipate future events. "This means he must develop a system in which the most unusual future can be anticipated in terms of a replicated aspect of the familiar past" (p. 118). To do this successfully a person must construct an image of the world that is workable. These images or templates Kelly calls "constructs"; modern cognitive theorists term them "schemas" or "schemata" (e.g., Dennett, 1991). Emotionally charged linkages between settings, constructs, and viewed actions evolve over time into scripts for action (Tomkins, 1979).

People differ in their construction of events and actions because they differ among themselves in temperament, experiences, and other characteristics. None-theless, individuals are not totally isolated from one another but must share a core understanding of their situation if coordinated action is to be possible. For Kelly,

When one does understand culture in terms of similarity of expectations, he can proceed from that point in one of two directions. He can consider the expectations of others as stimuli to which each person is subjected; or he can understand cultural similarity in what they perceive is expected of them (p. 93).

"A role," therefore, according to Kelly (1963, pp. 92–98),

is a psychological process based upon the role player's construction of aspects of the construction systems of those with whom he attempts to join in a social enterprise. . . . A role is an ongoing pattern of behavior that follows from a person's understanding of how others who are associated with him in his task think. . . . [It] is a position that one can play on a certain team without even waiting for the signals.

Whereas Kelly generally focuses upon the individual and his or her construc-tions, as befitting the interests of a psychologist, Burke was interested in the play. Dramaturgical analysis aims at providing an interactional analysis of all of the multiple and hierarchical systems of which the individual is a part. "Dra-matism," Burke's term to describe his approach,

centers on observations of this sort: for there to be an *act,* there must be an *agent.* Similarly, there must be a *scene,* the agent must employ some means, or *agency.* And it can be called an act in the full sense of the term only if it involves a *purpose* (that is, if a support happens to give way and one falls, such a notion on the agent's part is not an act, but an accident). These five terms (act, scene, agent, agency, purpose) have been labelled the dramatic pentad. (1969, p. 135)

Each of the terms of this pentad have somewhat elastic denotations, and, for Burke, this flexibility in meaning is natural and necessary.

For a man is not only in the situation peculiar to his era or to his particular place in that era. . . . He is also in a situation extending through centuries; he is in a "generally human" situation. In confronting this wide range in the choice of a circumference for the location of an act, men confront what is distinctively the human freedom and the human necessity. (Burke, 1969, p. 167)

The heuristic power of dramaturgical analysis should be obvious. It allows such questions as "What is the act?" "Who has committed it?" "To what purpose?" "What is the agent's motivation?" "Is there an audience?" "Is the audience there to approve or disapprove, take an active role or be passive?" "Do actors follow scripts or *ad lib?*" "Is the role enacted convincing to the agent, to the audience, to the other actors?" "Does the play have a plot?" "Is it a drama or comedy?" "Does it have a preconceived ending?" "How and by whom is it being staged?" "Does it have a director?" "Could it have been better written, better played?"

In Peter Berger's (1963) view, the dramaturgical perspective can also guide us to an ecstatic view of the human circumstance.

By this we refer not to some abnormal heightening of consciousness in a mystical sense, but rather, quite literally, to the act of standing or stepping outside (literally *ekstasis*) the taken-for-granted routine of society. . . . Looking at society through the medium of this dramatic model greatly changes our general sociological perspective. Social reality now seems to be precariously perched on the cooperation of many individual actors—or perhaps a better simile would be that of acrobats engaged in perilous balancing acts, holding up between them the swaying structure of the social world. . . . Acting out the social drama we keep pretending that these precarious conventions are eternal verities. (Berger, 1963, pp. 14–16)

Even though the belief that action may be altered is implicit, the dramaturgical perspective recognizes that doing so might indeed prove difficult. If the act to be changed is scripted and central to the actor's and the scene's meaning, few actors would dare omit it.

PREVENTION

There are fine distinctions to be made between the *prevention* of family violence, *deterrence* toward a more positive family script when violence is signaled or begins to unfold, and *treatment* for family members to contain and break cycles of repetition once a violent incident occurs. These slightly different goals and orientations are referred to as primary, secondary, and tertiary prevention (Macht, 1978). In primary prevention, the aim is to reduce the incidence of the problem by counteracting the forces that lead to its development. Parent effectiveness training and education designed to substitute more responsible behavior in relationships for rage-driven violence would be examples. Secondary prevention programs endeavor to be curative; their goals are to find cases early, shorten the duration, and limit the effects of problematic behavior. Such activities involve intervention before escalation, while family problems have done little damage, are manageable, and a return to normalcy is in sight. Successful early mediating efforts of relatives, friends, and professionals fall into this category. Tertiary prevention programs are ameliorative; their intent is to lighten the effects of damaging violence that has already occurred. Shelter programs for battered women and children that remove and protect them from further assault and offer services to alleviate residual psychological and physical effects are examples.

Any policy maker must make difficult decisions in allocation of resources among programs aimed at regulating a large general population sharing a few risk characteristics and intensive interventions aimed at changing sets of individuals whose circumstances are endangering or dangerous, but singular. For example, treating a child-batterer may reduce the incidence of his or her child being battered but will not reduce child-battery in the society as a whole, as child-battering is related to such variables as the social isolation of the family, whether the child was wanted, and the incidence of "broken homes" (Naroll, 1983; Rohner, 1975). In the more general case, if social and individual mechanisms of self-control are intact, a change in social policies and norms toward decrying violence, calling in to play peer and self-regulation, and containing a "stage direction" as to what is acceptable behavior may have broadly general primary prevention effects. Such rewriting of the drama of culture must, of course, be attempted with humility and wisdom, rare qualities in those varied constituencies that demand, lobby for, create, and implement policy change. Whenever one alters the fundamental power and regulatory relationships that structure a society, "the law of unintended consequences" must be considered and steps taken to ensure matters are not made worse by "reforms" (e.g., Campbell, 1988).

From an ethological perspective, agonistic behaviors, a more inclusive term than aggression, have long been held to have a crucial role in *maintaining* family, and by extension societal, relationships. Established dominance hierarchies and threat displays routinely *prevent* the occurrence of active fights, fights that may disrupt ongoing social life or result in injuries that compromise the genetic fitness of individual participants. Threat displays and other rituals of social behavior may disperse the species members over territory so that conflicts over the resources necessary to maintain life (food, safety) and preserve the species (mate selection) are reduced (Silverberg & Gray, 1992). Recently many ethologists have been forced by the results of their research to an even broader view of the role played by aggressive and agonistic behaviors. It is now obvious that agonistic behaviors serve a multitude of social purposes not easily explained as promoting the sociobiologists' kin selection or inclusive fitness—correcting juveniles from making social blunders, for example. Furthermore, biologically rooted affiliation and altruism have taken on a larger importance in an individual's adaptation to and position in social life. Selection of alpha or dominant members may, in some species and even in preschool children (Strayer, 1992), occur as much through establishment of broad friendship patterns as through violent acts or displays.

Bowlby (1984), the eminent developmental psychiatrist, to cite one instance, identifies the origins of family violence as arising from disorders within caregiving and attachment systems, which are anchored to the reproductive system. In these systems anger can be highly functional: "At the right time, and in the right degree, anger can serve to maintain . . . vitally important long-term relationships" (Bowlby, 1984, p. 12). Anger can serve to "drive off a rival," "deter dangerous behavior," or "coerce a partner" to perform reciprocal role behaviors in service of protection of a spousal, parent-child, or child-parent relationship.

Anger in intimate relationships, in Bowlby's view, is not a self-perpetuating emotion that once started must run to its end (a mythology common to some constructions of sex and violence, Thorne-Finch, 1992); instead he sees it as a subsystem in service of, and under the control of, preservation of long-term committed attachments. When operating properly, the caregiving-attachment systems, to cite a developmental example, lead to a child's developing "confidence that others will be helpful when appealed to and in his becoming increasingly self-reliant and bold in his explorations of the world, cooperative with others, and also—a very important point—sympathetic and helpful to others in distress" (Bowlby, 1984, p. 13). In contrast, the anxiously attached child will be apprehensive about receiving care, reluctant to leave the caregiver, "unwillingly and anxiously obedient, and unconcerned about the troubles of others." The rejected child will be conflicted between escape-avoidance and a desire for proximity, with angry behavior likely to become prominent. Such childhood experiences, in Bowlby's system, form the template for later romantic and parental attachments and competencies.

Of course, to indicate that anger and its accompanying potential for eliciting intrafamilial aggression may have evolutionary underpinnings and social significance does not argue that the aggression or threat may not be misdirected, misused, or that other actions cannot be substituted that would produce better, more prosocial, more sophisticated scripts. In fact, over the course of time, in the more "developed" societies there appears to be a general tendency, punctuated by retrogressions, toward the development of self discipline and a rechannelling of more "primitive" emotion-action sequences into socially programmed behaviors, into a cultural script. As Elias (1982, p. 230) has stated,

It has been shown . . . how constraints through others from a variety of angles are converted into self restraints, how the more animalic human activities are progressively thrust behind the scenes of men's communal social life and invested with feelings of shame, how the regulation of the whole instinctual and affective life by steady self-control becomes more and more stable, more and more all embracing. . . . This basic tissue resulting from many single plans and actions of men can give rise to change and patterns that no individual person has planned or created. From this interdependence of people arises an order sui generis, an order more compelling and stronger than the will and reason of the individual people among it.

General cultural scripts must of necessity address fundamental issues such as the nature of interpersonal relationships, including aggression and its tolerable limits. Each age writes its play; each culture its own script. For instance, the psychiatrist and historian team Stearns and Stearns (1986) have noted the restraint of anger is a significant theme in current U.S. American culture. It has been so, in different forms, for two hundred years. In its twentieth-century version, they suggest, "Americans have shifted in their methods of controlling social behavior toward greater reliance on direct manipulation of emotions and, particularly, of anger" (p. 2). They place in contrast attempts to regulate *behavior* without attack on their emotional bases.

Regulation of aggression is necessary for all cultures. Whether aggression in interpersonal affairs springs directly from our biological nature or the intrinsic demands of the social structure is moot. What is not arguable is that role relationships and the ties that one member of a culture shares with another influence the expression of violence in general and intrafamilial violence in particular. Dahrendorf (1981) labels these ties *ligatures*. Naroll (1983) attends to a subset of these that he calls *moral nets*. A moral net, according to Naroll (1983, p. 19), is "a primary group that serves as a normative reference group. The archetypical moral nets are the extended family or the primeval hunting band." Naroll has amassed considerable cross-cultural evidence that weak or attenuated moral nets (or ligatures, if Dahrendorf's terminology is used) are associated with murder, theft and fraud, hard drinking, drug abuse, suicide, brawling, wife beating, child battering, neurosis, and psychosis.

Familial moral nets can reduce marital violence in many ways. One is by making possible and instituting customs analagous to "bride price."

Bride wealth is wealth—money or cattle, for example—given by the groom or his family to the bride's family as part of the marriage contract. In most societies in which a man must find bride wealth to marry, what he buys is a *wife,* not a chattel. His wife may leave him if she feels basely abused—though this may not be easy for her. In many bride price societies, if the husband abuses the wife and she leaves him, he may lose the wealth that he gave her. Among the Thonga of South Africa, if a wife feels mistreated, she is free to go home to her parents. Then her husband must come humbly to her and her parents and beg her to come back. Otherwise, the couple, though still married, are separated. (Naroll, 1983, p. 229)

There are, of course, others. In general each depends on a resource base offered to the marriage partners that serves to strengthen ties to extended kin and move the balance of power between the couple to a broader and stronger base.

If increased family strength is the key to lowering family violence, it is incumbent upon us if we are serious about the primary prevention of violence,

Naroll argues, to identify the characteristics of strong families—those less troubled by violence, homicide, suicide, and crime—and to foster policies that support their development and maintenance. He summarizes cross-cultural research that suggests that strong families tend to have over five household members, delay first births (e.g., after six years of marriage, to women over 35), and delay marriage for women (average age at marriage higher). Weaker families are smaller, have higher divorce rates (especially within the first three years of marriage), and have higher birthrates among teenage mothers. They also produce more extramarital births. Drawing on Howard's (1978) description of families, Naroll describes strong families as developing their own heroes and folklore, celebrating rituals, treasuring posterity, and honoring elders. Such families are affectionate, communicative, problem centered, and realistic; have a sense of place and home; and are hospitable. They do not attempt to be everything to everyone but "foster outside interests and work." Citing cross-cultural studies of child abuse, Naroll finds parental rejection diminished in homes in which children are wanted and several interested adults (e.g., grandparents rather than cowives) share the work of child care, providing respite and guidance for the primary caretaker. In contrast, child abuse tends to occur in families that are socially isolated (Light, 1973; Naroll, 1983), as does violence against wives (Nielsen, Endo, & Ellington, 1992). Working against the development of strong families, Naroll cites three "tradeoff" processes. (1) Economic development weakens extended families, as it induces family members to move to centers of economic development; the accompanying specialization and bureaucracy increases mobility further by pulling individuals to where they are needed. (2) The ligatures of extended families often engender a "tug of family authority against individual freedom," one that frequently ends in favor of the latter. (3) Some social welfare programs direct their aid to individuals and thus weaken family units (e.g., nineteenth-century workhouses segregated husbands, wives, and children).

Strong moral net ties are not necessarily familial, but they are functionally familial. The army or church may regulate life to some degree, but no current or emerging U.S. American social organizations have the early and continuous influence throughout the life span that families do.

Naroll's work has obvious implications for social policy directed at supporting strong families or their surrogates: provide day or respite care; discourage teenage pregnancy; arrange leaves, aid, and incentives that support family life; provide visiting child-care helpers and good parent models to at-risk homes; reduce the social isolation of the nuclear family; and so forth. The impact on family violence of these promising suggestions, of course, has not been tested. Our society has not yet adopted programmatic legislation designed to support family life in the way Naroll envisioned. Moreover, even when legislation intended to be helpful is enacted, the assessment of its effects often does not proceed far enough along the causal chain. Do we know, for example, what influence easing divorce restrictions or providing birth control education has on child abuse? We do not even know whether the many group and individual interventions designed to reduce family violence, described in the literature, work (Hanks, 1992). Steps are now being taken to change this situation.

Due to record levels of violence in the 1970s and late 1980s, research into the prevention of violence has recently become a U.S. American national priority (Earls, 1991) and violence has been defined as a national health problem. The Centers for Disease Control and Prevention recently joined mental health and social service systems in a charge to *prevent* interpersonal violence, for example.

Legislators have not waited for the results of applied prevention research before acting, however (Besharov, 1990). "During the late 1970s and early 1980s, states began passing legislation aimed at specially protecting the battered mate. These provisions included civil and criminal penalties for violating protective orders, record keeping on family violence for those agencies interfacing with abusive families, and funding for shelters, as well as other services for violent families" (Hendricks, 1992, p. 213). In the succeeding ten years, a signal change in police practice occurred: Domestic violence was removed from the private sphere and criminalized. By June 1988 thirty-nine states had legislated probable cause warrantless arrest when domestic misdemeanor battery was suspected (Hendricks, 1992).

In a well-designed, random assignment field experiment the efficacy of this approach to secondary prevention was tested. Three hundred fourteen legally eligible subjects were assigned to one of three police responses to simple assault: arrest, advice (sometimes including informal mediation), or an order to leave for eight hours. Recidivism was tracked for six months. Arrested individuals committed significantly less subsequent violence than individuals in the other two treatment groups (Sherman & Berk, 1984).

Broadly instituted educational programs designed to reduce violence might also prove effective. The goal of such a primary prevention program would be teaching a set of easily learned scripts for productive and controlled anger in intimate relations. (In large families of the past, such education for parenting took place informally; children had the opportunity to observe the caregiving techniques of parents, grandparents, aunts and uncles.) These scripts would anticipate how family systems are likely to go awry. In one scenario, for example, an unskilled parent might perform a behavior that he or she expects would elicit positive responses from the child. The child—because of illness, irritability, or the parent's incorrect choice of actions—would not return the desired and expected response. In such an interaction, the child's *purpose* can be seen as blameworthy, the *agent*—the child—could be seen as defective, or the *act* of the parent could be seen as unworkable. Each of these attributions leads to the unfolding of slightly different plots or stories. If the *scene* were open to an audience that would approve and regulate the well-being of children and caregiving partners, how would the problem be solved? Education could be presented in the classroom, by models, or in interactive groups. Such training would not only address the "usual" situations of parenthood, spousal relations, and elder care but also deal with the management and normalization of "difficult" relations (e.g., with irritable infants, stepfamilies, or elders with cognitive deficits). Respite and sharing for relationships requiring a large caregiver contribution would also be addressed. Positive rather than aversive management techniques would be emphasized.

It would seem a component of any effectiveness training for intimate relations must be an effort to increase the problem-solving repertoire of individuals for even routine conflicts and arguments. Essentially, actors must learn new lines and motions for new scripts. The requirements for such problem solving are often cognitively complex, however, and require detachment, reflection, and objectivity (Ackoff, 1978; Polya, 1957). They may be beyond the reach of many individuals. The actors or their coagents become moral scientists. Ackoff's formulation of problem solving dictates that parties be able to state each other's positions, be able to state the conditions under which they would adopt the other's position, search facts for whether or not those conditions exist or could be provided, and if no facts or provisions are available, be able to form a regret matrix, essentially an analysis of the cost of the social consequences of adopting each viewpoint *and turning out to be wrong*. Further, as Coombs (1987) has pointed out, something must hold parties in a conflict together until a resolution can be effected. "It may be threats or benefits offered by a third party, or reframing relationships to emphasize cooperation and mutual interests. This recasts a conflict from unrelated individuals competing to related individuals settling" (Krauss & Krauss, 1989, p. 14). The latter conflict, in Coombs's typology of conflict, is easier to solve than the former. Stylistically, it occurs when a family defines itself as a unit.

The emphasis of this chapter has been on primary and secondary prevention through higher-level interventions. Individual and group therapy with perpetrators and victims of family violence has not been addressed. Although principles guiding such interventions have been described in the literature (e.g., Hanks, 1992), convincing systematic evaluations of their outcomes are not yet available. At best, results are mixed. No one believes that therapy for such problems is a simple process or that modifications of cognitions and behaviors that underlie familial violence are easily achieved. There are clear reasons for this. Some domestic violence is an outcome of predisposing biological forces for which no known remediation is available. Another reason is that cognitions are organized into hierarchical patterns of thought. A request for movement of change at a subordinate level may threaten superordinate constructs. A man who is asked to give up behaviors he construes as preventing him from being pushed around may subsume these ideas under a notion of what it means to be strong and manly. These notions may be further maintained by cultural sources, friendship networks, movies, TV, and songs. As Kelly (1963, p. 9) explains, "Frequently his personal investment in the larger system, or his personal dependence upon it, is so great that he will forgo the adoption of a more precise construct in substructure."

Although difficult, successful role change can be negotiated if several conditions are met. Among them are

a. a realistically achieved alternative role whose benefit/cost ratio is more favorable;

b. extent of structural autonomy of role setting, freedom from close observation, or weakening of [prior] normative controls over role performance;

c. extent to which the role incumbents are unified in desire for role change and mobilized to promote change;

d. extent to which there is a mobilized client demand for services this role provides or would under a new pattern;

e. cultural credibility of the potential new role pattern;

f. success in gaining institutional support for new patterns (Turner, 1990, p. 107).

Clearly, to act in the play as written is easier than to rewrite it. A shift from one worldview to another is unsettling and chaotic, without cultural collaboration.

No comprehensive framework or research program explicates how family violence would be addressed at the multiple interacting levels necessary for general change. Dramaturgical analysis has been suggested as a metaphor for these linked interactions.

REFERENCES

Ackoff, R. (1978). *The art of problem solving*. New York: John Wiley.

Bandura, A. (1973). *Aggression: A social learning analysis*. Englewood Cliffs, NJ: Prentice Hall.

Berger, P. (1963). Sociological perspectives—society as drama. In D. Brissett & C. Edgley (Eds.), *Life as theater: A dramaturgical sourcebook (1975)* (pp. 13–22). Chicago: Aldine.

Besharov, D. J. (1990). Family violence: Research and public policy issues for the '90's. *Response of the Victimization of Women and Children, 13,*(1), 6–7.

Biglan, A., Lewin, L., & Hops, H. (1990). A contextual approach to the problem of aversive practices in families. In G. R. Patterson (Ed.), *Depression and aggression in family interaction* (pp. 103–130). Hillsdale, NJ: Lawrence Erlbaum.

Blood, R. O., & Wolfe, D. M. (1960). *Husbands and wives: The dynamics of married living*. Glencoe, IL: Free Press.

Bowlby, J. (1984). Violence in the family as a disorder of the attachment and caregiving systems. *American Journal of Psychoanalysis, 44,* 9–27.

Brenton, M. (1977). What can be done about child abuse? *Today's Education, 66,* 51–55.

Burke, K. (1969). *On symbols and society*. J. R. Garfield (Ed.). Chicago: University of Chicago Press.

Burrowes, K. L., Hales, R. E., & Arrington, E. (1988). Research on biologic aspects of violence. *Psychiatric Clinics of North America, 11,* (4), 499–509.

Campbell, D. T. (1988). *Methodology and epistemology for social science.* Chicago: University of Chicago Press.

Carroll, J. (1980). The intergenerational transmission of family violence: The long term effects of aggressive behaviors. *Advances in Family Psychiatry, 2,* 171–181.

Coombs, C. H. (1987). The structure of conflict. *American Psychologist, 42,* 355–363.

Counts, D. A., Brown, J. K., & Campbell, J. C. (1992). *Sanctions and sanctuary: Cultural perspectives on the beating of wives.* Boulder, CO: Westview Press.

Dahrendorf, R. (1981). *Life chances: Approaches to social and political theory.* Chicago: University of Chicago Press.

Dennett, D. C. (1991). *Consciousness explained.* Boston: Little, Brown.

Denno, D. W. (1990). *Biology and violence from birth to adulthood.* New York: Cambridge University Press.

Dobash, R. E., & Dobash, R. P. (1979). *Violence against wives.* New York: Free Press.

Dodge, K. A., & Frame, C. L. (1982). Social cognitive biases and deficits in aggressive boys. *Child Development, 53,* 620–635.

Earls, F. (1991). Understanding and controlling violence. *Journal of Health Care for the Poor and Underserved, 2,* 156–164.

Elias, N. (1982). *Power and civility: The civilizing process* (Vol. 2). New York: Pantheon.

Elliot, F. A. (1988). Neurological factors. In V. Van Hasselt, R. L. Morrisoon, A. S. Bellack, & M. Hersen (Eds.), *Handbook of family violence* (pp. 359–382). New York: Plenum Press.

Gadlin, H. (1977). Structure of marriage in four US eras. In G. Levinger & H. Raush (Eds.), *Close relationships.* Amherst, MA: University of Massachussetts Press.

Garbarino, J. (1977). The human ecology of child maltreatment: A conceptual model for research. *Journal of Marriage and the Family, 39,* 721–735.

Gelles, R. J. (1983). An exchange social theory. In D. Finkelhor, R. J. Gelles, G. T. Hotaling, & M. A. Strauss (Eds.), *The dark side of families: Current family violence* (pp. 151–165). Beverly Hills, CA: Sage.

Gelles, R. J. (1990). Methodological issues in the study of family violence. In G. R. Patterson (Ed.), *Depression and aggression in family interaction* (pp. 49–74). Hillside, NJ: Lawrence Erlbaum.

Gray, J. P. (1985). *Primate sociobiology.* New Haven, CT: HRAF.

Hanks, S. E. (1992). Translating theory into practice: A conceptual framework for clinical assessment, differential diagnosis, and multi-modal treatment of maritally violent individuals, couples, and families. In E. Viano (Ed.), *Intimate violence: Interdisciplinary perspectives* (pp. 157–176). Washington, DC: Hemisphere.

Hendricks, J. E. (1992). Domestic violence legislation in the United States: A survey of the states. In E. Viano (Ed.), *Intimate violence: Interdisciplinary perspectives* (pp. 213–226). Washington, DC: Hemisphere.

Howard, J. (1978). *Families.* New York: Berkeley.

Kelly, G. A. (1955). *The psychology of personal constructs* (2 vols.). New York: W. W. Norton.

Kelly, G. A. (1963). *A theory of personality: The psychology of personality constructs.* New York: W. W. Norton.

Kelly, G. A. (1969). The autobiography of a theory. In B. Maher (Ed.), *Clinical psychology and personality: The selected papers of George Kelly* (pp. 40–65). New York: John Wiley.

Krauss, B. J., & Krauss, H. H. (1989). Interpersonal conflict. In J. B. Gittler (Ed.), *The*

Annual Review of Conflict Knowledge and Conflict Resolution (Vol. 1, pp. 1–31). New York: Garland.

Krauss, H. H., & Krauss, B. J. (1994). Anxiety and time. In B. B. Wolman & G. Striker (Eds.), *Anxiety and related disorders: A handbook.* New York: Wiley. Pp. 132–157.

Levinson, D. (1989). *Family violence in cross-cultural perspective.* Newbury Park, CA: Sage.

Light, R. J. (1973). Abused and neglected children in America: A study of alternative policies. *Harvard Educational Review, 43,* 556–598.

Lloyd, S. A. (1987). Conflict in premarital relationships: Differential perceptions of males and females. *Family Relations, 36,* 290–294.

Macht, L. B. (1978). Community psychiatry. In J. A. M. Nicholi (Ed.), *The Harvard guide to modern psychiatry* (pp. 627–699). Cambridge, MA: Harvard University Press.

McLoughlin, E., Lee, D., Letellier, P., & Salber, P. (1993). Emergency department response to domestic violence—California, 1992. *Morbidity and Mortality Weekly Report, 42* (32), 617–619.

Martin, D. (1976). *Battered wives.* San Francisco: Glide.

Maxwell, R. J. (1972). Anthropological perspectives. In H. Yakes, H. Osmond, & F. Cheek (Eds.), *The future of time: Man's temporal environment* (pp. 36–72). Garden City, NY: Anchor.

Miller, M. M., & Potter-Efron, R. T. (1989). Aggression and violence associated with substance abuse. *Journal of Chemical Dependency Treatment, 3* (1), 1–36.

Murty, K. S., & Roebuck, J. B. (1992). An analysis of crisis calls by battered women in the City of Atlanta. In E. C. Viano (Ed.), *Intimate violence: Interdisciplinary perspectives* (pp. 61–70). Washington, DC: Hemisphere.

Naroll, R. (1983). *The moral order: An introduction to the human situation.* Beverly Hills, CA: Sage.

Ney, P. G. (1992). Transgenerational triangles of abuse: A model of family violence. In E. C. Viano (Ed.), *Intimate violence: Interdisciplinary perspectives* (pp. 15–25). Washington, DC: Hemisphere.

Nielsen, J. M., Endo, R. K., & Ellington, B. L. (1992). Social isolation and wife abuse: A research report. In E. C. Viano (Ed.), *Intimate violence: Interdisciplinary perspectives* (pp. 49–60). Washington, DC: Hemisphere.

O'Leary, D. K. (1988). Physical aggression between spouses: A social learning theory perspective. In V. B. Van Hasselt (Ed.), *Handbook of family violence* (pp. 31–55). New York: Plenum Press.

Patterson, G. R., Capaldi, D., & Bank, L. (1991). An early starter model for predicting delinquency. In D. J. Pepler. & K. H. Rubin (Eds.), *The development and treatment of childhood aggression* (pp. 139–168). Hillsdale, NJ: Lawrence Erlbaum.

Pepler, D. J., & Rubin, K. H. (1991). *The development and treatment of childhood aggression.* Hillsdale, NJ: Lawrence Erlbaum.

Polya, G. (1957). *How to solve it.* Garden City, NY: Doubleday Anchor.

Retzinger, S. M. (1991). *Violent emotions: Shame and rage in marital quarrels.* Newbury Park, CA: Sage.

Rohner, R. P. (1975). *They love me, they love me not.* New Haven, CT: HRAF.

Rubin, K. H., Bream, L. A., & Rose-Krasnor, L. (1991). Social problem solving and aggression in childhood. In D. J. Pepler. & K. H. Rubin (Eds.), *The development and treatment of childhood aggression* (pp. 219–248). Hillsdale, NJ: Lawrence Erlbaum.

Sherman, L., & Berk, R. (1984). The specific deterrent effects of arrest for domestic assault. *American Sociological Review, 49,* 261–272.

Silverberg, J., & Gray, J. P. (1992). Violence and peacefulness as behavioral potentialities of primates. In J. Silverberg & J. P. Gray (Eds.), *Aggression and peacefulness in humans and other primates* (pp. 1–36). New York: Oxford University Press.

Soeffing, M. (1975). Abused children are exceptional children. *Exceptional Children, 42,* 126–135.

Sperry, R. W. (1993). The impact and promise of the cognitive revolution. *American Psychologist, 48,* 878–885.

Stearns, C. Z., & Stearns, P. N. (1986). *Anger: The struggle for emotional control in America's history.* Chicago: University of Chicago Press.

Straus, M. (1978). Wife-beating: How common and why? *Victimology, 2,* 443–459.

Straus, M. A. (1991). Physical violence in American families: Incidence rates, causes and trends. In D. D. Knudsen & J. L. Miller (Eds.), *Abused and battered: Social and legal responses to family violence* (pp. 17–34). New York: Aldine de Gruyter.

Straus, M. A., & Gelles, R. J. (1986). Societal change and change in family violence from 1975 to 1985 as revealed by two national surveys. *Journal of Marriage and the Family, 48,* 465–479.

Strayer, F. F. (1992). The development of agonistic and affiliative structures in preschool play groups. In J. Silverberg & J. P. Gray (Eds.), *Aggression and peacefulness in humans and other primates* (pp. 150–171). New York: Oxford University Press.

Telch, C. F., & Lindquist, C. U. (1984). Violent versus nonviolent couples: A comparison of patterns. *Psychotherapy, 21* (2), 242–248.

Thorne-Finch, R. (1992). *Ending the silence: The origins and treatment of male violence against women.* Toronto: University of Toronto Press.

Tomkins, S. S. (1979). Script theory: Differential magnification of affects. *Nebraska Symposium on Motivation, 26,* 201–236.

Turner, R. H. (1990). Role change. *Annual Review of Sociology, 16,* 87–110.

Veyne, P. (1987). The Roman empire. In P. Aries & G. Duby (Eds.), *A history of private life* (pp. 5–233). Cambridge, MA: Belknap Press.

Viano, E. C. (1992). Violence among intimates: Major issues and approaches. In E. C. Viano (Ed.), *Intimate violence: Interdisciplinary perspectives* (pp. 3–14). Washington, DC: Hemisphere.

Wilson, E. O. (1975). *Sociobiology: The new synthesis.* Cambridge, MA: Harvard University Press.

Wolfgang, M., & Ferracuti, F. (1967). *The subculture of violence: Toward an integrated theory of criminology.* London: Tavistock.

11

Gender Stereotypes and the Problem of Marital Violence

Gwendolyn L. Gerber

Violence by husbands toward their wives is a serious problem in our culture that is only now becoming fully recognized. Such violence has been linked with a variety of factors, including ones that are social, economic, familial, and psychological (Finkelhor, Gelles, Hotaling, & Straus, 1983; Gelles, 1972; Straus, Gelles, & Steinmetz, 1981; Walker, 1984). What has generally gone unrecognized, however, is the role the gender-stereotyped personality traits play in fostering and perpetuating men's violence toward women.

Most people believe that women and men have different personalities. Studies have shown that people think women are high in "communion"—personality traits that express warmth, concern, and connection with others (Bakan, 1966; Bem, 1974; Rosenkrantz, Vogel, Bee, Broverman, & Broverman, 1968; Spence, Helmreich, & Stapp, 1975). They also believe that men are high in "agency"—personality traits that enhance one's own self through self-assertion and exerting one's will on others. These traits not only are considered typical but also are believed to be desirable for each sex (Bakan, 1966; Bem, 1974; Rosenkrantz et al., 1968). If a woman is to be truly "feminine," many people think that she must be high in communion; if a man is to be really "masculine," he must be high in agency.

Since these gender-stereotyped traits are assumed to constitute the essence of masculinity in men and femininity in women, both sexes feel pressured to conform to them. They feel they must manifest the characteristics desirable for their sex in order to have an appropriate gender identity (Gerber, 1989a).

In the process of conforming to these cultural expectations, men and women generally do not realize that they are also perpetuating traditional relationships between the sexes—ones in which men have more power than women. The reason that they are not aware of this connection is because the gender-stereotyped traits are usually viewed in isolation from their context. They have become dissociated from their roots so that they are no longer connected with the roles in which they originate. When we define the essence of masculinity as agency and the essence of femininity as communion, we are not aware that we are implicitly sanctioning traditional relationships between the sexes. We do not realize that the roles associated with such traditional relationships are reflected and embedded in the personality traits we expect both sexes to express.

In traditional relationships between the sexes, men exercise more power than women, generally through persuasion and influence (Blood & Wolfe, 1960; Raven, Centers, & Rodrigues, 1975; Scanzoni, 1979). Here, the man's ability to exercise power is dependent on the mutual responsiveness of both sexes. However, men can also exercise power through the use of violence, which is expressed through coercion and control (Finkelhor, 1983; Straus et al., 1981).

This chapter is concerned with examining the connections between the gender-stereotyped traits and power and violence. It will focus on how the need to conform to gender stereotypes may sometimes lead to marital violence. This need can impel men and women to engage in behaviors that are disruptive and destructive to family relationships as well as to the self.

CONNECTIONS BETWEEN THE GENDER-STEREOTYPED TRAITS AND POWER AND VIOLENCE

Recent research has been concerned with finding out what factors underlie gender stereotyping (Spence, Deaux, & Helmreich, 1985). What gives rise to the belief that women and men have different personality attributes? The answer is that the roles women and men enact in their everyday life lead to stereotypes about gender. People repeatedly observe men and women interacting together within the marriage relationship (Parsons & Bales, 1955). Here, one of the fundamental differences in their roles involves power, with husbands usually exercising more power than wives (Scanzoni, 1979). On the basis of such observations, people assume that these roles are typical for the two sexes. Furthermore, they conclude that men and women are characterized by the personality attributes associated with their respective roles (Secord & Backman, 1961).

According to this formulation, it is the roles that the two sexes generally enact with each other that underlie the belief that men are high in agency and women are high in communion. The dominant person in a relationship is highly self-assertive and makes decisions, whereas the subordinate person accommodates to these decisions (Denmark, 1977, 1980; Hollander, 1980). In other words, the dominant person is high in agency and the subordinate is correspondingly high in communion (Gerber, 1987, 1988). In traditional marriages men play the role of the dominant person and women play the role of the subordinate, and so both sexes manifest the personality traits associated with these roles.

Even when people are *not* explicitly told that the two sexes are in a traditional relationship, they *implicitly* make this assumption. For example, when college students are asked to describe the characteristics of the typical man and women, they assume that the two sexes are in a traditional relationship and describe them as having the personality characteristics associated with this type of relationship (Gerber, 1989b). Without being aware of what they are doing, they assume that the man is dominant in the relationship and the woman is subordinate to him. They then describe the man as high in agency and the woman as high in communion.

In order to test whether power is the critical variable that underlies gender stereotyping, it is necessary to override these implicit assumptions by giving people *explicit* information about men's and women's roles. Research has shown that such explicit information then determines the way in which both the man and the woman are perceived—even when the two sexes are depicted in roles that are *not* conventional (Locksley, Borgida, Brekke, & Hepburn, 1980).

A number of studies have examined whether differences in the power associated with women's and men's marital roles can account for the belief that they have different personality attributes (Gerber, 1987, 1988, 1991). One study focused on the type of power that is expressed through leadership (Gerber, 1988). People were asked to read descriptions of married couples and then rate both persons on the agentic and communal personality traits. The results were as predicted. When the man was described as the leader in the marriage, both he and the woman were perceived in a traditionally stereotyped way. When the conventional power relationship was reversed and the *woman* was described as the leader, the gender stereotypes were also totally reversed: The woman was perceived as high in agency and low in communion, whereas the man was seen as high in communion and low in agency. Thus, the critical factor underlying gender stereotyping was shown to be power, *not* gender. Reversing the traditional roles between the sexes also reversed the gender stereotypes associated with each sex.

Most people think of gender stereotypes as referring to the socially *desirable* aspects of agency and communion examined in the previous study. These characteristics have been the focus of most of the research and theorizing about personality differences between the sexes (Spence et al., 1985). However, there are other aspects of communion and agency that are socially *undesirable* (Helmreich, Spence, & Wilhelm, 1981; Kelly, Caudill, Hathorn, & O'Brien, 1977; Spence, Helmreich, & Holahan, 1979). The positive form of agency involves enhancing one's self and expressing one's own needs. In its negative form, agency reflects an excessive self-concern that has as its goal the mastery, subjugation, and even destruction of others (Bakan, 1966). The positive form of communion involves warmth and accommodation to the needs of other persons. In its negative form, communion reflects an excessive selflessness in which the individual sacrifices the self for others, thereby becoming emotionally and personally vulnerable (Bakan, 1966).

The previously described study focused on a socially acceptable form of power, namely, leadership (Gerber, 1988). However, there are other kinds of power that can be expressed in traditional relationships between the sexes. Husbands can exercise more power than wives in socially acceptable ways, such as leadership, as well as in ways that are *not* considered acceptable (French & Raven, 1968; Raven et al., 1975). If power is one of the crucial dimensions in gender stereotyping, it would be expected that marital violence, a form of power involving coercion and control, would also account for gender stereotyping.

Statistics have shown that when victimization occurs in marriage, it is the wife who is injured approximately 95 percent of the time (Berk, Berk, Loseke, & Rauma, 1983; Bureau of Justice Statistics, 1980). Such acts of violence are generally carried out by the husband in order to establish and maintain his power over the wife (Dobash & Dobash, 1979; Finkelhor, 1983). Since wives are usually the less powerful victims of violence and husbands are the more powerful aggressors, wives would be perceived as highly communal and husbands as highly agentic.

A subsequent study tested whether marital violence could also explain gender stereotyping (Gerber, 1991). This research examined the negative, as well as the positive, aspects of agency and communion. Again, people were given descriptions of married couples and then rated both individuals on the gender-stereotyped personality traits. As predicted, when the man was described as violent toward his wife, both he and the woman were perceived in a traditionally stereotyped way. When the *woman* was described as violent toward her husband, the gender stereotypes were totally reversed, with the violent woman perceived as high in agency and low in communion and the abused man as high in communion and low in agency. In other words, when the conventional power relationship between the sexes was reversed, the gender-stereotyped traits associated with each sex were also reversed. The violent woman was then perceived as having the personality attributes of the "typical male" and the abused man was perceived as having the characteristics of the "typical female."

To describe these results in another way: A violent person of either sex was seen as having the agentic personality traits traditionally associated with men; an abused person of either sex was viewed as having the communal personality traits associated with women. Furthermore, this study found that information about violence affected not only the *negative* forms of agency and communion but also their *positive* forms. In their acts of violence, aggressors were perceived as manifesting negative agentic traits involving the domination of others, as one might expect. However, they were also seen as having the positive agentic traits involving self-assertion and decisiveness.

The results from this perception study correspond with those found in research on *actual* aggressors, for example, studies in which aggressors or other family members have been interviewed. Aggressors are frequently violent not only to obtain compliance with their demands but also to elicit respect and approval from others (Berkowitz, 1983; Finkelhor, 1983). When aggressors are violent toward their spouse, they can appear to be positively self-assertive (Gelles, 1972). Furthermore, research has shown that people do *not* necessarily think aggression between couples is deviant; many people still believe that certain forms of marital violence are at least somewhat necessary, normal, or good (Straus et al., 1981, p. 47).

The abused person was also perceived as having negative as well as positive gender-stereotyped traits. Not only was the abused person perceived as having *negative* communal traits involving helplessness and vulnerability; he or she was also seen as having *positive* communal traits involving warmth, concern, and consideration for others. Again, this corresponds with clinical observations. Victims have been found to react to acts of aggression by manifesting the negative communal traits (Koss, 1987; Symonds, 1982; Walker, 1977–78). However, they have also been observed to show the accommodation and concern for the aggressor's welfare that are manifestations of the positive communal traits (Dutton & Painter, 1981; Finkelhor, 1983; Graham, Rawlings, & Rimini, 1988; Symonds, 1982).

One of the critical findings in this research is that violent husbands and battered wives are perceived as having personality traits that correspond with cultural ideals. The violent husband is seen as having the valued agentic traits associated with masculinity, and the abused wife is seen as having the desirable communal traits associated with femininity. This has important implications for our understanding of husbands' violence toward their wives.

GENDER STEREOTYPES AND HUSBANDS' VIOLENCE TOWARDS THEIR WIVES

Most people are not aware that the crucial factor in gender stereotyping is power. This is because the gender-stereotyped traits have become dissociated from their roots and are generally viewed in isolation from their original context. People do not connect them with the power-related roles in which they originate. Instead, they see them as personal attributes associated with individual women and men.

There is a further problem associated with the gender-stereotyped traits. Not only do people think these traits are *typical* of the two sexes; they also see them as *ideal* characteristics. They believe that both sexes must demonstrate sex-typed attributes in order to have an appropriate gender identity. A women who is "truly feminine" must show that she is high in communion; a man who is "really masculine" must demonstrate that he is high in agency.

Even some of the feminist writers reinforce the belief that the gender-stereotyped traits represent ideal characteristics for each sex. They describe women's connectedness with others as the defining characteristic of femininity (Belensky, Clinchy, Goldberger, & Tarule, 1986; Gilligan, 1982; Miller, 1988). Communion is presented as the fundamental principle that operates in women's approach to learning, morality, and relationships. For men, the defining characteristic of masculinity is said to involve the enhancement of their own self or agency.

There is an inherent contradiction here, which conflicts with the fundamental definition of feminism—that women and men are equal. In relationships where both sexes manifest such "ideal" characteristics, men are high in agency and women are high in communion. As shown by research, these are basically *un*equal relationships in which men play the dominant role and women enact the subordinate role (Gerber, 1988). Thus, giving sanction to stereotyped differences between the sexes perpetuates traditional relationships in which men have more power than women. It is only when men and women manifest *both* agency and communion that they have equality in their interactions with each other.

Feminist writers who subscribe to these sex-typed ideals are simply providing a more current, socially acceptable rationale for long-standing beliefs about the two sexes. They are merely reinforcing long-established social norms that promote traditional relationships between men and women.

These social norms are particularly strong within the marriage relationship. They are supported by imposing penalties on married couples who act in socially deviant ways and do not conform with the expected behaviors for their sex. Members of couples who do not conform with traditional expectations are stereotyped as having a less appropriate gender identity than those who conform (Gerber, 1989a). The strongest sanctions are imposed on couples who totally reverse the conventional roles for the two sexes. When the wife is dominant, she is perceived as having the least feminine gender identity and her husband the least masculine gender identity in comparison with all other types of couples.

Social norms that prescribe that the husband have more power than the wife are also bolstered by the way in which society is organized. A primary source of power derives from the possession of superior resources involving income and occupational status. Within society, the husband is assigned the role of breadwinner and the wife the role of homemaker. Consequently, the husband generally posseses greater economic resources and higher occupational status than the wife (Parsons & Bales, 1955; Scanzoni, 1979). This gives him a legitimate right to exercise power over his wife and to manifest the positive agentic traits that are expected of him. The wife can comfortably accept her husband's authority and defer to his wishes, thereby manifesting the positive communal characteristics expected of her.

A problem arises when the man does *not* possess the external resources that would enable him to exercise power. If he has a low-status occupation and a low-income level, he may not be able to adequately provide for his family. He would not be able to demonstrate that he has a legitimate right to exercise power over his wife on the basis of his competence and achievement. The only way he might feel he is able to exercise power would be to turn to violence. If he is physically abusive toward his wife, he would be perceived as manifesting negative agentic traits and being dominating and dictatorial. However, he would also be perceived as having positive agentic traits and being self-assertive and decisive (Finkelhor, 1983; Gelles, 1972).

The wife, who is the target of the violence, would be perceived as having the communal traits associated with femininity (Straus et al., 1981, p. 191). She would have the negative communal traits of helplessness and vulnerability. However, she would also have positive communal traits of warmth and concern—even for her aggressor.

Clinical observations of violent families and research support this formulation. Men are often violent when they fail to have the external status and skills expected of their position in the family (Gelles, 1972). Violence is most likely to occur in families where the husband has few external resources that would give him a legitimate right to exercise power, so that the greatest amounts of violence occur at the lowest levels of income and occupational status (Straus et al., 1981).

As a consequence, battering husbands often have deep feelings of inadequacy (Finkelhor, 1983). Their violence can sometimes be a reaction to a real or fancied put-down by the wife (Gelles, 1972). It is an attempt to regain the control that is expected of them. When such a husband has fundamental questions about his adequacy as a man, he cannot afford to exhibit any compassion or concern for his wife (communion) because this would be perceived as a sign of weakness and a confirmation of his lack of manliness.

Wives in such families frequently rationalize their husband's violence toward them and see it as justified (Gelles, 1972). Women who are the victims of violence often report that they can ''understand'' their husband's aggression and, furthermore, that they feel it ''just isn't right'' for a woman to hit back· (Gelles, 1972, p. 81). In some cases, wives have been observed to provoke the husband's violence in order to get him to prove he is really a man (Gelles, 1972; Straus et al., 1981).

Such wives are caught in a web of social expectations, some of which involve their fundamental identity as women. One of their alternatives would be to fight back, but this would raise questions about their basic femininity. By ''understanding'' their husband's aggression and showing compassion for him, they can manifest the positive communal traits that are desirable for their sex.

Outside observers frequently ask why battered wives remain in abusive marriages. There are a variety of economic and social factors that make it difficult for many of them to leave (Finkelhor et al., 1983; Gelles, 1976). Furthermore, these women feel passive and helpless as a result of the violence they have experienced and unable to initiate any actions for themselves (Walker, 1979). However, an additional factor is that by leaving, they would promote their own personal well-being and ''self-centered'' interest—something that is culturally associated with stereotypes about masculinity. A battered woman who already blames herself for the abuse and questions her adequacy as a woman could not afford to act in her own self-interest because this might raise questions for her about whether or not she is really feminine. In an abusive relationship, women's frequently demonstrated concern for their aggressor's welfare conforms with cultural ideals for them as women and reinforces their sense of themselves as feminine.

SUMMARY AND CONCLUSION

Conventional norms involving gender stereotyping can lead men and women to engage in behaviors that have tragic and destructive consequences. When we expect men to be high in agency and women to be high in communion, we do not realize that we are thereby perpetuating traditional relationships between the sexes. Not only are these traditional marriages less happy than more egalitarian forms of marriage (Gerber, 1989a); they also have the potential for greater amounts of violence (Straus et al., 1981).

The need to present oneself as meeting cultural standards for one's gender identity is very deep seated. Men feel strong pressures to demonstrate that they are masculine, even when this necessitates that they engage in violence toward their wives (Pleck, 1981). Once the violence starts, women can feel ensnared by their own need to demonstrate that they are feminine. Since they frequently blame themselves for their husband's aggression and hold themselves responsible for the success of the marriage, women can begin to question their own adequacy as women. What better way is there for them to demonstrate that they meet cultural standards for femininity than to show empathy, warmth, and concern, especially for their aggressor?

As we have seen here, abused women and violent men represent the extremes of stereotyped femininity and masculinity. They are perceived as possessing the *desirable* traits associated with their sex, in addition to the *undesirable* traits.

The positive forms of agency and communion are both valuable characteristics. It is the cultural assignment of communion to women and agency to men, however, that restricts the full psychological development of both sexes. At the highest levels of ego development, men and women do *not* have different personalities (Bakan, 1966; Block, 1973; Hefner, Rebecca, & Oleshansky, 1975; Pleck, 1975). Instead, they have been able to integrate the communal *and* agentic traits.

What is needed in our culture is a realization of the limiting and potentially destructive aspects of gender stereotyping for both sexes. We need to develop new cultural norms and beliefs that foster and promote the full development of women and men so that they both feel free to express the human traits of agency as well as of communion.

NOTE

I would like to express my appreciation to Joan Einwohner, Carol J. Geisler, Marianne Jackson, Deborah Tanzer, and Fred B. Wright for their very helpful comments on an earlier version of this chapter.

REFERENCES

Bakan, D. (1966). *The duality of human existence*. Chicago: Rand McNally.
Belensky, M. F., Clinchy, B. M., Goldberger, N. R., & Tarule, J. M. (1986). *Women's*

ways of knowing: The development of self, voice, and mind. New York: Basic Books.

Bem, S. L. (1974). The measurement of psychological androgyny. *Journal of Consulting and Clinical Psychology, 42,* 155–162.

Berk, R. A., Berk, S. F., Loseke, D. R., & Rauma, D. (1983). Mutual combat and other family violence myths. In D. Finkelhor, R. J. Gelles, G. T. Hotaling, & M. A. Straus (Eds.), *The dark side of families: Current family violence research* (pp. 197–212). Beverly Hills, CA: Sage.

Berkowitz, L. (1983). The goals of aggression. In D. Finkelhor, R. J. Gelles, G. T. Hotaling, & M. A. Straus (Eds.), *The dark side of families: Current family violence research* (pp. 166–181). Beverly Hills, CA: Sage.

Block, J. (1973). Conceptions of sex role: Some cross-cultural and longitudinal perspectives. *American Psychologist, 28,* 512–526.

Blood, R. O., & Wolfe, D. M. (1960). *Husbands and wives: The dynamics of married living.* New York: Free Press.

Bureau of Justice Statistics (1980). *Intimate victims: A study of violence among friends and relatives* (U.S. Department of Justice). Washington, DC: U.S. Government Printing Office.

Denmark, F. L. (1977). Styles of leadership. *Psychology of Women Quarterly, 2,* 99–113.

Denmark, F. L. (1980). Psyche: From rocking the cradle to rocking the boat. *American Psychologist, 35,* 1057–1065.

Dobash, R. E., & Dobash, R. (1979). *Violence against wives.* New York: Free Press.

Dutton, D., & Painter, S. L. (1981). Traumatic bonding: The development of emotional attachments in battered women and other relationships of intermittent abuse. *Victimology, 6,* 139–155.

Finkelhor, D. (1983). Common features of family abuse. In D. Finkelhor, R. J. Gelles, G. T. Hotaling, & M. A. Straus (Eds.), *The dark side of families: Current family violence research* (pp. 17–30). Beverly Hills, CA: Sage.

Finkelhor, D., Gelles, R. J., Hotaling, F. T., & Straus, M. A. (Eds.). (1983). *The dark side of families: Current family violence research.* Beverly Hills, CA: Sage.

French, J. R. P., Jr., & Raven, B. (1968). The bases of social power. In D. Cartwright & A. Zander (Eds.), *Group dynamics: Research and theory* (3rd ed., pp. 259–269). New York, Harper & Row.

Gelles, R. J. (1972). *The violent home: A study of physical aggression between husbands and wives.* Beverly Hills, CA: Sage.

Gelles, R. J. (1976). Abused wives: Why do they stay? *Journal of Marriage and the Family, 38,* 659–668.

Gerber, G. L. (1987). Sex stereotypes among American college students: Implications for marital happiness, social desirability and marital power. *Genetic, Social, and General Psychology Monographs, 113,* 413–431.

Gerber, G. L. (1988). Leadership roles and the gender stereotype traits. *Sex Roles, 18,* 649–668.

Gerber, G. L. (1989a). Gender stereotypes: A new egalitarian couple emerges. In J. Offerman-Zuckerberg (Ed.), *Gender in transition: A new frontier* (pp. 47–66). New York: Plenum Medical Book Co.

Gerber, G. L. (1989b). The more positive evaluation of men than women on the gender-stereotyped traits. *Psychological Reports, 65,* 275–286.

Gerber, G. L. (1991). Gender stereotypes and power: Perceptions of the roles in violent marriages. *Sex Roles, 24,* 439–458.

Gerber, G. L. (1992). Gender stereotypes and the change toward greater personal maturity in psychotherapy. In J. C. Chrisler & D. Howard (Eds.), *New directions in feminist psychology: Practice, theory, and research* (pp. 46–57). New York: Springer.

Gilligan, C. (1982). *In a different voice: Psychological theory and women's development.* Cambridge, MA: Harvard University Press.

Graham, D. L. R., Rawlings, E., & Rimini, N. (1988). Survivors of terror: Battered women, hostages and the Stockholm syndrome. In K. Yllo & M. Bograd (Eds.), *Feminist perspectives on wife abuse* (pp. 217–233). Beverly Hills, CA: Sage.

Hefner, R., Rebecca, M., & Oleshansky, B. (1975). The development of sex-role transcendence. *Human Development, 18,* 143–158.

Helmreich, R. L., Spence, J. T., & Wilhelm, J. A. (1981). A psychometric analysis of the personal attributes questionnaire. *Sex Roles, 7,* 1097–1108.

Hollander, E. P. (1980). Leadership and social exchange processes. In K. J. Gergen, M. S. Greenberg, & R. H. Wills (Eds.), *Social exchange: Advances in theory and research.* New York: Plenum Press.

Kelly, J. A., Caudill, M. S., Hathorn, S., & O'Brien, C. G. (1977). Socially undesirable sex-correlated characteristics: Implications for androgyny and adjustment. *Journal of Consulting and Clinical Psychology, 45,* 1185–1186.

Koss, M. P. (1987). Women's mental health research agenda: Violence against women. *Women's Mental Health Occasional Paper Series.* National Institute of Mental Health: Office of the Associate Director for Special Populations.

Locksley, A., Borgida, E., Brekke, N., & Hepburn, C. (1980). Sex stereotypes and social judgment. *Journal of Personality and Social Psychology, 39,* 821–831.

Miller, J. B. (1988). Connections, disconnections and violations. *Work in progress,* No. 33. Wellesley, MA: Wellesley College.

Parsons, T., & Bales, R. F. (1955). *Family, socialization and interaction process.* Glencoe, IL: Free Press of Glencoe.

Pleck, J. H. (1975). Masculinity-femininity: Current and alternative paradigms. *Sex Roles, 1,* 161–178.

Pleck, J. H. (1981). *The myth of masculinity.* Cambridge, MA: MIT Press.

Raven, B. H., Centers, R., & Rodrigues, A. (1975). The bases of conjugal power. In R. E. Cromwell & D. H. Olson (Eds.), *Power in families* (pp. 217–232). New York: Halsted Press.

Rosenkrantz, P., Vogel, S., Bee, H., Broverman, I., & Broverman, D. M. (1968). Sex-role stereotypes and self-concepts in college students. *Journal of Consulting and Clinical Psychology, 32,* 283–294.

Scanzoni, J. (1979). Social processes and power in families. In W. R. Burr, R. Hill, F. I. Nye, & I. L. Reiss (Eds.), *Contemporary theories about the family: Research-based theories* (Vol. 1, pp. 295–316). New York: Free Press.

Secord, P. F., & Backman, C. W. (1961). Personality theory and the problem of stability and change in individual behavior: An interpersonal approach. *Psychological Bulletin, 68,* 21–32.

Spence, J. T., Deaux, K., & Helmreich, R. L. (1985). Sex roles in contemporary American society. In G. Lindzey & E. Aronson (Eds.), *Handbook of social psychology: Vol. 2. Special fields and applications* (pp. 149–178). New York: Random House.

Spence, J. T., Helmreich, R. L., & Holahan, C. K. (1979). Negative and positive components of psychological masculinity and femininity and their relationships to self-reports of neurotic and acting out behaviors. *Journal of Personality and Social Psychology, 37,* 1673–1682.

Spence, J. T., Helmreich, R. L., & Stapp, J. (1975). Ratings of self and peers on sex-role attributes and their relation to self-esteem and conceptions of masculinity and femininity. *Journal of Personality and Social Psychology, 32,* 29–39.

Straus, M. A., Gelles, R. J., & Steinmetz, S. K. (1981). *Behind closed doors: Violence in the American family.* Beverly Hills, CA: Sage.

Symonds, M. (1982). Victim responses to terror: Understanding and treatment. In F. M. Ochberg & D. A. Soskis (Eds.), *Victims of terrorism* (pp. 95–103). Boulder, CO: Westview Press.

Walker, L. E. (1977–78). Battered women and learned helplessness. *Victimology, 2,* 525–534.

Walker, L. E. (1979). *The battered woman.* New York: Harper & Row.

Walker, L. E. (1984). *The battered woman syndrome.* New York: Springer.

12

Women and Crime

Barbara Cowen

The majority of crimes are committed by men. Only a small percentage of crimes are committed by women. However, when women commit crimes, particularly violent crimes, the reasons given for their criminal behavior vastly differ from those associated with men. It is not unusual to have the "inherent nature of women" cited as the root cause of female criminality. This "inherent nature" refers to a woman's sexuality, her biology, and her psyche. Economic, social, and political forces are usually considered peripherally. On the other hand, reasonable explanations for male criminality have often been placed within the framework of economic, social, or political factors. Furthermore, when men's "inherent nature," that is, aggression, is considered, it is usually viewed as an attribute. Recently feminist psychologists, sociologists, and criminologists have begun to challenge these traditional views, views that are laden with sex and gender biases. As we shall see, these biases have victimized women for over a century.

To appreciate the effect of sex and gender on women and crime we must begin with a historical overview of theories that have explained the etiology of female crime from this perspective. From the turn of the century until the 1970s, many theorists and researchers saw the offending woman in terms of stereotypical "female characteristics," that is, those characteristics associated with menstruation, childbirth, and menopause or psychological dispositions such as hysteria or narcissim. Each one of these characteristics has been woven into a theory that has at its core one of these physiological or psychological traits as a causal factor in female crime (Freud, 1933; Lombroso, 1920; Pollak, 1950; Thomas, 1923).

VICTIMS OF THEIR BIOLOGY

Most prominent is the characterization of a woman as a victim of her own biology. Biological processes were, and still are, believed to cause women to behave either irrationally or irresponsibly or both; consequently, biological events such as menstruation, childbirth, or menopause were thought to be the most likely reasons to explain female criminality.

Male criminality, in contrast, was only briefly viewed in biological terms and then lost favor with researchers when in the 1930s they began to identify social causes. Violent aggressive behavior in men was approached by criminologists in terms of social causation and subculture (Heidensohn, 1985). Even now, when testosterone figures prominently in some theories, it is not only considered biologically intrinsic to man's nature but often perceived as a desirable attribute. No such shift in thinking has occurred for women. As one shall see, biological theories continue to be popular explanations for female criminal deviant behavior to the exclusion of either social or economic causation. One such popular theory is the linking of the menstrual cycle with violent behavior.

Menstruation and Violence

The linking of menstruation with a lack of judgment, insanity, and violent behavior has a long history. The belief continues to be that females are most likely to commit acts of violence during their premenstrual and menstrual periods. Edwards (1984), a leading English criminologist, points out that so ingrained is this alleged connection between menstruation and aggressive behavior in our psyche that Mrs. Thatcher's decision regarding the Falklands was seen by many as a loss of control because she was subject to her menstrual cycle.

This use of the menstrual cycle as the contributing factor in a crime was used as early as 1833 to defend a women accused of pyromania. The defense claimed amenorrhea as the explanation for criminal behavior. In 1845 a woman was charged with "willful murder" of a child. The evidence presented in her defense was that she was suffering from a disordered menstruation and was found not guilty on grounds of insanity (Edwards, 1984). In 1882 Richard von Kraft-Ebbing wrote in his classic *Psychosis Menstrualis:*

The menstruating women has a claim to special consideration by the judge because she is at this period unwell and more or less psychologically disturbed. Abnormal irritability, attacks of melancholia, feelings of anxiety, are common phenomena. Inability to get along with husband and domestics, ill-treated of otherwise tenderly cared for children, emotional explosions, libelous acts, breach of peace, resisting authority, scenes of jealousy, craving for alcoholic beverages, because of physical pain, neurotic anxiety conditions are everyday experiences with numerable individuals. (*Australian Law Journal, 56* [1982], as cited in Edwards, 1984, p. 99)

The alleged relationship between menstruation and antisocial and violent behavior continues to this day. The new version of this theory is known as the PMS, or the premenstrual stress syndrome. Katherine Dalton has earned a reputation as a pioneer in this field, and her research findings are often cited as evidence of a connection between menstruation and crime. Dalton examined the influence of the menstrual cycle on crimes carried out by 156 adult female prisoners after they were incarcerated in an English prison. On the basis of interviews Dalton (1964) reported that 49 percent of all crimes were committed either during the premenstrual period or during menstruation; 63 percent of the women committed their crimes during the premenstrual phase. Dalton concludes: "The analysis shows that there is a highly significant relationship between menstruation and crime. This could mean that the hormonal changes cause women to commit crime during menstruation and the premenstruum and/or that women are more liable to be detected in their criminal acts during this time" (p. 1753). So convincing was this research that several legal cases in England were won on the basis of premenstrual tension as the causal factor in violent crimes (Edwards, 1984).

Feminist criminologists have criticized the use of PMS as an explanation for criminal deviant behavior on the grounds that this theory covers criminal acts influenced during the premenstrual, menstrual, and postmenstrual periods. This equals one half of any given month. They argue that chance alone could put women in this time frame (Pollock-Byrne, 1990). Furthermore, Dalton's data when carefully examined showed that it was self-reporting data, colllected retrospectively and, therefore, unreliable. The women who were doing the reporting also held to the common notion that women act differently during their menstrual cycle (Morris, 1987; Pollock-Byrne, 1990). The overall feeling of feminist criminologists is that PMS continues to perpetuate the myth that women are prone to deviant behavior as the result of their biology.

Childbirth and Violence

A popular myth in the late 1800s presumed that women were biologically driven to secure a husband. This drive was assumed to be so strong that a female would commit a serious crime to achieve marital status. When a woman found herself unwed and with child, it was thought that the instinct for wedlock was so strong that a woman would kill the baby to improve her chances of finding a husband (van deWarker, 1875, as cited in Pollock-Byrne, 1990).

In 1950 Otto Pollak, a widely quoted criminologist whose views remained uncriticized for over twenty years (Heidensohn, 1985), elaborated on this myth by explaining that a woman was capable of concealing her pregnancy and killing her infant because she was inherently deceitful. Pollak believed that the evidence for deceitfulness lay in a woman's ability to fake orgasms, whereas a man could not. Further evidence of deceitfulness, according to Pollak, was that a woman was trained from birth to conceal menstruation. In *The Criminality of Women* (1950) Pollak stated, "The inclination to concealment is perhaps nowhere more clearly expressed than in crime [infanticide]" (p. 27).

However, it is now generally known that many of the women and teenagers who kill their newborn infants today are mainly poor and unmarried. They have usually felt the need to conceal their pregnant state. There has been no physical care either for the pregnant woman or her unborn child, for the energy usually directed to the care of the expectant mother and her unborn infant is directed toward concealment. It is not uncommon for the delivery of the child to be carried out unassisted and in secrecy.

Postpartum depression and psychosis notwithstanding, it is now widely conceded among the medical and the legal profession that social and economic factors are related to infanticide and child killing. However, when this has been extended to paternal filicide, the unsupported father is likely to receive more sympathy than the unsupported mother. The unsupported mother is presumed to have "natural resources of maternal instincts to help her survive adverse social conditions" (Edwards, 1984, p. 101). Here again we find women victimized because of presumed biological traits. Feminists explain this as evidence that the ideology of normal motherhood both guides and informs society's intolerance and rejection of women who are engaged in infanticide or child abuse, whereas men's acts of violence have often been tolerated, accepted, and even mandated under certain conditions.

Menopause and Violence

Although no evidence or theory links menopause with violence, menopause has been linked with shoplifting and kleptomania in psychiatric literature, in books, and in film. Subconscious motivations and depression resulting from the menopausal experience serve to explain shoplifting (Moore, 1976; Russell, 1973). Men, in contrast, are understood to shoplift because they are either responding to peer group pressure and/or searching for excitement (Belson, 1975). Widom (1979) reports that despite the expectation that women have greater opportunity to shoplift, the frequency of shoplifting arrests across all categories of shoplifting—supermarkets, drugstores, discount stores—are male juveniles, not women. Nevertheless, the image of the middle-aged menopausal woman engaged in shoplifting is alive and well, recently characterized as such on a recent episode of the popular television program "Murder, She Wrote."

VICTIMS OF THEIR SEX

Early theories on female criminality concentrated on not only biological theories but psychological theories as well. The psychological theories tended to see women as primarily sexual beings ruled by their drives and impulses. Of all the theories, Sigmund Freud's (1933) view of women had the most far-reaching effect on causal explanations of female criminality, particularly delinquency and treatment. In Freud's view, a woman is anatomically inferior; the root of this inferiority is her sexual organs. When a little girl discovers that she lacks a penis, according to Freud, she experiences grave disappointment, severe trauma, and intense envy. According to Freud, the girl assumes she has lost her penis as a result of castration and so grows up envious and revengeful. The result is that women learn to compensate for their inferior organs through narcissism, that is, by concentrating on appearing beautiful and well dressed. The original penis wish is, according to Freudian theory, transformed into a desire for a baby, with a man as bearer of the penis and provider of the baby.

The deviant woman, engaged in overt sexual activity, in Freudian terms has not learned to compensate appropriately for her inferior organ. She is motivated to behave as such because she has not adjusted to her role as wife and mother. Her criminal behavior, particularly if it involves aggression, is perceived as a rebellious act against her sex role, and she is as a consequence considered a maladjusted misfit.

Freud's theories had a profound effect on criminologists, researchers, psychologists, social workers, and the criminal justice system. Influenced by Freud, professionals in these disciplines tended to view female criminality, and delinquency in particular, as blocked access or maladjustment to the normal feminine role. Often high rates of delinquency were attributed to a lack of "healthy narcissism" (Klein, 1973).

For example, according to Cowie, Cowie, and Slater (1968), adolescent girls entered into criminal activities as a form of rebellion against strict standards of sexual behavior. Peter Blos (1969) stated that "in the girl, it seems delinquency is an overt sexual act or to be more correct, a sexual acting out." He further stated that "female delinquency is far more profoundly self-destructive and irreversible in its corrosive consequences than is male delinquency" because it violates the caring and protective maternal role, thus affecting the female and subsequently her offspring (p. 109). Likewise, Herskovitz (1969) claimed that "predominant expression of delinquency among girls in our society is promiscuous sexual behavior" (p. 89).

All the while delinquency among boys was considered the result of a lack of opportunity for creative success. Rehabilitation for boys was an opportunity to develop skills. Girls, on the other hand, were viewed as psychological misfits. Therapy was what was needed to help them adapt to their socially appropriate roles of wife and mother or, at the very least, to become pretty and sociable women. Economic, political, and social factors during this time were usually ignored (Klein, 1973). Vedder and Sommerville (1978) encapsulated this prevailing view in the following quotation: "The female offender's goal, as any woman's is a happy and successful marriage; therefore her self-image is dependent on the establishment of satisfactory relationships with the opposite sex. The double standard for sexual behavior on the part of the male and female must be recognized" (p. 153).

Victims of a Double Standard

As we have seen, psychologists, sociologists, and criminologists have traditionally viewed women who commit crimes as having betrayed womanhood; to the degree that they have done so, they are viewed as having deviated from being a good mother and wife. Once having engaged in criminal activity, a woman was considered no longer honest, decent, moral, or feminine.

The effect of this thinking on the criminal justice system was to see the crimes of women as crimes of the psychologically troubled who required therapeutic intervention. If they committed a violent crime, women were considered "masculine," suffering from chromosomal deficiencies, penis envy, or atavism. If they conformed, committing acts of prostitution and shoplifting, "ladylike crimes," women were considered manipulative, sexually maladjusted, and promiscuous (Klein, 1973, p. 59). Consequently, the woman offender was dealt with in accordance with the degree to which her criminal behavior deviated from society's expectation of her gender role.

The result was that courts upheld longer sentences for females on the grounds that women constitute a reasonable class for discrimination. The rationale for confining females to either longer sentences or to unspecified time was that they were deemed to be more amenable than males to psychological treatment, their crimes understood solely on a psychosexual basis. Women were therefore confined until cured, even if this meant that they were institutionalized for greater lengths of time than their male counterparts (Kurowitz, 1969 [*Women and law.* Alberquerque: University of New Mexico Press], as cited in Pollock-Byrne, 1990). This practice continued until the late 1960s (*Commonwealth v. Daniel,* 1968; *Robinson v. York,* 1986, as cited in Pollock-Byrne, 1990).

The differential sentencing for adolescent girls was in effect even longer. It was not overturned in New York State until 1972. The rationale of protection under the New York Persons Need Supervision Law was finally deemed unconstitutional because it permitted the court to have jurisdiction over female adolescents two years longer than over male adolescents (Pollock-Byrne, 1990). The difference was based on the age of majority: 18 years for boys, 21 years for girls. Conceivably, a 12-year-old girl could have been held in a correctional facility until she was 21 whereas a 12-year-old boy could have been released at 18 years of age or even earlier.

Victims Twice

The lack of protection for battered wives is the most glaring of all the gender inequities. The battered woman is victimized not once, but twice: once by her abusive husband, whom she cannot leave because of a lack of economic or legal solutions to battering; a second time by the judicial system, which punishes her for taking the law into her hands when acting in self-defense.

Women may kill their partners after years of suffering physical violence by their hand. Such women have usually exhausted all available resources within the criminal justice system. Wilson and Daly (1992) hypothesize that men escalate domestic violence through continued coercive acts, acts not necessarily reported to police. After years of entrapment the woman may resort to violence. The police viewing the murder scene make the decision that determines who is the offender. The police's labeling of the offender is based solely on the woman's one violent act, with little consideration for the ongoing abusive behavior on the part of the husband. Consider the following example. A husband accused his wife of giving money to another man. While she was making breakfast, he attacked her with a milk bottle, then a brick, and finally a piece of concrete block. Having had a butcher knife in hand, she stabbed him with it during the fight (Widom, 1984).

The research clearly shows that women are victimized by their husbands long before they resort to violence. Often these husbands have had arrest records for disorderly conduct, drunkenness, or domestic difficulty. Ewing reports that 40 percent to 78 percent of women who kill their husbands or boyfriends have been abused (Pollock-Byrne, 1991). Browne (1987) found that battered women who killed their abusing husbands often had husbands who used drugs and alcohol and were frequently intoxicated. The men used threats and had exhibited assaultive behavior. Those assaults were not only on the wife but on her children or other family members. Many of these men had also abused the children. Wilson and Daly (1992) suggest that women kill "specifically when they feel the need to defend their children of former unions against their current mates" (p. 209).

With few celebrated exceptions, many of the women who have killed their abusing spouses are serving long prison sentences. Some courts continue to refuse to allow expert witnesses to testify to the psychological state of a woman who has been victimized by an abusing husband over a period of time (Pollock-Byrne, 1990). Browne found in her research that women who killed their husbands were absolutely certain that their husbands would have killed them. It was just a matter of time. Usually this conviction was based on specific threats by their husbands (Browne, 1987). Yet this kind of testimony is not admissible in court, particularly when no obvious external threat is detected. The law does not have a provision for a slow building up of terror.

It is often very difficult for a woman to claim self-defense because the victimized wife is more likely to strike when her abusive husband is asleep or is caught off guard. Unlike men, women rarely strike in the heat of an attack. The law requires that a person be in imminent danger and defend himself or herself using equal force. In the eyes of the law the husband is often viewed as defenseless because in most instances his wife has used a weapon to kill him when he was unarmed, often incapacitated by alcohol or asleep. Thus, according to the law it is the wife who has used unequal force and is therefore the guilty party.

CHANGING CONCEPTS

Researchers are now beginning to seriously challenge the sexually biased theories discussed in the preceding sections. These gender-biased theories have now given way to new theories and research that include social and economic realities. For example, the prostitute, once perceived as a fallen women or a "good girl gone bad," whose behavior was understood only in terms of female sexuality, is now seen by researchers as a person who is attempting to work out an economic solution (Heidensohn, 1985). James (1977) found in her research that a desire for income and an independant life were the major motivating factors for most prostitutes.

Other shifts away from sexuality and toward social reality and circumstances are the studies of runaway girls. Once thought of as disturbed girls who often gave way to sexual urges, runaway girls are now understood as girls who are escaping from intolerable conditions. The American Correctional Association (1990) reports that the average female offender has likely been a victim of sexual abuse (36 percent), a minimum of three to eleven times or more (55 percent) between the ages of 5 to 14 (57 percent). She was most likely sexually abused by a male member of the immediate family, such as a father or stepfather (49 percent). However, reporting the incident resulted in no change or made things worse (49 percent). By all accounts most women in prison have a history of physical and/or sexual abuse with little help or intervention.

Victims Again: Four Ounces = Life

While traditional theories are being discounted and new social and economic theories have begun to take their place, the harsh sentencing of females for minor drug offenses has resulted in a meteoric rise in the rate of incarceration for women. The arrest of women for minor crimes continues to victimize women in much the same manner as the old sentencing procedures that were rooted in sex and gender bias. Ironically, it was the lifting of the indetermined sentence laws that is partly responsible for the placing of more women in jail and in prison than ever before. This differs from past policy, when only women who committed murder were sent to prison.

This increase is attributed to mandatory sentencing laws that include minor drug violations. The Correctional Association of New York (1992) reports the following: A woman arrested because of possession of four ounces of an illegal narcotic drug gets the same prison time as someone brought in for murder (fifteen years to life). Thus, a significant number of women who are minor participants in the drug trade or wrongly accused are receiving life sentences (cited in Price & Sokoloff, 1994). One such woman is Nina from Jamaica, whose husband, unbeknownst to her, hid narcotics in a loaf of bread, which Nina then proceeded to transport to New York. She was arrested immediately upon her arrival at Kennedy Airport. Nina is now serving a fifteen-year sentence.

The incarcerated female drug offender is likely to be poor and a member of a minority. To support her habit she often resorts to the following three crimes: prostitution, with African-American women more prone to arrest for prostitution that whites; shoplifting; or assisting a male drug dealer, the most common form of arrest. Women generally commit nonviolent crimes to support their habit.

When arrested they are usually convicted of possession and sale of an illegal substance as well as the participation in income-generating crimes such as prostitution or shoplifting.

The story is very different for male addicts. They are often involved in violent crimes such as burglary, robbery, and assaults as a means of supporting their habits; they are also often involved in murders associated with bad drug deals (Anglin & Hser, 1988).

Perpetuating the Cycle

A fallout of judicial harsh sentencing of women for minor crimes is that the majority of the women sent to prison today are mothers who are often the sole support of their children. Their imprisonment often destroys the family unit. Many times the children are placed in foster care, a placement that devalues the individual, reduces any existing support system, and carries a risk for potential physical and sexual abuse.

A Baltimore study found that four times the number of substantiated cases of sexual abuse occurred in foster care as in the general population (Wexler, 1993). Likewise, in a Pacific Northwest foster-care facility, reported to be a model foster-care program, 24 percent of the girls said that they were victims of actual or attempted sexual abuse in their foster homes (Wexler, 1993).

Stanton (1980) found in her studies that the incarceration of the mother caused serious negative effects for her children. The disruption of their lives was significant. The children often had difficulty learning in school and were often reported disciplinary problems, as well as withdrawn and sad. Children of incarcerated women have been known to experience shame and demoralization. Such was John's case. John was an adolescent serving time at Rikers for car theft. He was reduced to tears because he was fearful and embarrassed that the other adolescents would find out that his mother was incarcerated for a drug-related crime. John expressed feelings of utter shame. In contrast, he was willing to tell the others that his father was incarcerated for murder (at the same time as his mother). His father's imprisonment did not cause John to feel either ashamed or humiliated.

It is evident that children suffer when their mothers are incarcerated. Boys of 12 to 14 years of age whose mothers are imprisoned often engage in antisocial activities; girls are known to run away or take drugs. Carlen (1988) found that the four factors that correlated with women's criminality were placement in foster care or state care as a child or a teenager, drugs, poverty, and the quest for excitement (often masking underlying depression). Thus, the incarceration for minor offenses of women who are the sole support of their children results in the dissolution of the family. The placement of the children within the foster-care system, with its accompaning risks, and the propensity for the older children to act out or become involved in drugs strongly suggest that the criminal justice system has unwittingly become a partner in the cyclical perpetuation of criminal behavior.

The incarcerated man's family does not suffer as profoundly as the family of the incarcerated woman. The man often has a wife or a family member who takes care of his children during his time in prison. His family remains relatively intact, waiting for him upon his release.

New Breed of Female: Reality or Myth?

Freda Adler (1975), a leading criminologist, proposed that as women gained equality in all spheres, they will also become more violent. She proposed that the liberation of women will cause women to behave more like men, even in the area of criminal activity. The media seem to have adopted this view of the "new breed of female" with such movies as *Thelma and Louise.* Statistics from crime data prove otherwise, however. Females have represented only 10 percent of arrests for violent crimes. This has been consistent for well over a decade (Pollock-Byrne, 1990). Furthermore, most studies have shown no relationship between "the masculinizing of women" and offending women (Pollock-Byrne, 1990; Widom, 1979).

Smart (1979) argues that female liberation is irrelevant to poor minority women, who are the majority of the women in prison. The main issue for them is economics. This view is also expressed by Pollock-Byrne (1990):

Women in prison are a notably poor audience for liberation sentiments. They typically hold very traditional stereotypes of female and male roles and their goals tend to focus on home and family. . . . Some argue, in fact, that women in prison need to be liberated from their poverty, from their typically dysfunctional relationships with men, and from their tendencies to get involved in relationships that lead to criminal involvement. (p. 26)

ROOT CAUSE OF FEMALE CRIMINALITY REEXAMINED

The root cause of female criminality was thought to be the result of a woman's flawed "inherent nature." It was theorized that her sexuality, biological processes, and psyche conspired under particular circumstances to produce criminal behavior. These theories victimized women for over a century.

Recent studies have shown that economic and social factors figure prominently in our understanding of the causation of female criminality. Most women in prison are poor. They have limited skills and economic opportunity. Most are imprisoned for minor drug offenses. They receive long sentences, often on par with murder. When they are in prison, their families are dissolved and their children are placed within the foster-care system. Those sentenced for murder have usually killed after years of physical abuse, moved to do so when their lives have been threatened. Those charged with infanticide have often killed because of social and economic factors. Prostitution, a victimless crime, continues to be one of the primary reasons women are arrested, despite the fact that it has been demonstrated that in most instances prostitution is an economic and viable solution for women with limited skills, particularly in times of low employment.

Many women in prison have suffered from abuse as children from male relatives or caretakers, and as adults from their husbands. A clear connection exists between the victimization of women and the offenses of women. In *Men, Women, and Aggression* (1993) Anne Campbell offers this explanation for the all too frequent acceptance of male violence: She proposes that society is accepting violence in men because of social conditioning. Society views men's violence as a necessity. It accepts this violence as a legitimate reason for the imposing of self-control over others.

Female crime, particularly violent crime, is often the response to the degradation and despair in the lives of those who are poor, helpless, and at the bottom of the underclass. Constructive change in the form of economic parity and the lessening of social attitudes responsible for promoting male violence is necessary before one can end the connection between the victimization of women and female criminality.

REFERENCES

Adler, Freda. (1975). *Sisters in crime.* New York: McGraw-Hill.

American Correctional Association. (1990). Washington, DC: St. Mary's Press.

Anglin, M., & Hser, Y. (1988). Addicted women and crime, *Criminology, 25*(2), 359–394.

Belson, W. (1975). *Juvenile theft: The causal factors.* New York: Harper & Row.

Blos, Peter. (1969). Three typical constellations in female delinquency. In O. Pollak (Ed.), *Female dynamics and female sexual delinquency* (pp. 229–249). Palo Alto, CA: Science and Behavior Books.

Browne, A. (1987). *When battered women kill.* New York: Free Press.

Campbell, A. (1993). *Men, women, and aggression.* New York: Basic Books.

Carlen, P. (1988). *Women, crime and poverty.* Philadelphia: Open Press.

Commonwealth v. Daniel. (1990). Legal issues of incarcerated women. In J. Pollock-Bryce, *Women, prison and crime.* Belmont, CA: Wadsworth Press.

Cowie, J., Cowie, V., & Slater, E. (1968). *Delinquent girls.* London: Heinemann.

Dalton, K. (1964). *The premenstrual syndrome.* Springfield, IL: Charles C. Thomas.

Davis, K. (1961). Prostitution. In Robert K. Merton & Robert A. Nisbet (Eds.), *Contemporary social problems.* New York: Harcourt Brace Jovanovich.

Edwards, S. (1984). *Women on trial.* Dover, NH: Manchester University Press.

Freud, S. (1993). *New introductory lectures on psychoanalysis.* New York: Worton.

Heidensohn, F. (1985). *Women and crime.* New York: New York University Press.

Herskovitz, H. (1969). A psychodynamic view of sexual promiscuity. In O. Pollak (Ed.), *Family dynamics and female sexual delinquency.* Palo Alto, CA: Science and Behavior Books, 1969.

James, J. (1977). Motivation for entrance into prostitution. In L. Crites (Ed.), *Female offender.* Lexington, MA: D. C. Heath.

Jones, E. (1961). *The life and works of Sigmund Freud.* New York: Basic Books.

Klein, D. (1973). The etiology of female crime. *Issues in Criminology, 8,* 3–30.

Konopka, G. (1966). *The adolescent girl in conflict.* Englewood Cliffs, NJ: Prentice Hall.

Lombroso, C. (1920). *The female offender.* New York: Appleton.

Moore, G. (1976, March 20). Publications review. *Security Management,* p. 60.

Morris, A. (1987). *Women, crime and criminal justice.* London: Basil Blackwell.

Pollak, O. (1950). *The criminality of women.* Philadelphia: University of Pennsylvania Press.

Pollock-Byrne, J. (1990). *Women, prison and crime.* Belmont, CA: Wadsworth Press.

Price, B., & Sokoloff, N. (1982). *The criminal justice system and women.* New York: Clark Boardman Company.

Price, B. & Sokoloff, N. (1994). *The criminal justice system and women: Offenders, victims, and workers.* New York: McGraw-Hill.

Russell, D. (1973). Emotional aspects of shoplifting. *Psychiatric Annals, 3,* 77–86.

Smart, C. (1976). Women, crime and criminology. Boston: Routledge & Kegan.

Smart, C. (1979). The new female criminal: Reality or myth? *British Journal of Criminology, 19*(1), 50–57.

Stanton, A. M. (1980). *When mothers go to jail.* Lexington, MA: Lexington Books.

Thomas, W. (1923). *The unadjusted girl.* Boston: Little, Brown.

Wexler, R. (1993, July 3). OP-ED page of the *New York Times.*

Widom, C. (1979). Female offenders. *Criminal justice and behavior, 6,* 365–382.

Widom, C. (1984). Sex roles, criminality, and psychopathology. In C. Widom (Ed.), *Sex roles and psychopathology.* New York: Plenum.

Wilson M., & Daly, M. (1992). Who kills whom in spouse killings? *Criminology, 30*(2), 189–209.

Vedder, C., & Sommerville, D. (1978). *The delinquent girl.* Springfield, IL: Charles C. Thomas.

13

Prevention of Family Violence for the Female Alcoholic

Jean Cirillo

There are an estimated six million women with alcohol-related problems in the United States today. More women drink alcohol than ever before, and alcohol dependence among women has grown steadily. About one-third of all persons with drinking problems are female. Thirty-four percent of Alcoholics Anonymous (AA) members are women. There is no typical alcoholic female. The problem appears to transcend age, social conditions, and economic background.

One of the most famous studies conducted by Sharon Wilsnack (1980) found that whereas men appear to do their heaviest drinking during young adulthood (21–34), the rate of drinking among women continues to climb into midlife (34–49). This study also found that the characteristics of women showing the highest rates of alcoholism varied according to age. Risk factors for those in the youngest group (21–34) were being single, childless, and not employed full time. These were young women who had failed to assume expected adult roles. Among the women aged 35 to 49, the highest rates of alcoholism were found among those who were divorced or separated, were unemployed, or had children who did not live with them. These women had assumed, but lost, some of the adult roles. The oldest women in the study, aged 50 to 64, showed the most alcohol problems among those who were married, not employed outside the home, and had children no longer living with them. These women may have been experiencing feelings related to the empty nest syndrome.

Women who drink heavily face some special social, emotional, and physical risks that differ from those of men. Many researchers refer to the "vanishing differences" between the sexes, in both alcohol and drug use, yet there remains a double standard in the United States. The man who drinks heavily or uses illicit drugs is often accepted, whereas the woman who engages in these behaviors is strongly criticized. This criticism dates back to the ancient belief that alcohol and other chemicals can make a woman sexually promiscuous. As a result, women tend to hide their alcohol or drug use, making them less likely to seek help and more seriously ill before the disease is diagnosed.

Alcoholism's physical problems are different for women, too. The disease appears to progress more rapidly among women. Prescription drugs are also more likely to be combined with alcohol, thus increasing the effect. Women reach higher peak levels of alcohol in the blood than men, even when size and body weight are matched. Women also show greater variability in peak blood level because of the menstrual cycle. Not surprisingly, the highest peaks occur in the premenstrual phase.

Important differences have also been noted in women's vulnerability to the physical problems associated with the later stages of alcoholism. Alcoholic women develop cirrhosis of the liver, hepatitis, high blood pressure, anemia, and ulcers at lower levels of alcohol intake than do men. Strong relationships have also been found between heavy drinking and frigidity, infertility, and gynecological problems. It is also interesting to note that although women may report higher levels of sexual arousal after ingesting alcohol, increasing levels of blood alcohol have been found to decrease the ability to climax and the intensity of orgasms.

Other physical effects of alcohol unique to women include fetal alcohol symdrome (FAS). FAS is characterized by mental retardation, very low birth weight, and birth defects. It occurs about 1 in every 700 births. More common in women with lower alcohol intake is fetal alcohol effect (FAE). Its effects range from repeated miscarriages to low birth weight and minor birth defects.

There is still a great deal of uncertainty about the personality traits that may increase some women's vulnerability to alcoholism. Beckman (1978) found that a sex-role conflict between unconscious masculinity and conscious femininity is more prevalent among alcoholic women than among nonalcoholics. Female alcoholics also show lower self-esteem and have a higher incidence of an absent parent during childhood than nonalcoholic females. Compared to male alcoholics, female alcoholics appear to experience more neurotic symptoms such as anxiety and depression and a greater number of suicide attempts. They are less likely than male alcoholics to experience job problems or trouble with the law. Alcoholic women are more likely than men to be divorced when they enter treatment or to be married to or living with an alcoholic "significant other." A 1980 study conducted by the New York City Affiliate of The National Council on Alcoholism found that whereas only 10 percent of male alcoholics are left by their wives, 90 percent of female alcoholics are left by their husbands.

Alcohol or drug abuse is involved in 75 percent of child abuse cases. In those cases dealing with severe abuse causing serious injury or death, 95 percent were preceded by the excessive use of alcohol or illicit drugs on the part of the abuser.

A young child first learns about the world through physical and emotional contact with the primary caretaker, most often the mother. Even if the alcoholic mother is not actively drinking, she often creates an atmosphere devoid of touching, hugging, or other forms of affection. She is most often unable to give and receive affection openly. This may have a profound impact on the children's later abilities to engage in intimacy.

Mothers are the dominant force and role model in the life of most young women. Frustration grows from attempting to live up to impossible or ambiguous expectations. This turns into increasing anger and guilt as the daughter's perceptions of failure and inadequacy are confirmed. Stammer (1991) describes a typical scenario wherein a daughter rushes home from school to finish her household chores before her mother arrives to begin her daily inspection of the house. The daughter cleans the bathroom thoroughly, hoping against hope that maybe, just maybe, this time her mother will say it looks good. The mother arrives home, enters the bathroom, and goes over the floor with a clean cloth. Finding no dirt, she further inspects, until her eyes fall upon a single hair. With that the alcoholic mother shoves her daughter against a wall, holds the hair under her nose and laments the ''filth,'' saying that next time the bathroom had better be clean. The mother further announces that the daughter will not get dinner tonight and then returns to the kitchen to pour herself a drink. The scenario ends with the daughter crying as she examines her rough, red hands. Anyone familiar with *Mommie Dearest* (Christina Crawford, 1984) can recall similar incidents in which the alcoholic Joan Crawford becomes hysterical and abusive when her young daughter fails to clean the bathroom perfectly, places her expensive dresses on wire hangers, or gets her hair tangled.

Whereas a codependent mother often protects her children from their alcoholic father's wrath, if only by keeping them away from him, the codependent husband is often away from home when the children need him most. It is a rare father who assumes the role of primary caretaker, even if his wife is dysfunctional.

In the 1950s and 1960s more men than women were known to be having problems with alcohol. The woman's role was to keep the family together and meet the needs of others. Mother was usually the chief enabler, often involving the children in keeping the family secret, that is, Dad's alcoholism.

Today drinking is more acceptable among women. It is likely that children growing up today will have a mother and a father who are alcoholic. Children from homes where both parents drink cannot benefit, then, from interaction with one nonalcoholic parent. This leaves the older children in the family with awesome responsibilities. Often these same children are unable to handle the unfair load dropped upon them. They escape through engaging in the behaviors they have witnessed at home; when the going gets tough, they turn to alcohol or drug abuse.

When Mother is an alcoholic, the daughter is also more likely to feel rejected and begin to question her own worth and value. Neglect is almost certain in families where the mother is alcoholic, although it occurs to some degree in all alcoholic households. Often a parental child assumes the role of primary caretaker for younger siblings. Resentful of this additional responsibility and angered by possible history of abuse, older siblings often repeat the mother's pattern of abuse when dealing with younger siblings. The same may be true of the code-pendent father. He often turns resentment against the wife's disease into acting-out behavior against the children.

A common pattern is the father who comes home after a long day at work to find the house in disarray, the children unruly, uncombed, and unscrubbed, the shopping undone, no dinner on the table, and the wife in an alcoholic or drug-induced state. This situation may be worsened by the likelihood that the codependent male may blame the children, at least in part, for their mother's condition. Already in denial, the alcoholic woman usually welcomes the excuse that her family's misbehavior, rather than her disease, is responsible for the abuse and neglect in the home.

Sexual abuse is also more common when the mother's judgment is incapac-itated by the use of alcohol or drugs. Since a great number of female alcoholics are left by their husbands, the children may be abused by stepparents or live-in or occasional boyfriends. In recent years this trend has shifted somewhat, since a greater number of fathers are awarded custody when the mother is found to be unable to care for the children. In some cases, this fear of losing her children provides a woman with the strongest motivation to overcome her drug or alcohol problem.

Another common phenomenon found in the families of female alcoholics is the battered husband syndrome. Men's rights groups have arisen to question the notion that the abused spouse is always the female. Although the abusive female often inflicts less serious injury than her male counterpart, a great percentage of violent incidents are initiated by the alcoholic or drug-addicted woman. Such incidents often go unreported because the male is ashamed to admit to his vic-timization or to bring attention to his partner's problem. He may displace his anger onto the children, especially the female parental child who may be seen as a stand-in for her mother.

Roy Schenck (1990) claims that society has a strong tendency to treat physical violence as much more serious than psychological violence. Thus, when two people are exchanging insults, that is not considered serious. But the first person to strike a physical blow is viewed as the aggressor or the wrong-doer. Schenck further states that since men are usually larger than women and have perhaps more intense and more suppressed rage, they will usually be the first to do physical violence and so are viewed as the aggressors. Further, according to Schenck, recent studies show that men and women initiate physical violence about equally.

Often, though, if the person who strikes the first blow is a woman and the recipient is a man, there is still a strong tendency to blame the man and excuse the woman. Even intense acts of violence if committed by a woman are more likely to be treated as defensive and so as justified. Schenck's research cites three recent highly publicized spouse murders in Wisconsin. In all three cases, two involving a dead man and one a dead woman, the man had been portrayed as the violator and the woman the innocent victim.

A consequence of this type of thinking is that men are reluctant to discuss openly the violence they encounter from the women in their lives for fear of being condemned. Whereas physical violence against women has become a thoroughly discussed subject in recent years, as the man who comes to work with obvious injuries inflicted by his wife knows, violence against men by women has not been seriously explored. A man who has been physically assaulted by a woman, it is commonly believed, deserves the abuse. Such a man may feel less of a man because he cannot control the woman in his life. As a result, the battering of men by women is one of the best-kept secrets in our society.

John Gordon (1982) suggests that males and females are equally capable of viciousness, violence, and cruelty, and to the same degree. Women's forms of violence, however, often differ from that men do to women. According to Gordon, men's violence tends to be more open and physical, whereas women's violence tends to be more subtle, more psychological and emotional. Many abusive situations involve a woman heaping verbal and psychological abuse upon a man, and the man striking back physically. This situation is even more likely when the woman is under the influence of alcohol or drugs. She becomes less able to exercise judgment in controlling her own negative behavior while at the same time being too intoxicated to defend herself or convince others of her need for protection.

Schenck (1991) challenges the notion that women are more often than men the victims of physical violence in a marital relationship. Men's macho compensation for their presumed spiritual inferiority creates an image of men as physically invincible. This may make it psychologically difficult for a man to acknowledge having experienced physical violence from a woman. With women more often seem as victims, the physical violence they do to men may be seen as defensive and thereby be excused or ignored. Men can then become trapped, unable to escape from ongoing physical violence. When this violence is combined with alcohol or drug abuse on the part of the woman, the man is doubly ashamed and may invest all his effort in concealing his partner's problem rather than obtaining help.

Women are more vocal about the violence they experience and the problems created when the man in their life has a substance abuse problem. As a result, the violence alcoholic men do to women receives more publicity than does the violence alcoholic women do to men. Since this violence is also more likely to be verbal and emotional, rather than physical, it is often less visible.

Susan Steinmetz (1986) states that the most underreported form of violence in the United States is husband abuse. Her studies indicate that close to half of spouse abuse is experienced by men. In spite of these findings, there do not appear to be any shelters for abused men.

The clinician who works with the female alcoholic in early recovery should be prepared to deal with the additional shame related to social disapproval, poor performance in the parenting role, and the double handicap faced in seeking employment, that of being both female and alcoholic. Membership in a minority group may add a third disadvantage. Detoxification may also have to include withdrawal from prescription drugs, as women are frequently also addicted to these. If the alcoholic woman is a single parent, the clinician may have to assist her in finding responsible child care. Spouses and children should be involved in family therapy and self-help groups. Whether the alcoholic woman is single or married, if children are in the picture she must know that their safety is ensured. The children must also be informed that mother has not "deserted" them but is getting necessary help. Where signs of abuse or neglect are evident, the clinician should be prepared to alert the appropriate outside agencies. The therapist must take a clear moral position on the unacceptability of violence within the family.

Since women are often socialized to put the needs of others before their own, the task of sobriety may be particularly difficult. The alcoholic female may need to detach temporarily from the demands of family members to avoid excess stress in the early stages of recovery. The clinician must help the alcoholic woman realize that she will be unable to cope with her family's problems if she begins drinking again. Therefore, in the beginning the recovering alcoholic must learn to put her own needs first. As she becomes stronger, the alcoholic woman must be helped to reassume her duties as wife and mother, often in conjunction with returning to the workforce.

Many women today are driven to excel in all areas, which may include a desire to "drink like the boys" in order to fit in socially in a work situation. Since her physiology is different from a man's, the woman often experiences earlier physical indications that she is overdoing alcohol. A woman in this situation may feel driven to conceal the "fatal flaw of her imperfection," that being her inability to drink as much socially as others. As her dependence on alcohol to cope with feelings of inadequacy and low self-esteem increases, a woman may feel compelled to compensate. Trying to be Superwoman, she makes impossible demands of herself, her coworkers, and her family. "Hitting bottom" for these women often means getting fired from work, losing their husbands, and realizing that they have alienated their children. Through the slow, painful process of climbing back up to functioning, these women must learn to reevaluate priorities, accepting less lofty goals rather than using alcohol to cope with their stressful lifestyle.

It is extremely important for the recovering female alcoholic to take whatever time she needs to go to A.A. meetings, get a sponsor, and continue in aftercare therapy. She will be of little help to her family or job if she is not sober. Many women report that over time they hear pride in the voices of their family as they discuss their recovery. Forgiveness for past wrongdoing may be a rather slow process, but it does occur.

Making the transition from the closed treatment community to the home and workplace is often very frightening. Some women are fortunate enough to find their home and family intact. Where the husband also has an alcohol problem, he may decide to get help for himself. In some cases the man may not seek help, and the woman may find that she can no longer live with an alcoholic man. Divorce or other life changes may be necessary to maintain sobriety. Some women discover that they cannot immediately handle the stress of returning to work, so that adjustment to economic difficulties may be necessary while the mother regains her health.

In some cases, women may return to an extremely troubled environment. The husband may have deserted the woman emotionally if not physically. The children are often angry. The woman may feel that her power as mother of the household is gone. Often the alcoholic mother's most difficult task is facing up to the fact that she has been a less than perfect parent. She must be willing to hear her children express their anger and disappointment over her past transgressions. Only after this process is complete will the recovered alcoholic begin to regain the closeness and trust of family members.

REFERENCES

Beckman, L. J. (1978). "Six-role conflict in alcoholic women: Myth or reality." *Journal of Abnormal Psychology, 84,* 408–417.

Crawford, Christina. (1984). *Mommie dearest.* Berkeley, CA: William Morrow.

Gordon, John. (1982). *The myth of the monstrous male, and other feminist fables.* Madison, WI: Bioenergetics.

Jones, M. C. (1971). "Personality antecedents and correlates of drinking patterns in women." *Journal of Consulting and Clinical Psychology, 36,* 61–69.

National Council on Alcoholism. (1980). *Facts on alcoholism and women.* New York: Affiliate.

Schenck, Roy. (1990). *The other side of the coin: Causes and consequences of men's oppression.* Madison, WI: Bioenergetics.

Schenck, Roy. (1991). *On sex and gender.* Madison, WI: Bioenergetics.

Stammer, Ellen. (1991). *Women and alcohol: The journey back.* New York: Gardner.

Steinmetz, Susan. (1986, September). "Studies of spouse abuse." *Family Therapy Networker.*

14

Elder Violence (Maltreatment) in Domestic Settings: Some Theory and Research

Margot B. Nadien

Violence against the elderly, often referred to as elder abuse, emerged as a serious concern only in the late 1970s and early 1980s. At that time, the first set of published research and governmental findings revealed that maltreatment, while only 4 percent among the well elderly, reached 10 percent among the frail or impaired elderly (Anetzberger, 1987).

Today elder maltreatment is thought to be six times greater than these figures suggest (U.S. Congress, 1980). One reason for underestimates is that suspected elder maltreatment often goes uninvestigated because of the prevailing view that "the family" is sacrosanct and should not be interfered with (Kosberg, 1988). Widespread underreporting of elderly abuse also traces to the fact that, when confined to private dwellings, it is hidden from public scrutiny. Then, too, many elderly are unwilling to report their abuse by relatives (Lau & Kosberg, 1979). Finally, many of the professionals who work with the aged are unaware of the need to detect, record, and report abuse (Lau & Kosberg, 1979; Rathbone-McCuan, 1980), even in states where there are laws mandating these procedures.

Even if elder abuse were limited to 10 percent of the frail or impaired elderly, the need to identify and remedy elder abuse takes on urgency in the light of a burgeoning of the aged population, who currently make up almost 13 percent of the U.S. population (U.S. Bureau of Census, 1984) and who are projected to account for over 20 percent of the population by the year 2020, with 21 percent of all males and 24 percent of all females expected to be 65 years or older (Pegels, 1988). In addition to being the fastest-growing age segment (Cantor & Little, 1985), today's elderly are living much longer. Indeed, among U.S. residents who reached age 65 during the 1980s, males can expect to live until age 80, and females to age 84 (National Center for Health Services, 1986). Thus, it is important to find ways of detecting and checking the maltreatment of impaired old-agers.

Two phases distinguish the course of published elder maltreatment research in the United States. Before 1982 ten major investigations had identified the existence, nature, and scope of elder maltreatment (Anetzberger, 1987, p. 6). But by 1982 major investigations started to examine the etiology of abuse and to grapple with a number of methodological flaws, including overly broad definitions. Thus we begin our review of elder maltreatment in domestic settings with differing definitions of elder abuse. We then examine research that points to factors in domestic settings that increase the risk of elders becoming victimized and of caregivers becoming victimizers. Finally, we explore some theories that have been proposed to explain the differing intrapersonal, interpersonal, and situational factors that may underlie the abuse and neglect of elders in domestic settings.

THE NATURE OF ABUSE

Violence against the elderly assumes different forms. Although all forms entail suffering for the victim, the source of that pain may derive either from something inflicted or something withheld.

Inflicted pain clearly inheres in *physical abuse,* which occurs when frail or ill elderly are pushed, shoved, grabbed, hit, or assaulted with a gun, knife, or other weapon (Pillemer & Finkelhor, 1988). However, inflicted injury or pain may also stem from *psychological abuse,* as occurs in (1) verbal aggression (e.g., insults, blame, ridicule), (2) threats where no weapon is involved (Pillemer & Finkelhor, 1988), or (3) some form of coercion, abandonment, or confinement. Finally, inflicted pain may derive from *legal* or *material abuse,* the misuse or misappropriation of an elder's real property (e.g., cash or other resources) (Hall, 1989).

Suffering is often associated with physical or emotional injury, but it may be equally great when needed care is lacking. This may trace to *physical neglect,* the deprivation or absence of needed food, rest, hygiene, or medical care; or from *psychological neglect,* the deprivation of social stimulation or of emotional support; or from *legal* or *material neglect,* the deprivation of needed information or privacy or supervision (Johnson, 1991).

The impact of elder maltreatment also varies according to perceptions of the perpetrator's intentions. Seemingly intentional intimidation or manipulation, as when caregivers falsify or withhold needed information or misappropriate the elder's personal resources, appears more abusive than when caregivers deprive elders of personal control over their finances because their fraility or ill health is mistakenly viewed as a sign of mental incompetence.

Further complicating the analysis of elder maltreatment is the fact that investigators often differ in their emphasis (Johnson, 1991). When investigators focus on the perpetrator's acts, abuse is treated as a cause of suffering; but when the focus is on the victim's suffering, abuse is conceptualized as the effect of the perpetrator's acts. Thus, to avoid this confusion we shall designate the overall condition *maltreatment* and shall reserve the terms *abuse* and *neglect* to denote two broad means wherby the actions of caregivers eventuate in suffering in the elderly.

One further distinction relates primarily to the elders. Whether or not caregivers' acts are experienced as maltreatment depends on the elder's subjective perception of the caregiver's behavior, with such perceptions varying according to the elder's prior expectations, threshold for experiencing physical or emotional pain, and cognitive capacity for considering the caregiver's motives.

Thus far we have briefly noted forms of maltreatment (abuse and neglect), factors relative to perpetrators (whether or not their abuse or neglect was intended), and factors relative to the perceptions of elders (their expectations, pain thresholds, and cognitive appraisals). Now let us consider (1) factors that contribute to the vulnerability of elders to maltreatment by others, (2) factors that predispose caregivers to becoming abusive or neglectful of their charges, and (3) environmental factors that seem to permit or even foster elder maltreatment. For purposes of analysis, these factors will sometimes be treated as if they were separate. However, readers should bear in mind that the maltreatment of elders results from interactions among the victim, perpetrator, and environment.

WHICH ELDERLY PERSONS ARE MOST VULNERABLE TO MALTREATMENT?

In some instances elder maltreatment may be independent of the victim's behavior. However, in many instances the traits, gender, or life situation of elders may increase their risk of being abused or neglected.

Traits. Of all the traits of old-agers that predispose them to maltreatment, *dependency* is perhaps the most pervasive one. Dependency may come about for elders who (1) become physically or mentally impaired as they grow older (Anastasio, 1981; Fulmer & O'Malley, 1987; Kosberg, 1988), especially following a period of physiological decline (Anastasio, 1981; Godkin, Wolf, & Pillemer, 1989); (2) suffer from the combined effects of aging and substance abuse (Fulmer & O'Malley, 1987; Kosberg, 1988); or (3) are unable to handle their finances and daily problems (Kosberg, 1988).

Other traits of the aged may invite maltreatment or allow its continuation once it has begun. Excessive demandingness, complaints, ingratitude, and aggression are behaviors that may provoke abuse or neglect from overburdened or overstressed caregivers (Douglass, Hickey, & Noel, 1980; Kosberg & Cairl, 1986). Then, too, elders with such personality traits as intropunitiveness, self-depreciation, stoicism, and timidity may fail to report instances of maltreatment (Johnson, 1991; Kosberg, 1988).

Gender issues. The dominant group of dependent elderly are women, especially those over age 75. One reason is that women in most cultures are more apt than men to live to advanced old age (Giordano & Giordano, 1983; Wolf, Strugnell, & Godkin, 1982), perhaps because of genetic factors (Turner, 1982). Moreover, when very old, women are more apt to suffer physical and cognitive impairments that render them more dependent and more prone to maltreatment by abusive or neglectful caregivers (Kosberg, 1988).

Elderly women are constitutionally less able than elderly males to resist sexual molestation, medical maltreatment, and other types of abuse by caregiving relatives or homecare workers in a domestic setting (Kosberg, 1988; Pillemer, 1988).

Although impaired elderly women are more prone than elderly men to physical abuse, gender interacts with maltreatment in subtle ways. In a study in which Pillemer and Finkelhor (1988) made separate analyses of physical abuse, psychological abuse, and physical neglect, male elders were found to be much more vulnerable to *verbal* abuse than were female elders; but of the female elders who lived alone, over 70 percent reported much more neglect than did the male elders (Kosberg, 1988).

Situational factors. The living situation of impaired old people influences the possibilities for their maltreatment. When residing with others, elders are as likely to be abused by a spouse as an adult child (Pillemer & Finkelhor, 1988) and are three to four times more likely to be abused than are old-agers who live alone because of widowhood, divorce, or never having been married (Pillemer & Finkelhor, 1988; Wolf, Godkin, & Pillemer, 1984, 1986). On the other hand, when living alone the elderly may be protected against abuse but may also be neglected because of being geographically and socially isolated from potential helpers (Pillemer & Finkelhor, 1988; Quinn & Tomita, 1986; Rathbone-McCuan & Hashimi, 1980).

Thus far we have focused on the characteristics of the aged that increase their susceptibility to maltreatment. But what factors may lead caregivers to abuse or neglect the elderly?

WHO ARE AT RISK FOR BECOMING MALTREATORS OF THE ELDERLY?

In domestic settings maltreaters of the elderly are more apt to be family members than neighbors or homecare workers. And these maltreating caregivers, when contrasted with nonmaltreating ones, are more often males (usually husbands and sons) than females. Consider, for example, the study by Godkin and his colleagues (1989). Over 70 percent of the abusive caregivers were men, with husbands representing 25 percent, and adult sons, 23 percent. By contrast, adult daughters accounted for only 18 percent of the acts of maltreatment.

What about the personality characteristics of perpetrators? Whether based on random samples or comparisons of maltreating caregivers with nonmaltreating ones, research shows that some of the same characteristics found in the victims of maltreatment are also found in the victimizers (Godkin et al., 1989; Pillemer & Finkelhor, 1988, 1989).

A major characteristic of perpetrators is *dependency*. When financially dependent on the elderly, caregivers may appropriate or misuse their funds (Anastasio, 1981; Anetzberger, 1987; Fulmer & O'Malley, 1987; Hwalek & Sengstock, 1986; Kosberg, 1988). When dependent on alcohol or drugs, angry caregivers may displace their negative feelings onto those in their custody and may distort or disregard the impact of their behavior (Fulmer & O'Malley, 1987; Kosberg, 1988; Wolf et al., 1982).

Mental impairment, a trait in some elderly victims, is also found in some victimizers. When suffering mental illness, senile dementia, or confusion, caregivers may unintentionally neglect or even harm their elderly charges because they do not understand the effects of aging (Kosberg & Cairl, 1986; Wolf et al., 1982). For example, some adult caregivers rebuke and threaten retaliation against aging parents who are incontinent.

As is true for elderly victims, so too may victimizers may be influenced by a past history of abuse. The wish to abuse an elder may reflect learned behavior, unconscious hostility, or intentional retaliation by a caregiver who (as a child or a spouse) had been abused by the now-dependent but previously abusive person (Kosberg, 1988; Sengstock & Hwalek, 1985).

In some instances caregivers may maltreat the elderly when severely stressed or "burnt out" by intolerable frustration, tension, or depression, with such stress often linked with feelings of being unable or unwilling to function as a caregiver (Kosberg, 1980) or with resentment over the toll of caregiving on the person's time, energy, financial resources, and opportunities for independent activity outside the caregiving situation (Anastasio, 1981; Fulmer & O'Malley, 1987; Kosberg, 1988; O'Brien, 1971).

Elder maltreatment is often found among psychopaths, perhaps because such caregivers can lie, exploit, coerce, or assault elders without feelings of guilt (Fulmer & O'Malley, 1987). Yet neglect or abuse is also characteristic of caregivers who tend to blame others for their dissatisfactions or who, because of immaturity or egocentrism, lack understanding and empathy for the plight of the elder (Kosberg, 1988).

ENVIRONMENTAL INFLUENCES

Beyond the factors that incline people to become perpetrators or victims of maltreatment, what are some environmental conditions that may foster elder abuse or neglect?

One feature is inadequate social support (Anastasio, 1981), which may occur along with social and/or geographical isolation (Breckman & Adelman, 1988; Kosberg, 1988; Pillemer, 1986). A second feature is the lack of privacy caused when the aged live with their family (Breckman & Adelman, 1988).

The most pervasive environmental influence, however, may be *ageism,* which is the stereotyped, societal view of the aged as being physically and psychosocially incompetent (Quinn & Tomita, 1986). This negative stereotype may unconsciously foster the belief in immature or psychopathic caregivers that their society condones the maltreatment of the elderly.

Thus far we have reported on empirical indications of some factors that may place people at risk for becoming the victims or perpetrators of elder abuse or neglect. Now we turn to a number of different theories that seek to explain some of the antecedent conditions that might lead people to become perpetrators or victims of abuse.

THEORETICAL UNDERPINNINGS OF RISK FACTORS

Several theories have been proposed to explain factors that increase the likelihood of elder maltreatment. Psychoanalysis and social learning theory suggest that personality disorders or psychopathology may increase the risk of caregivers becoming elder abusers and of elders becoming victims. Social exchange and conflict theories may explain the roles of dependency and power imbalances between caregivers and elders. Symbolic interactionism has been advanced to show how elder maltreatment may grow out of the perception of caregiving as a stressful condition. Role-learning theory is a basis for ascribing elder maltreatment to insufficient knowledge, skill, or maturity. Finally, two additional theories, situational theory and functionalism, attribute elder maltreatment to environmental factors.

Psychoanalysis: A Proposed Explanation of Psychopathology

Maltreatment, if traceable to psychopathology or personality disorders of the victim or perpetrator, may be explained in terms of psychoanalysis. Suppose, for example, that disturbed biochemical or mental processes stir a dependent elder to incessant complaints, denunciations, or attacking behavior. Such provocation, if perceived by caregivers as highly threatening or stressful, may trigger abusive responses. As for caregivers, when they are schizophrenic, depressed, or paranoid, they may project hostility onto elders, suddenly striking out at them during periods of uncontrollable violence. Perhaps this occurred in the case of a middle-aged son who, when gripped by uncontrollable rage, would assault his mother, often causing her such severe bone fractures that she would have to be hospitalized (Johnson, 1991).

Critique. Some depressives and paranoics can control their psychopathological tendencies; and in some situations, both the caregiver and elder have mental health problems and sometimes exchange roles of victim and victimizer (Johnson, 1991).

Social Learning Theory: A Proposed Explanation of Violent Behavior

Psychopathology in abusive caregivers may also stem from *transgenerational violence,* the violence in adult children who model the abusive behaviors they had learned as young children from their own abusive parents. Such adult children have been seen to shake and shove their incontinent or hard-of-hearing elderly parents so as to compel their "good behavior." Abusive behavior is said to be "transgenerational" if it was learned from the aged parents and was used to discipline aged parents who had become childlike (Phillips, 1986).

Critique. Social learning theory has limited generality in that not all victims of childhood abuse become adult abusers, just as some people who had loving parents nevertheless become elder abusers.

Social Exchange Theory: A Proposed Explanation of Dependency

Dependency, broadly conceptualized, is perhaps the most pervasive quality found in both abusers and victims. The effects of such dependency can be explained by social exchange theory, which proposes that all social interaction depends on the exchange of resources, such as money, love, respect, knowledge, or power (Homans, 1961; Blau, 1968). Since all parties to a social interaction seek personal gain, social exchanges persist only so long as they are perceived to be profitable; they end once the costs seem to outweigh the benefits (Gelles, 1983). Thus the theory predicts that dependent elders cling to abusers only so long as salient need-satisfactions exceed the costs of their maltreatment. Conversely, abusers gratify their victims' needs only when the benefit-cost ratio remains a favorable one.

Johnson (1991) cites one case involving the mutual dependency needs of an unemployed, alcoholic niece and the disabled aunt with whom she lived and for whom she had been appointed as guardian. Instead of providing the aunt with personal and household care, the niece was absent most of each day and night and misspent much of her aunt's income on her own pleasures. The relationship's benefits clearly outweighed the costs for the niece. Indeed, the niece's greater resources gave her the power to establish the rate of the exchange between herself and her aunt. By contrast, the dependent aunt had to endure the maltreatment until she could find another caregiver.

In one of the first applications of exchange theory to gerontology, Dowd (1975) suggested that as people age, their power diminishes while that of younger adults increases. For example, as people grow functionally old, their skills and knowledge become outdated by technological change and they become replaced by younger persons whose more advanced skills and recent knowledge enable them to fulfill occupational roles in less costly and more efficient ways. Old age may bring other declines in power—declines in attractive appearance, physical strength, influential friends, and, often, financial resources (Crandall, 1991), although a small segment of wealthy old-agers may enjoy greater economic power than do younger adults.

Critique. Social exchange theory may explain why an abusive relationship, once begun, can persist owing to the dependency of elders and caregivers. But the initial basis for dependency may be traced to early childhood training. Specifically, tendencies toward habitual dependency may have been instilled (1) through direct conditioning because of the positive reinforcing of dependency behaviors and the punishment of independence and assertiveness, (2) through the indirect conditioning of modeling, or (3) through identification with and internalization of a model's dependency behaviors. In other words, dependent behaviors can also be explained in terms of behavioral, social learning, or psychoanalytic positions.

Conflict Theory: A Proposed Explanation of Coercion

A variant of exchange theory, conflict theory holds that the unequal distribution of scarce, desired resources (e.g., power, wealth, or prestige) enables those who control such resources to dominate and exploit those who lack them (Johnson, 1991). Thus, when in need of help with the activities of daily life, the elderly may become subjugated by those upon whom they depend.

In this connection Johnson (1991) cites the case of a social worker who sought to mislead a mentally competent but wheelchair-bound older adult into believing that her son could no longer care for her in her own home and that for purposes of safety she would have to enter a nursing home. When the older woman protested, the social worker then falsely claimed that as the representative of adult protective services, she could force the woman's entry into a nursing home. Fortunately, the social worker's attempted misuse of her authority was discovered. Hence the old woman was able to remain in her home and to continue to receive care from her loving son, along with some outside help (Johnson, 1991).

Critique. Studies have revealed significantly more interpersonal conflict and coercion by caregivers among abused elders as opposed to nonabused ones (Godkin et al., 1989). But are the conflict and coercion in these cases attributable solely to the unequal distribution of resources? For example, in the case noted above, might the social worker's misuse of her authority indicate a personality problem?

Symbolic Interactionism: A Proposed Explanation of Stress

To explain how stress may contribute to the behavior of both maltreators and their victims, Suzanne Steinmetz (1988) draws on symbolic interactionism to theorize that the way a situation is *defined* determines whether or not it is experienced as stressful. Since people vary in their perception of stress and their threshold for tolerating it, the tending of elders may be intolerably stressful for some caregivers but relatively easy for others. Similarly, dependence on caregivers, while stressful for elders who cannot relinquish any independence, is tolerable to elders who can acknowledge and accept the losses in personal control that sometimes accompany old age.

By way of illustration, Johnson (1991) cites the case of an adult daughter who was suddenly thrust into the role of primary caregiver of her suddenly disabled mother. The daughter felt that the proper care of her mother required that she move into her mother's home, relinquish her job, neglect her college-bound children, and abandon her friendships so as to devote all her energy to caring for her mother. Having thus defined the situation as requiring total self-sacrifice, the daughter placed herself under extraordinary stress. The effect was to heighten the likelihood of intolerable anger—and, hence, of future abuse of the mother.

Critique. The value of this theory remains to be verifed because abuse has been studied not in terms of *subjective* experiences of stress but only according to external events identified by objective observers as stressful, such as recent changes in living arrangements (e.g., a new residence), economic status (short- or long-term financial problems), or family relationships (e.g., the loss of a spouse through death or divorce or separation).

Role Theory: A Proposed Explanation of Insuffient Knowledge or Maturity

Insufficient skill or knowledge may sometimes be the basis for inadequate or inappropriate caregiving. For example, when unaware that organic changes may cause involuntary incontinence in some old-agers, caregivers may misinterpret an elder's soiling as a sign of willfulness or noncooperation. In other instances, immaturity underlies the unwillingness of some caregivers to endure the inevitable inconvenience and personal sacrifice entailed in caring for elderly relatives.

Whatever the case, abuse and neglect can be avoided if both caregivers and elders learn about and play their expected roles. An illustrative case is the one cited by Johnson (1991) in which a son promised to care for his father if he were to become disabled. But the son also warned that he could not tend his father in his own home because to do so would undermine his own identity and cause such resentment as to impede him from caring properly for his father. By giving this advance explanation of the conditions under which care would be given, the son avoided the potential for maltreating his father and provided advance assurance of good care of his father should he become ill or impaired.

Critique. In a caregiving situation the avoidance of perceptions of maltreatment by elders and of stressfulness by caregivers requires a prior understanding not only of the roles of elder and caregiver, but also of the way cultural and personal standards can affect expectations about those roles. For example, what affluent persons may view as cramped, crowded conditions with many unmet needs may be viewed by impoverished persons as luxurious conditions and abundant need gratification (Johnson, 1991). In other words, people's perception of maltreatment varies according to all the features of their past experiences that might influence their expectations.

Situational Theory: A Proposed Explanation of Isolation

Focusing less on intrapersonal factors and more on the way external events affect people regardless of their individual differences, situational theory (see Linda Phillips, 1986) and empirical studies (see Phillips, 1983; Wolf et al., 1984) suggest that isolation may be a situational basis for elder maltreatment. When socially isolated, caregivers lack the emotional and social support that can help to defuse the tension that might otherwise culminate in elder maltreatment. When living alone, elders may feel neglected because of being disconnected from the significant figures in their lives. Moreover, social isolation minimizes the possibility of intervention or prevention of elder maltreatment by caring outsiders (Anetzberger, 1987; Johnson, 1991).

Critique. There are several reasons why social isolation has limited generality as an explanation of elder maltreatment. First, isolation cannot be equated with loneliness or disrupted communication. Some people actually prefer to live alone; those who do not can maintain meaningful contact with significant others by phone or letter. Second, the mere presence of a social network does not assure emotional support nor guarantee protection against loneliness (Johnson, 1991). Indeed, as noted earlier, comparisons of maltreated with nonmaltreated elders found more physical abuse among elders living with a caregiver than among those living alone (Godkin, Wolf, & Pillemer, 1989; Pillemer & Finkelhor, 1988, 1989). Moreover, nonabused elders who lived alone did not suffer neglect if they had extensive social support networks (Anetzberger, 1987).

Functionalism: A Proposed Explanation of Ageism

The functionalism theory ascribes elder maltreatment to *ageism,* stereotyped views of the aged as weak, foolish, and mentally and physically incompetent. These negative stereotypes spring from institutional policies that tacitly approve and perpetuate elder maltreatment because it is functional for a society to maintain its existing practices. Hence, elder prejudice and discrimination, once introduced, are preserved until such time as age integration proves more "functional" than age discrimination (Johnson, 1991).

Critique. Ageism may explain why society tolerates or condones acts of elder maltreatment. Certainly a society's tacit support of negative stereotypes of the elderly may explain why some caregivers feel free to displace their anger and aggression onto elder dependents and why some of the aged passively accept maltreatment by their caregivers.

CONCLUSIONS

How is our understanding of research on elder maltreatment furthered by the above theories? Taken together, the theories offer dissimilar explanations of the diverse influences suggested by the empirical studies. Elder maltreatment is ascribed to contextual features in *situational theory,* with its emphasis on the adverse impact of social isolation or too little privacy on caregivers and elders, and also to *functionalism,* which attributes elder maltreatment to ageism.

Other theories, however, suggest that elder maltreatment springs from the effects on caregivers and elders of their intrapersonal states, that is, their mental or physical impairment, dependency, personality problems, or psychopathology. Thus the theories of *social exchange* and of *conflict and coercion* help to explain why the inevitable dependency of ill or frail elders renders them powerless and hence vulnerable to maltreatment by their caregivers. Yet, though the dependency of elders may predispose them to maltreatment, actual acts of caregiver abuse or neglect come about only because of the characteristics of caregivers (e.g., their dependency or immaturity or pathology) in conjunction with environmental influences (e.g., social isolation and ageism).

Thus, it seems likely that elements of more than one theory are needed to explain elder maltreatment. For example, elder maltreatment might initially arise when caregiver feelings of intolerable stress suddenly erupt in a violent and uncontrollable outburst, with such perceptions of intolerable stress influenced by contextual factors, such as too little privacy or insufficient emotional support (the view of situational theory), and/or because the perpetrators have a low tolerance of stress owing to such personality factors as dependency, immaturity, or psychopathology (the view of psychoanalysis, social learning theory, role theory, or behaviorism).

Moreover, once elder abuse has been initiated, its persistence may also be explained by elements of different theories. Thus, as social exchange and conflict theories predict, the perpetrator-victim relationship would continue so long as it proved profitable for the perpetrator and so long as the victim was powerless to oppose the violence—a condition that obtains when victimizers are insulated against harmful repercussions either because social isolation ensures that their violent acts go undetected (a position advanced by situational theory) or because the society's ageistic views leave abusive caregivers and their victims with the impression that elder maltreatment is condoned (a viewpoint consistent with functionalism).

In sum, when seeking to explain empirical findings of elder maltreatment within a theoretical framework, one cannot rely on any one theory. Instead, what is needed is an overarching theoretical position, one that takes into account the combined impact of (1) *intrapersonal* factors such as impairment, dependency, immaturity, personality problems, or psychopathology; (2) *interpersonal* factors involved in the caregiver-elder relationship, including, for example, the subjective perceptions of stress, of costs-gains ratios, and of relative degrees of power versus powerlessness in the relationship; and (3) *contextual* factors such as the inaccessibility of help, respite care, and emotional and social support, as well as social stereotypes that allow or even foster elder maltreatment.

REFERENCES

Anastasio, C. J. (1981). Elder abuse: Identification and acute care intervention. In *First National Conference on Abuse of Older Persons.* Cambridge, MA: Legal Research and Services for the Elderly.

Anetzberger, G. J. (1987). *The etiology of elder abuse by adult offspring.* Springfield, IL: Charles C. Thomas.

Blau, P. (1968). Social exchange. In D. L. Sills (Ed.), *International Encyclopedia of the Social Sciences, 7,* 452–458. New York: Macmillan.

Breckman, R., & Adelman, R. (1988). *Helping elderly victims of abuse and neglect.* Beverly Hills, CA: Sage.

Cantor, M., & Little, V. (1985). Aging and social care. In R. H. Binstock & E. Shanas (Eds.), *Handbook of aging and the social sciences* (2nd ed.). New York: Van Nostrand Rheinhold.

Crandall, R. C. (1991). *Gerontology.* New York: McGraw-Hill.

Douglass, R. L., Hickey, T., & Noel, C. (1980). *A study of maltreatment of the elderly and other vulnerable adults.* Ann Arbor, MI: University of Michigan, Institute of Gerontology.

Dowd, J. J. (1975). Aging as exchange: A preface to theory. *Journal of Gerontology, 30,* 584.

Fulmer, T. T., & O'Malley, T. A. (1987). *Inadequate care of the elderly: A health care perspective on abuse and neglect.* New York: Springer.

Gelles, R. J. (1983). An exchange/social control theory. In D. Finkelhor, R. J. Gelles, G. T. Hotaling, & M. A. Strauss (Eds.), *The dark side of families: Current family violence research.* Beverly Hills, CA: Sage.

Giordano, N. H., & Giordano, J. A. (1983, November). Family and individual characteristics of five types of elder abuse: Profiles and predictors. Paper presented at the meeting of the Gerontological Society of America, Chicago, IL.

Godkin, M. A., Wolf, R. S., & Pillemer, K. A. (1989). A case comparison analysis of elder abuse and neglect. *International Journal of Aging and Human Development, 28*(3), 207–225.

Hall, P. A. (1989). Elder maltreatment items, subgroups, and types: Policy and practice implications. *International Journal of Aging and Human Development, 28*(3), 191–205.

Homans, G. (1961). *Social behavior: Its elementary forms.* New York: Harcourt, Brace & World.

Hwalek, M. A., & Sengstock, M. C. (1986). Assessing the probability of abuse of the elderly: Toward development of a clinical screening instrument. *Journal of Applied Gerontology, 5*(2), 153–173.

Johnson, T. F. (1986). Critical issues in the definition of elder mistreatment. In K. A. Pillemer & R. S. Wolf (Eds.), *Elder abuse: Conflict in the family.* Dover, MA: Auburn House.

Johnson, T. F. (1991). *Elder mistreatment: Deciding who is at risk.* Westport, CT: Greenwood Press.

Kosberg, J. I. (1980, November). *Family maltreatment: Explanations and interventions.* Paper presented at the meeting of the Gerontological Society of America, San Diego, CA.

Kosberg, J. I. (1988). Preventing elder abuse: Identification of high risk factors prior to placement decisions. *The Gerontologist, 28*(1), 43–50.

Kosberg, J. I., & Cairl, R. E. (1986). The cost of care index: A case management tool for screening informal care providers. *The Gerontologist, 26,* 273–278.

Lau, E. E., & Kosberg, J. I. (1979, September-October). Abuse of the elderly by informal care providers, *Aging,* 10–15.

National Center for Health Services. (1986). Health US, 1985. In Public Health Service, DHHS Pub. No. PHS 86-1232. Washington, DC: U.S. Government Printing Office.

O'Brien, J. (1971). Violence in divorce prone families. *Journal of Marriage and the Family, 33,* 692–698.

Pegels, C. C. (1988). *Health care and the older citizen (economic, demographic, and financial Aspects).* Rockville, MD: Aspen.

Phillips, L. R. (1983). Abuse and neglect of the frail elderly at home: An exploration of theoretical relationships. *Journal of Advanced Nursing, 8,* 379–392.

Phillips, L. R. (1986). Theoretical explanations of elder abuse: Competing hypotheses and unresolved issues. In K. A. Pillemer & R. Wolf (Eds.), *Elder abuse: Competing hypotheses and unresolved issues.* Dover, MA: Auburn House.

Pillemer, K. A. (1986). Risk factors in elder abuse. In K. A. Pillemer & R. S. Wolf (Eds.), *Elder abuse: Conflict in the family.* Dover, MA: Auburn House.

Pillemer, K. A. (1988). Maltreatment of patients in nursing homes: Overview and research agenda. *Journal of Health and Social Behavior, 29*(3), 227–238.

Pillemer, K., & Finkelhor, D. (1988). The prevalence of elder abuse: A random sample survey. *The Gerontologist, 28,* 51–57.

Pillemer, K., & Finkelhor, D. (1989). Causes of elder abuse: Caregiver stress versus problem relatives. *American Orthopsychiatric Association, 59*(2).

Quinn, M. J., & Tomita, S. K. (1986). *Elder abuse and neglect: Causes, diagnostics and intervention strategies.* New York: Springer.

Rathbone-McCuan, E. (1980). Elderly victims of family violence and neglect. *Social Casework, 61,* 296–304.

Rathbone-McCuan, E., & Hashimi, J. (1980). *Isolated elders: Health and Social Intervention.* Rockville, MD: Aspen.

Sengstock, M. C., & Hwalek, M. (1985). *Comprehensive index of elder abuse.* Detroit, MI: Wayne State University.

Steinmetz, S. K. (1988). Elder abuse by family caregivers: Processes and intervention strategies. Special issue: Coping with victimization. *Contemporary Family Therapy in an International Journal, 10*(4), 256–271.

Turner, B. F. (1982). Sex-related differences in aging. In B. B. Wolman (Ed.), *Handbook of developmental psychology.* Englewood Cliffs, NJ: Prentice Hall.

U.S. Bureau of Census. (1984, May). Projection of the population of the U.S. *Current Population Reports.* Series P-25, No. 952. Washington, DC: U.S. Government Printing Office.

U.S. Congress, House Select Committee on Aging. (1980). *Elder abuse: The hidden problem.* Washington, DC: U.S. Government Printing Office.

Wolf, R. S., Godkin, M. A., & Pillemer, K. A. (1984). *Elder abuse and neglect: Final report from three model projects.* Worcester: University of Massachusetts Center on Aging.

Wolf, R. S., Godkin, M. A., & Pillemer, K. A. (1986). Maltreatment of the elderly: A comparative analysis. *Pride Institute Journal of Long-Term Home-Health Care,* 5(4), 10–17.

Wolf, R. S., Strugnell, C. P., & Godkin, M. A. (1982). *Preliminary findings from three model projects on elderly abuse.* Worcester: University of Massachusetts Center on Aging.

Epilogue: Traditional Buddhist Ladakh—A Society at Peace

Uwe P. Gielen

> In traditional Ladakh, aggression of any sort is exceptionally rare: rare enough to say that it is virtually nonexistent. . . . I have hardly seen anything more than mild disagreement in the traditional villages.
> —*Norberg-Hodge*, 1991

Psychologists such as Fromm (1973) and Gielen and Chirico-Rosenberg (1993) and anthropologists such as Briggs (1970), Howell and Willis (1989), and Montagu (1978) have studied the nature of small-scale, traditional, nonviolent societies in various parts of the globe. Examples of reputedly nonviolent societies include the Semai Senoi of Malaysia, certain Zapotec communities in Mexico (Fry, 1992), the Mbuti Pygmies of Zaire (Turnbull, 1961, 1965), the Inuit (Eskimos) of Canada (Briggs, 1970), and the Zuni Pueblo Indians of New Mexico. Students of these societies have tended to focus on worldviews, value systems, cognitive scripts, and child-rearing practices that they have held responsible for the prevailing low rates of violent behavior.

The anthropological study of peaceful societies took as one of its origins the famous book of Ruth Benedict (1934), *Patterns of Culture*. In this book Benedict contrasted the peaceful way of life of the Zuni Pueblo Indians with the power-oriented ethos of the Kwakiutl Indians on America's northwest coast and the prevailing attitudes of mistrust, paranoia, and treachery among the Dobu of Melanesia. Benedict's book is a monument to *cultural relativism*, that is, the idea that value systems, moralities, and worldviews differ radically from society to society. The book not only had a strong impact on the anthropological profession—cultural relativism became the reigning ideology of U.S. American anthropology under the influence of Franz Boas, Ruth Benedict, Melville Herskovits, and Margaret Mead—but it also shaped the imagination of countless college students and the educated public. More than 800,000 copies of her book were sold over the years.

Benedict's book played an important role in the battle of cultural anthropologists, behaviorists, and social learning theorists against the "instinctivists." Instinctivists such as the psychoanalyst Sigmund Freud, the hormic psychologist William McDougall, and the ethologist Konrad Lorenz have claimed that there exists an innate, universal core of human characteristics among which aggression, hostility, and self-seeking tendencies are prominent. By showing that there exist peaceful societies, the anthropologists also sought to demonstrate that there are no universal and innate aggressive drives or instincts. This argument was forcefully advanced by Ashley Montagu (1978) in his edited book *Learning Non-aggression: The Experience of Non-literate Societies.* A similar but more recent and less ideologically oriented collection by Howell and Willis (1989) also contains studies of peaceful societies. The studies are based on the premise that sociality rather than aggression is the psychological basis on which humans have built their societies and created satisfying religious and moral frameworks for living.

Although psychologists have conducted numerous studies concerning the prosocial, altruistic, and cooperative behavior of individuals, they have played only a very limited role in the study of peaceful societies. One important exception is Erich Fromm's (1973) survey of thirty "primitive" (i.e., preliterate) tribes, which he divided into life-affirmative societies, nondestructive-aggressive societies, and destructive societies. Among the life-affirmative societies he placed the Zuni Indians, the Mountain Arapesh, the Aranda, the Semangs, the Todas, the Polar Eskimos, and the Mbuti Pygmies. Relying on evidence collected by anthropologists, he claimed that in these societies

there is a minimum of hostility, violence, or cruelty among people, no harsh punishment, hardly any crime, and the institution of war is absent or plays an exceedingly small role. Children are treated with kindness, . . . [and] there is little envy, covetousness, greed, and exploitativeness. There is also little competition, . . . a general attitude of trust and confidence . . . ; a general prevalence of good humor, and a relative absence of depressive moods. (Fromm, 1973, P. 194)

This chapter investigates how well Fromm's generalizations apply to the society of Ladakh, a Tibetan society located in northwest India that until recently was relatively isolated from Western contacts. The chapter centers on the nonviolent ethos and worldview of traditional Ladakh, an ethos based upon Buddhist conceptions of "no-self," religious merit and demerit, karma, compassion with all sentient beings, and the undesirability of mental poisons such as greed, aggression, jealousy, envy, and spiritual ignorance. The nonviolent ethos of Ladakh culminates in the ideal of the *bodhisattva,* a religious savior figure embodying the ideals of compassion, altruism, nonviolence, and "karmic interconnectedness." Our interviews suggest that most Ladakhis have deeply internalized the Buddhist "Ethos of Peace."

Finally, the chapter compares the ethos of Ladakh to the worldview and competitive ethos of the modern United States. It is argued that the aggressive individualism prevailing in the United States stands in stark contrast to the restrained, synergistic, cooperative forms of social interaction found in Ladakh and other peaceful societies.

SETTING

Ladakh is located in the northwestern area of India and forms a part of the state of Jammu and Kashmir. About half as large as England, it has approximately 130,000 inhabitants. More than 99 percent of the land is a high-altitude mountain desert, but barley, buckwheat, potatoes, turnips, and walnut and apricot trees are planted in the valleys. Ladakh borders on Pakistan and on Tibet, the latter now forming part of China. There is one town, Leh, which has about 9,500 inhabitants. The other Ladakhis live in villages, but some nomadic pastoralists roam the more remote, high areas. Most Ladakhis are farmers, craftsmen, small-business men, government officials, or members of the Buddhist clergy. They speak Ladakhi, a Tibetan language. Hindi, Urdu, "high Tibetan," and English are spoken by some Ladakhis in business or government transactions or by the Buddhist clergy. Literacy levels vary greatly by region, social class, gender, and age. The author estimates that perhaps 35–45 percent of all adults in the central Leh region are literate to varying degrees. The majority of children in Leh and surrounding villages are now attending primary school.

About 60 percent of Ladakh's population profess the Buddhist faith while most other inhabitants of Ladakh belong to the Sunni and Shiite traditions of Islam. Among the Muslims are Baltis and Ladakhis. The Baltis share their culture, language, and religion with the Baltis of neighboring Baltistan, a province of Pakistan. Pervasive cultural differences and certain political tensions separate the Baltis from the Buddhist Ladakhis. In contrast, the Muslim Ladakhis are often rather similar in their cultural habits and personality traits to the Buddhist Ladakhis, although the two groups differ in their religions. The present chapter confines itself to the Buddhist population and is based on interviews conducted with seventy-two Buddhist children, men, women, and monks during 1980–81.

The upper Indus valley forms the cultural center of Buddhist Ladakh. Here are located many of the monasteries that have traditionally dominated the spiritual life of Buddhist Ladakh. The monasteries belong to a variety of Tibetan lineages such as the Gelugpa ("Yellow Hat"), the Kargyupa (including Digunkpa and Dukpa), the Nyingmapa, and the Sakyapa.

METHOD

Sample

The sample of seventy-two respondents included eight boys and eight girls, ages 10–12; eight boys and eight girls, ages 14–16; ten men and ten women, ages 25–73; and twenty monks, ages 20–72. All respondents were Buddhists and came from Leh and surrounding villages. The twenty monks were affiliated with a wide variety of monasteries throughout Ladakh. Their educational attainments and ranks within their monastic communities varied considerably, and some of the monks had in the past gone to Tibet for higher religious studies. Four *rinpoches* (abbots) were included in the sample. A large majority of the interviewees spoke little or no English. They came from a considerable variety of backgrounds and included farmers, village workers, shopkeepers, small government officials, and their wives and children. Some prominent citizens from Leh were also included in the interviews. Educational levels of respondents varied from no schooling at all to college education.

The sample included a highly varied cross-section of Ladakhis from Leh and surroundings, but compared to the rest of Ladakh the sample was better educated, had been more influenced by exposure to the "modern world," and included a smaller percentage of farmers.

Questionnaire and Interview Procedure

The questionnaire included two moral decision stories taken from Colby and Kohlberg (1987) and two social reasoning dilemmas taken from Selman (1979). The author presented to his Ladakhi informant, Nawang Tsering Shakspo of J & K Cultural Academy, Leh, a selection of moral and social decision stories and asked him to select those stories that appeared to him to be especially appropriate for Ladakhi settings. The stories were translated into Ladakhi, and some of their details were changed. Each of the four stories described a hypothetical dilemma where the actions and expectations of the fictitious adults and children clash with each other. The following is an example of a dilemma:

Should desperately poor Stobdan steal *dakjun* (a difficult-to-attain, traditional type medicine) from a doctor-druggist in order to save his deathly ill wife? (An adaptation of Kohlberg's Heinz story)

The four vignettes were followed by an extensive series of standard questions that attempted to elicit the reasoning behind the interviewee's decisions. The questions were designed to raise issues such as the value of life, property, theft, mutual role taking, interpersonal expectations and duties, punishment, guilt, promise and trust, conceptions of the subjective nature of persons (thoughts, feelings, motives), self-awareness and self-reflection, personality traits, self-esteem, dyadic relationships, anger, and friendship. Depending on a person's answer to these issues, numerous additional questions were introduced.

In addition to the decision stories described above, three new dilemmas were constructed with the help of Wangchuk Shalipa. Sixteen of the interviews included the three new dilemmas. The three stories described a son who wanted to become a monk against the wishes of his mother, a young couple who got married against the determined opposition of the husband's parents, and a woman who felt cheated after buying a shawl from a Kashmiri shopkeeper. Thirty-eight respondents were given an abbreviated version of Fowler's (1981) faith interview. In this interview a person was asked about his or her life story, the meaning of life, the nature of his or her religious commitments, and various values and attitudes that constituted the person's faith. The faith interview included a wide variety of broad, open-ended questions used to elicit a person's overall outlook on life.

The interviews took place in schools, monasteries, the author's guesthouse and hotel, or occasionally in the fields. They usually lasted one and a half to three hours and were taperecorded. Several interpreters were used throughout the research. The interviewees were typically unfamiliar with the whole interview procedure, and some among them, especially children, made comments about the difficulty of the questions. More details about the research procedures and findings may be found in Gielen and Chirico-Rosenberg (1993).

Constructing the Ethos of Ladakh

Based on the interviews with seventy-two Ladakhis, the author's daily interactions with Ladakhis over a time period of six months, his participation in religious festivals, and a review of sacred writings, mythology, folk songs, and poetry, themes felt to reflect the prevailing ethos of traditional Ladakh were identified. By *ethos* is meant here the characteristic spirit or "genius" of a people; this includes characteristic value systems, forms of moral reasoning, attitudes, and the overall worldview.

The author's observations were condensed into an "ideal-type" (Max Weber) representation of Ladakh's Buddhist ethos, which in a purified and exaggerated way sums up the guiding spirit of Ladakh's traditional culture. The ideal-typal representation of Ladakh's ethos is then contrasted with an equally purified and exaggerated representation of the ethos of modern, liberal America. By contrasting the worldviews and moral conceptions of two such highly different societies, the inner coherence and spiritual beauty of Ladakh's ethos are highlighted. The comparison also points to the enormous psychological and spiritual distance between the Buddhist vision of inner and outer peace and the competitive, individualistic assertive-aggressive vision of self-actualization that shapes modern North America.

THE WHEEL OF LIFE

Close to the entrance door of every large Ladakhi monastery one finds a painting of the "Wheel of Life" (*Bhavacakra*), which in a concrete, easily understandable form sums up the worldview of Tibetan (Vajrayana) Buddhism, the religion that shapes the worldview and ethos of Ladakh. The author has often seen simple farmers standing in front of the Wheel of Life while paying special attention to the part of the painting that depicts humans suffering in the Buddhist version of hell or purgatory.

The wheel shows various beings in the six zones of existence that together make up *samsara*, the realm of illusion, reincarnation, and suffering. Every sentient being is born with the possibility to reach enlightenment or Buddhahood, and thus to escape the wheel of suffering. Shinje (Yama), Lord of Death, holds the wheels in his claws and teeth, symbolizing that attachment to *samsara* represents a kind of spiritual death.

At the hub of the wheel one can see three theriomorphic symbols representing "mental poisons." These are said to drive the wheel—and thereby all existence—through the karmic stages of birth, death, and reincarnation. The three poisons are symbolized by a pig, a rooster or cock, and a snake. The pig symbolizes ignorance and illusion, the cock greed and lust, and the snake hate, envy, and jealousy. The three animals bite each other's tails, reflecting interconnections between the basic manifestations of evil, sin, and mental poisons. The symbolic nature of the three animals is easily understood, since they represent a kind of Buddhist Id. Similar to Freud's theory, a combination of blind sexual and agressive impulses together with ignorance or repression form the core of human nature. But unlike orthodox psychoanalysis, Tibetan Buddhism teaches that one can overcome the basic impulses of greed, hate, and attachment to egoistic goals so that one may reach one's own liberation and that of all sentient beings. This can be accomplished by following the basic teachings (*dharma*) of Buddhism, meditation, empathy for the suffering of others, nonattachment to the illusions of this world, and the fundamental insight that the self is a steadily shifting mixture of karmic factors no more solid in substance than the ever-shifting clouds that drift across the endless Tibetan sky. All life is transitory, and attachment to the goods of this world chain a person to *samsara* and the steadily turning wheel of life. Greed, hate, illicit lust, envy, jealousy, egoism, and ignorance make up the basic links of the chain.

Because human beings are weak, they need models of perfection. In Vajrayana Buddhism the savior figure of the *bodhisattva* serves as such a model. *Bodhisattvas* are enlightened beings who out of compassion for all sentient creatures forgo their chance to enter the blissful, timeless state of nirvana that would take them out of the wheel of life. *Bodhisattvas* frequently descend to the earthly realm where they become incarnated in *tulkus* and *rinpoches,* including the Dalai Lama and some of the abbots of Ladakh's monasteries. The Dalai Lama is a reincarnation of Chenrezig, patron deity of Tibet and manifestation of the principle of compassion, a principle that pervades the teachings of Vayrayana Buddhism. In daily life, the principle helps to soften relationships between people and serves as an emotional glue binding people together. Harsh self-assertion, insistence upon one's rights, and the expression of aggressive impulses are unlikely to occur when the principle of compassion holds sway.

Although certain details of the wheel of life can be understood only by the theologically trained monks, our interview results strongly suggest that the average Ladakhi has deeply internalized the basic vision of human nature underlying the wheel of life.

INTERVIEW RESULTS

The results of the interviews are summarized in Table E.1 where they are contrasted with the conceptions of human nature and goals of life prevailing among many modern, well educated, liberal Americans. When inspecting Table E.1 the reader is asked to keep the "ideal-typal" nature of the constructions of the two visions of life in mind.

In their interviews the Ladakhi respondents emphasized their faith in the Buddhist religion, the pervasiveness of karma, the importance of acquiring religious merit and avoiding religious demerit (sin), and the desire for a good reincarnation. These themes were especially emphasized by the older respondents, who tended to show a stronger orientation toward religious concerns than the younger respondents.

The traditional Ladakhi lives in a world where the Buddhist religion is universally accepted and provides a convincing explanation for human suffering. Karma, as an impersonal, objective system of retribution and reincarnation, connects all "sentient beings." By showing compassion with the suffering of others and of animals, a person can acquire religious merit while experiencing a feeling of karmic interconnectedness with the web of life. These feelings undercut "natural" tendencies toward self-assertion, selfishness, and acquisitiveness. Instead, conflicts between people are reduced and cooperation and interpersonal trust are emphasized. In the village communities the self is submerged in a network of concrete interpersonal obligations and reciprocal relationships. Little emphasis is placed on intimacy or romantic love in husband-wife relationships.

The Ladakhi admires emotional restraint, quiet dignity, serenity, a certain detachment from the affairs of the world, honesty, discretion in human relationships, and religious piety. Physical aggressiveness is extremely rare and confined to occasional and usually harmless fights between young men under the influence of the local beer, *chang*. Capital crimes are almost unknown. Feelings of envy do sometimes surface and are then externalized and projected in an unconscious process of ego defense onto outsiders, witches, demons, ghosts, and neighbors with the evil eye. On the whole, however, Ladakhis are remarkably cheerful and good humored in the face of troublesome situations and their harsh living conditions. Feelings of depression appear to be rare, although a few girls

Table E.1
Comparison of the Worldviews, Ethos, and Personality Characteristics of Traditional Ladakhis and
Modern Americans

	TRADITIONAL LADAKHIS	MODERN LIBERAL AMERICANS
ULTIMATE MEANING OF LIFE AND ROLE OF RELIGION IN PROVIDING MEANING:	Religion universally accepted; life means suffering, but is only a dream; death is relative, not final; not harming others leads to good reincarnation; meaning exists objectively and has been revealed; why questions and doubt are rare; mystic contemplation leads to ultimate truth beyond all conceptualization	Role of religion limited and frequently doubted; death often seen as final tragedy; meaning of life is subjectively chosen and never final (existentialism); doubt frequent and why questions encouraged; life in this world the only provable reality; mysticism seen as avoidance of the struggle of life
NATURE OF MORALITY:	Objective reality, facts, and rules revealed to rinpoches, saints, etc.; part of impersonal system of retribution (karma) and reincarnation embedded in religion; do not cause people and animals to suffer; moral relativism and self-conscious, ideological reflection on ethical systems are rare	Personal choice of competitive values that must be justified to self and others; morality more or less separate from religion; control of aggressive and sexual feelings
GUILT AND SHAME FEELINGS; SUPEREGO:	Unclear conception of guilt feelings; guilt feelings rare; little self-blame; tolerance for other people and worldviews; strong feelings of shame when breaking interpersonal norms or religious prescriptions	Guilt feelings commonly recognized and often strong; strong ambivalence about desirability of guilt feelings; frequent self-blame and blame of others; ambivalence about tolerance

CONSCIENCE:	Unclear or no conception of conscience; correctly analyzed actions rather than conscience are emphasized	Inner voice that guides and checks antisocial desires and produces guilt feelings
DRIVES:	Greed, selfishness, lust, ignorance are basic cause of suffering and lead to bad reincarnation; conflict between id and superego fairly low; drives are muted	Acquisitiveness, sex, toughness necessary for personal happiness and self-actualization, although they create intrapersonal and interpersonal conflicts; conflict between id and superego strong
EMOTIONALITY, ASSERTIVENESS, DEFENSIVENESS:	Generally low levels; emphasis on quiet dignity, detachment, serenity, assertiveness, aggressiveness, impulsivity, inner restlessness, emotional expressivity all considered undesirable; introversion, shyness, timidity fairly common: distinct sense of privacy and discretion with correlated lack of intrusiveness	High levels of emotionality, assertiveness, defensiveness; emotional expressivity is valued
INTRAPERSONAL AND INTERPERSONAL CONFLICTS; COOPERATION:	Strong avoidance of conflicts; very little interpersonal violence; intrapersonal conflicts weak; emphasis on cooperation, but undercurrent of envy and occasional "toughness" against others and self	Very frequent conflicts within self and between self and others; competition strongly emphasized; personal success emphasized as key to self-esteem
CONCRETE LIFE GOALS:	Long life, health, reasonable prosperity, happiness, acceptance from and convivial relationships with others	Long life, health, monetary success; achievement; good relationships and family life
SYNERGY (MASLOW):	High level of synergy: altruism leads to merit and better reincarnation (limited by pragmatic concern for immediate self-interests)	Low level of synergy; life often seen as approaching zero-sum game

Table E.1 (Continued)

ANOMIE AND DEVIANCE:	Very low levels of anomie and deviance	Fairly high levels of anomie; extremely high levels of deviance
SELF AND SELF-ESTEEM:	Little focus on self; self-esteem seen as selfishness and undesirable pride; self embedded in society; few basic identity conflicts; limited awareness of inner feelings and inner conflicts; little awareness of inner personality change	Extreme individualism and emphasis on self's autonomy and self-esteem; self-esteem precarious, but key to happiness; frequent redefinitions of self and identity conflicts
INDIVIDUAL CHOICE:	Not emphasized	Very strongly emphasized
INTERPERSONAL RELATIONSHIPS; ROMANTIC LOVE; DEPENDENCE FEELINGS AND RELATIONSHIP TO AUTHORITY:	Concrete reciprocity and obedience; ambivalence rare or not recognized; little emphasis on intimacy and romantic love in husband-wife relationships; dependence on religious leaders easily expressed; non-hostile belief in authority	Ambivalence in relationships frequent; relationships romanticized with strong emotional expectations that may not be met; obedience seen as inhibiting self-actualization; dependence feelings seen as weakness and debilitating; distrust of authority
HAPPINESS:	Frequent, though life is hard; feelings of depression and tragedy rare	Difficult to achieve; feelings of depression, emptiness, futility frequent
FAITH, TRUST, TRUTHFULNESS:	Very strong faith, considerable interpersonal trust; "naive" honesty and "innocence" combined with lack of ability to systematically manipulate others	Variable; faith and trust often uncertain; manipulation of others may be perceived as being necessary
IDEAL MODEL OF PERFECTION:	Compassionate saint who has conquered his selfish passions (greed, envy, anger, hate, lust) and fears and works for the welfare of all sentient beings	Well adjusted and self-actualized person who leads a full life

and women expressed feelings of unhappiness about extreme poverty, ill-treatment by stepparents, and misbehaving husbands.

Although the Buddhist metaphysical doctrine of "no-self" is not fully understood by many of Ladakh's villagers, on the psychological level the doctrine is widely accepted. In the interviews, there was little focus on the self and only limited awareness of inner feelings, conflicts, and systematic personality change over time. When asked to explain the meaning of self-esteem, only a very few Ladakhis fully understood this question. Instead, most respondents saw self-esteem as representing undesirable pride and selfishness. They saw little place for people with "big egos" in their village communities.

Tibetan societies such as Ladakh have traditionally assigned a relatively high status to women, especially when compared to their lower and more restricted status in the neighboring societies of Muslim Kashmir and Pakistan, Hindu India, and Confucian China (Gielen, 1985; 1993). Traditional Ladakh was—and to some degree still is—a center of traditional polyandry, a system of marriage in which a wife is married to two or more brothers. Such a system is simply unthinkable in the neighboring Muslim societies, since it assigns to the wife a central if delicate position in the web of family life. Relationships between Ladakh's men and women have always been more relaxed, open, cheerful, and egalitarian than corresponding relationships in other traditional peasant societies. This is not to say that there is true equality between Ladakh's men and women; such a situation is unknown in the world of peasants around the globe.

COMPARING LADAKH AND THE UNITED STATES

Our results show considerable agreement with Fromm's previously cited generalizations concerning the nature of peaceful, small-scale societies. Following Fromm, we find in Ladakh a minimum of hostility and violence among the people, very few serious crimes, a quiet but persistent disapproval of greed, covetousness, and exploitativeness, little competition and individualism, a good deal of interpersonal trust and cooperation, a general prevalence of good humor, a relative absence of depressive moods, a fairly easy going attitude toward sex (this is more fully discussed in Gielen, 1993), and relatively high levels of equality between the sexes. Whereas Fromm's investigation focused only on preliterate societies, the present study extends his findings to a semiliterate society with an upper stratum of highly trained monks.

As Table E.1 makes clear, the ethos of Ladakh presents a striking contrast to the ethos of the modern United States. The watchwords in the modern United States are competitive individualism, striving for status, monetary success and other achievement goals, extremely high rates of family disorganization, deviance and crime, an emphasis on self-actualization and self-esteem as the ultimate good, a pervasive emphasis on sexuality, rapidly increasing rates of depressive and antisocial personality disorders, and the pervasive presence of capitalistic goals such as consumption and profit seeking.

Whereas Buddhist doctrine has identified greed, hate, aggression, lust, envy, jealousy, pride, and spiritual ignorance as the ultimate sources of human unhappiness, modern North American society has been ambivalent about the acceptability of these "mental poisons." In return, it has paid a high price for this ambivalence: Among all fully industrialized nations, the United States has the highest rates of homicide, assault, and rape, the most serious drug problem, the greatest emphasis on competitive individualism and individual choice, and the weakest family system. A rapidly increasing number of children grow up in fatherless households and poverty, conditions that invariably lead to high rates of delinquent behavior during adolescence and early adulthood. The United States is the only major country to allow its citizens to buy a wide variety of weapons. It worships the gun, as shown in numerous movies and TV series. Modern North American culture emphasizes individual choice to such an extent that competing values of restraint, soberness, and responsibility have lost their guiding force among many segments of the population. The emphasis on individual choice is just as prevalent among liberal segments of the population as among conservative ones.

When Benedict published *Patterns of Culture* in 1934, she meant to be neutral about the basic values of the three societies she described. But this is not what many of her readers concluded because they correctly saw that Benedict's own value preferences "leaked through" her seemingly objective comparisons. Benedict as well as many of her readers preferred the peaceful lifestyle of the Hopis over the power-oriented lifestyle of the Kwakiutl and the fear-driven treachery of the Dobu.

In contrast to Benedict, this author makes no pretense at being value-neutral. In his opinion, the peaceful ethos of the Ladakhis has much to teach to modern North Americans whose comparatively violent way of life is morally suspect. The comparison between the Ladakhi and the North American ethos suggests that the North American ethos is inherently flawed. These flaws cannot be fixed by the currently popular prescriptions of liberal American psychology and social science: More multiculturalism, more freedom of choice for everybody, more autonomy for women, greater freedom to express one's sexual preferences, and more tolerance for alternative life styles. Following these prescriptions will do little to stop the social disorganization and violence-proneness of modern North American society—it may well make the situation worse. This is so because the prescriptions themselves reflect the extreme emphasis on freedom of choice and individualism that constitutes a root cause of social disorganization. The prescriptions are part of the problem, not part of the solution. This ironic if deeply disturbing conclusion is bound to displease many readers; however, the more important question to ask is: Could it be true?

NOTE

The author is grateful to the many Ladakhis who so patiently responded to difficult questions, to Donna Chirico-Rosenberg, who conducted some of the interviews, and to

Wangchuk Shalipa, who served as interpreter. The author also wishes to express his appreciation to the University Seminars at Columbia University for assistance in the preparation of the manuscript for publication. Material drawn from this work was presented to the University Seminar on Moral Education. This chapter builds upon an article previously published by Gielen and Chirico-Rosenberg (1993).

REFERENCES

Benedict, R. (1934). *Patterns of culture*. Boston, MA: Houghton Mifflin.

Briggs, J. L. (1970). *Never in anger: Portrait of an Eskimo family*. Cambridge, MA: Harvard University Press.

Colby, A., & Kohlberg, L. (1987). *The measurement of moral judgment*. New York: Cambridge University Press.

Fowler, J. (1981). *Stages of faith. The psychology of human development and the quest for meaning*. San Francisco, CA: Harper & Row.

Fromm, E. (1973). *The anatomy of human destructiveness*. Greenwich, CT: Fawcett.

Fry, D. P. (1992). "Respect for the rights of others is peace": Learning aggression versus non-aggression among the Zapotec. *American Anthropologist, 94*(3), 621–639.

Gielen, U. P. (1985). Women in traditional Tibetan societies. *International Psychologist, 27*, 17–20.

Gielen, U. P. (1993). Traditional Tibetan societies. In L. L. Adler (Ed.), *International handbook on gender roles*, ch. 29. Westport, CT: Greenwood Press.

Gielen, U. P., & Chirico-Rosenberg, D. (1993). Traditional Buddhist Ladakh and the ethos of peace. *International Journal of Group Tensions, 23*(1), 5–23.

Howell, S., & Willis, R. (1989). *Societies at peace: Anthropological perspectives*. London: Routledge.

Montagu, A. (Ed.). (1978). *Learning non-aggression. The experience of non-literate societies*. New York: Oxford University Press.

Selman, R. (1979). *Assessing interpersonal understanding*. Cambridge, MA: Harvard University, Judge Baker Social Reasoning Project.

Turnbull, C. M. (1961). *The forest people*. New York: Simon & Schuster.

Turnbull, C. M. (1965). *Wayward servants*. New York: Natural History Press.

Index

About the Contributors

LEONORE LOEB ADLER is the Director of the Institute for Cross-Cultural and Cross-Ethnic Studies and a Professor Emerita in the Department of Psychology at Molloy College, Rockville Centre, New York. Dr. Adler is active in many professional organizations and recently was elected to the American Psychological Association's Committee on International Relations in Psychology. Dr. Adler is currently, and has been for over 30 years, intensely involved in cross-cultural research. She has received both the Kurt Lewin Award and the Wilhelm Wundt Award from different divisions of the New York State Psychological Association, the Distinguished Contributions of the Decade Award from the International Organization for the Study of Group Tensions, and the Certificate of Recognition from the International Council of Psychologists, as well as the President's Medal from Molloy College. Dr. Adler has published over seventy professional papers and chapters and is the author, editor, or coeditor of fourteen books.

CHARLES V. CALLAHAN is a Professor of Psychology at Molloy College in Rockville Centre, New York. His primary field of interest and focus of professional activity is cognitive behavior therapy with children. He has only recently become interested in the cross-cultural aspects of psychology, especially as regards the delivery of modern clinical services in traditional cultures. Dr. Callahan has developed one of the first graduate programs in cross-cultural psychology in conjunction with Dr. Leonore Loeb Adler at Molloy College (the program is currently awaiting approval by the New York State Education Department).

JUNE F. CHISHOLM, a clinical psychologist, is an Associate Professor of Psychology at Pace University and an Adjunct Professor at New York University Medical Center providing supervision for psychology interns. She had been a Senior Psychologist in the out-patient department of Harlem Hospital Center providing psychological services to an ethnically diverse primarily poor population. Her research interests include issues in the psychological treatment of women of color, psychological assessment, and bias and prejudice in the theory and practice of psychology.

JEAN CIRILLO is president of the New York State Psychological Association's Division on Women's Issues. She is also New York State representative for the American Psychological Association's campaign for National Health Care Reform. She serves on the Executive Board of the Nassau County Psychological Association and co-chairs its Community Relations Committee. A neuropsychologist at Central General Hospital in Plainview, Long Island, Dr. Cirillo works with alcohol- and drug-dependent patients.

BARBARA COWEN is an Adjunct Assistant Professor of Psychology at John Jay College of Criminal Justice, City University of New York. She is also Secretary-Treasurer of the Academic Division of the New York State Psychological Association. Dr. Cowen's chapter is based on her work as a psychological consultant in the prison at Riker's Island in New York City. Her research interest is about incarcerated women.

FLORENCE L. DENMARK is the Robert Scott Pace Professor of Psychology at Pace University, where she is the Chair of the Department of Psychology. She was President of the American Psychological Association, 1980–81; the Eastern Psychological Association, 1985–86; the New York State Psychological Association, 1972–73; the International Council of Psychologists, 1989–90; and Psi Chi, the National Honor Society in Psychology, 1978–80. In addition, she served as vice-president for the New York Academy of Sciences and the International Organization for the Study of Group Tensions and is currently a member of the Advisory Board of the Institute for Cross-Cultural and Cross-Ethnic Studies, Molloy College. Dr. Denmark has been the Thomas Hunter Professor of Psychology at Hunter College of the City University of New York. She has authored or edited sixteen books and monographs and has written numerous chapters and articles. Dr. Denmark is the recipient of numerous awards including the American Psychological Association's Distinguished Contributions to Education and Training (1987) and, most recently, APA's Division 35 (Psychology of Women) Carolyn Wood Sherif Award (1991) and the APA's Award for Distinguished Contributions to Psychology in the Public Interest (1992).

GWENDOLYN L. GERBER is Professor of Psychology at John Jay College of Criminal Justice, City University of New York, and a psychotherapist in private practice in New York City, where she works with individuals and couples. In 1993, she received the Wilhelm Wundt award from the Academic Division of the New York State Psychological Association. She has held offices and served on the executive council of a number of professional organizations, including the Psychology of Women Division and the Division of Psychoanalysis of the American Psychological Association, and the New York State Psychological Association. Currently she is Chair of the Psychology Advisory Committee at the New York Academy of Sciences. She is the author of over thirty publications in professional journals and edited books and has presented papers and participated in over forty professional conferences and symposia.

UWE P. GIELEN is Professor of Psychology and International Cultural Studies at St. Francis College, Brooklyn, New York, and served as Chairman of its Psychology Department from 1980 to 1990. He is coauthor/coeditor of *The Kohlberg Legacy for the Helping Professions* (1991), *Psychology in International Perspective: 50 Years of the International Council of Psychologists* (1992), *Cross-cultural Topics in Psychology* (1994), and *Advancing Psychology and Its Applications: International Perspectives* (in press). During 1994–95, he will serve as President of the International Council of Psychologists (ICP), an organization of more than 1,500 members in eighty-three countries.

LISA GOODMAN is an Assistant Professor in the Clinical-Community Psychology Program at the University of Maryland at College Park. She was the James Marshall Public Policy Research Fellow at the American Psychological Association between 1991 and 1992. Dr. Goodman's primary areas of research are the consequences of physical and sexual violence against low-income, seriously mentally ill, and homeless women and the differential effects of various forms of traumatic events and conditions on community-based populations.

JACK L. HERMAN is a Professor of Psychology at Pace University, New York, in the Psy.D. Program in School and Community Psychology. He is a clinical psychologist and psychoanalyst, a former faculty member of the New York Society for Psychoanalytic Training, a member of the Adelphi Society for Psychoanalysis and Psychotherapy, and a Past President of the Nassau County Psychological Association. He is also an Adjunct Clinical Professor and Supervisor of Psychotherapy in the Gordon Derner Institute of Advanced Psychological Studies of Adelphi University. In his practice Dr. Herman works with children, adolescents, and adults and conducts workshops in child psychotherapy. He is particularly interested in the technique and practice of psychoanalytic psychotherapy with children and adolescents and in collateral work with parents.

MARY P. KOSS is a Professor of Family and Community Medicine, Psychiatry, and Psychology at the University of Arizona in Tucson. With Dr. Mary Harvey she is the author of *The Rape Victim: Clinical and Community Interventions*. She is the co-chair of the American Psychological Association Taskforce on Violence against Women and is a member of the National Institute of Mental Health Working Group on Violence. She is also the associate editor of the journals *Psychology of Women Quarterly* and *Violence and Victims* and is a consulting editor for the *Journal of Interpersonal Violence, Violence Update, Journal of Sexual Abuse,* and *Criminal Behavior and Law.* Dr. Koss has testified on the quality of federal rape statistics before the U.S. Senate Committee on the Judiciary and on rape of women in the military before the U.S. Senate Committee on Veteran's Affairs. The focus of her current research is recovery from rape.

BEATRICE J. KRAUSS is a Senior Project Director at the National Development and Research Institutes, New York. Dr. Krauss is also an Adjunct Associate Professor of Psychology at Hunter College, teaching courses in health psychology, personality, human development, and women's studies. She is currently implementing a Community AIDS Demonstration Project under contract to the Centers for Disease Control and Prevention. Her recent publications include a review on conflict resolution and a series of articles on adjustment to the HIV/AIDS epidemic.

HERBERT H. KRAUSS is Professor and Chair of Psychology at Hunter College, City University of New York. He is also Adjunct Associate Professor of Psychology in psychiatry, Cornell Medical College, and Adjunct Associate Psychologist, New York Hospital and Payne Whitney Clinic. Dr. Krauss directs the rehabilitation research program at the International Center for the Disabled (ICD). He considers himself a Boulder model clinical psychologist with wide-ranging interests, among them anxiety and its relationship to the experience of time, depression, and the biosocial construction of personality.

ROBERT S. LEE is Associate Professor of Marketing at the Lubin School of Business at Pace University in New York. Prior to this, he was at IBM corporate headquarters for many years where, as Research Advisor for Communications, he conducted national studies on attitudes toward automation, technological change, and computers. He also did research in the area of educational technology and on the climate of decision making within management. He has published many articles on these as well as methodological topics and is co-author of *The Road to H,* a book on narcotics, delinquency, and social policy. Dr. Lee has been a member of the executive council of the American Association for Public Opinion Research (AAPOR) for a number of years and was twice chairman of the annual AAPOR conference. His current research is on how people deal with time pressure situations.

JOAN M. REIDY MERLO is Professor of Sociology at Molloy College, Rockville Centre, New York, and is Adjunct Associate Professor of Sociology at Hofstra University. Dr. Merlo is currently the Chair of the Sociology and Social Work Department at Molloy and spent the 1993–94 academic year as institutional research consultant to the Director of Planning. Her personal research has centered on the role of women in the media, and she has presented many papers on this topic at the American Sociological Association conferences. In 1991, Dr. Merlo was awarded the Distinguished Service Medal for her outstanding contributions to Molloy College.

DAN MEYER holds the position of Clinical Director at Holy Cross Residential Treatment Center in Rhinecliff, New York. Holy Cross is a treatment center for adolescent boys. During a five-year period in the 1980s Dr. Meyer was the Director of SAFER (Sexually abusing families entering recovery) where services were provided to offenders and their spouses, and where he helped to coordinate services for victims. This work put him in contact with Social Services, the courts, probation officers, and attorneys.

BARBARA A. MOWDER is a Professor of Psychology and the Director of Graduate Psychology Programs at Pace University in New York City. She has written extensively in the areas of at-risk and handicapped children, consultation, and school psychology. Her research interests center on children, parents, and professional service provision. Most recently Dr. Mowder's writing focuses on parents, the parent role, and parenting activities.

LINDA MOY is currently a Graduate Student in the School-Community Psychology Program at Pace University, and a Psychology Extern at the New York Hospital, Cornell Medical Center Westchester Division. She is interested in issues related to early childhood and is in field placements in which she is gaining greater experience in working with children and adolescents.

MARGOT B. NADIEN has been a member of the full-time psychology faculty at Fordham University's Lincoln Center campus in New York City since 1973, where she serves as a life-span psychologist as well as the Director of the Gerontology Certificate Program. Dr. Nadien is the author of two textbooks—*The Child's Psychosocial Development* (1980) and *Adult Years and Aging* (1989)—in addition to journal articles, book chapters, and presentations at psychological societies. Along with Dr. Florence L. Denmark, she is currently preparing an edited volume dealing with life-span perspectives on autonomy and gender. Her professional memberships within psychology include six associations and societies.

JOSEPH O'DONOGHUE is Associate Professor of International Business at the City University of New York (CUNY). He has served as Editor or Coeditor for the *Journal of Merger and Acquisition Analysis* and the *International Journal of Case Studies and Research*. He is the author of *The World of the Japanese Worker* (1991) and with Dr. Donald Grunewald Coeditor of *How to Resist Hostile Takeovers* (1990). With Dr. Mary Ann O'Donoghue, Dr. O'Donoghue has published his research on the impact of violence in the *International Journal of Group Tensions* and in the series *Dimensions of International Terrorism* (1994).

He has been a consultant to Fortune 500 companies on trends in international trade and has presented seminars on anticipated developments in global trade at conferences in Europe and Asia.

NANCY FELIPE RUSSO is Professor of Psychology and Director of Women's Studies at Arizona State University. The first Administrative Officer for Women's Programs of the American Psychological Association (APA), she is also a former President of APA's Division of the Psychology of Women and Associate Editor of the *Psychology of Women Quarterly*. Dr. Russo currently serves on APA's new Board for the Advancement of Psychology in the Public Interest. She is author of more than 100 publications related to sex roles and the psychology of women. Dr. Russo is the recipient of the Distinguished Leadership Certificate of APA's committee on Women in Psychology.

LINDA SADLER has completed all requirements for the Psy.D. degree in School-Community Psychology from Pace University. Her doctoral internship is being completed at the Postgraduate Center for Mental Health, where she works with children, adolescents, parents, families, and couples. As an intern, she also serves as a psychological consultant to an elementary school in the New York City public school system.

HAROLD TAKOOSHIAN is currently Associate Professor in the Social Sciences Division of Fordham University. He was elected to serve as Eastern Vice-President of Psi Chi, the national honor society for psychology (1993–95). He was a U.S. Fulbright Scholar to the Soviet Union in 1987–88, and Visiting Professor of Psychology at the universities of Atacama and Talca (Chile). He occasionally consults for industry and government, using behavioral science methods to address social problems.

SERGEI V. TSYTSAREV is an Associate Professor of Clinical and Forensic Psychology at St. Petersburg State University, Russia, and is currently a Visiting Professor at Hofstra University in Hempstead, New York. His field is the psychology of addictive and criminal behavior. In 1988 he began his cross-cultural research as a visiting scholar at Osaka City University, Japan, and then continued his studies, working in 1991–93 as a Visiting Associate Professor at John Jay College of Criminal Justice of the City University of New York and as an Adjunct Professor at Hofstra University. Dr. Tsytsarev has participated in a number of international research projects and conferences. His research data have been summarized in two books and in more than forty articles, which were published in Russia, in the United States, and in Japan.

WILLIAM M. VERDI is a doctoral student in the Industrial-Organizational Psychology Program at Baruch College of the City University of New York, where he is doing research on downsizing in industry. He is a past president of the

Fordham University at Lincoln Center chapter of Psi Chi, the national honor society in psychology. He has done research and consulting with government and private industry.

LENORE E. A. WALKER is Executive Director of the Domestic Violence Institute in Denver, Colorado. She is an international lecturer who trains at the invitation of governments, private groups, and world health organizations. Dr. Walker has done research, clinical intervention, training, and expert witness testimony on the psychology of battered women and the dynamics of the battering relationship.

BENJAMIN B. WOLMAN has been affiliated with several academic institutions, including Columbia University, Yeshiva University, Adelphi University, and Long Island University. He also has a private practice of psychoanalysis and psychotherapy. Dr. Wolman has authored over 200 scientific papers and has written or edited thirty books in psychology and related fields. He is also the Editor-in-Chief of the thirteen-volume *International Encyclopedia of Psychiatry, Psychology, Psychoanalysis and Neurology*. A Fellow or Member of many professional associations, societies, and institutions, Dr. Wolman is an Honorary Professor at the Andres Bello Catholic University in Caracas, Venezuela, and the President of the International Organization for the Study of Group Tensions. Dr. Wolman is the recipient of the Distinguished Contributions Award from the American Psychological Association.

ISBN 0-275-94873-0

90000>

EAN

9 780275 948733

HARDCOVER BAR CODE